GEOPOLITICAL UNION

From the rise of China as a technological superpower, to wars on its eastern borders, and to the belief that the US is no longer a reliable ally, the European Commission sees the world as more unstable than at any other time in recent history. As such, the Commission has become the Geopolitical Commission, working to serve the interests of the Geopolitical Union. Central to many of these conflicts is technology – who produces it, where it is produced, and who controls it. These questions are central to the Commission's pursuit of digital/technological sovereignty: Europe's attempt to regain control of technology regulation. Focusing on topics such as setting technological standards, ensuring access to microchips, reining in online platforms, and securing rules for industrial data and AI, this book explores the EU's approach to lawmaking in this field, resulting in increased regulatory oversight and promotion of industrial policy at home, while exporting its rules abroad.

Benjamin Farrand is Professor of Law & Emerging Technologies at Newcastle University, UK. His research on technology regulation has been published in journals such as the *Journal of Common Market Studies* and *International Affairs*. He is also affiliated with the Newcastle University Academic Centre of Excellence in Cyber Security Research.

Geopolitical Union

EUROPE'S ATTEMPT TO TAKE BACK CONTROL OF TECHNOLOGY REGULATION

BENJAMIN FARRAND
Newcastle University

Shaftesbury Road, Cambridge CB2 8EA, United Kingdom

One Liberty Plaza, 20th Floor, New York, NY 10006, USA

477 Williamstown Road, Port Melbourne, VIC 3207, Australia

314–321, 3rd Floor, Plot 3, Splendor Forum, Jasola District Centre, New Delhi – 110025, India

103 Penang Road, #05–06/07, Visioncrest Commercial, Singapore 238467

Cambridge University Press is part of Cambridge University Press & Assessment, a department of the University of Cambridge.

We share the University's mission to contribute to society through the pursuit of education, learning and research at the highest international levels of excellence.

www.cambridge.org
Information on this title: www.cambridge.org/9781009691116

DOI: 10.1017/9781009691093

© Benjamin Farrand 2026

This publication is in copyright. Subject to statutory exception and to the provisions of relevant collective licensing agreements, no reproduction of any part may take place without the written permission of Cambridge University Press & Assessment.

When citing this work, please include a reference to the DOI 10.1017/9781009691093

First published 2026

Cover image: Jorg Greuel/Photodisc/Getty Images

A catalogue record for this publication is available from the British Library

A Cataloging-in-Publication data record for this book is available from the Library of Congress

ISBN 978-1-009-69110-9 Hardback
ISBN 978-1-009-69111-6 Paperback

Cambridge University Press & Assessment has no responsibility for the persistence or accuracy of URLs for external or third-party internet websites referred to in this publication and does not guarantee that any content on such websites is, or will remain, accurate or appropriate.

For EU product safety concerns, contact us at Calle de José Abascal, 56, 1°, 28003 Madrid, Spain, or email eugpsr@cambridge.org

For Lena, my wife, my co-author, and my constant companion, and for Francesca, my daughter, my star, and my number one pancake-making assistant. None of this would have meaning if not for you both.

Contents

Acknowledgements — page ix

Introduction: The Geopolitical Commission and Technology Control — 1

PART I REGULATORY MERCANTILISM AND THE GEOPOLITICS OF TECHNOLOGY CONTROL

1 Regulatory Mercantilism as a Means of Understanding the Actions of the Geopolitical Union — 19

2 The EU as a Technology Regulator — 50

3 The Geopolitics of Technology Control and the Crisis of Globalisation — 71

PART II TECHNOLOGY REGULATION IN THE VON DER LEYEN COMMISSION

4 Regulating Technological Systems — 95

5 Regulating Platform Content and Architecture — 120

6 Regulating Data and AI — 142

PART III THE FUTURE OF THE GEOPOLITICAL UNION

7 The von der Leyen II Commission and the Future of the Geopolitical Union — 167

Conclusions: The Geopolitical Union as an Approach to Governance and the Utility of Regulatory Mercantilism for Regulation and Governance Studies — 190

Index — 199

Acknowledgements

Writing an acknowledgements section for a book is both an opportunity to thank everyone involved in the writing process and an opportunity to worry that you may have inadvertently left someone out. On that basis, I want to begin by pre-emptively apologising and by making it very clear that this account is non-exhaustive. If you think you should be listed here and you weren't, please let me know in case I'm fortunate enough to be asked to write a second edition after the end of the von der Leyen II Commission!

First and foremost, I'd like to thank Helena Carrapico (Northumbria University), my co-author and life partner. When I was developing the regulatory mercantilism concept and was going down rabbit holes on seventeenth-century mercantilist thought, she was hugely supportive, if occasionally mystified by my interest in the subject, and was happy for me to develop it further in a co-authored article we wrote that marked the starting point of this research project. On that point, I would also like to thank Rocco Bellanova (Vrije Universiteit Brussel), Denis Duez (UC Louvain), and Helena Carrapico (again) as editors of the *European Security* special issue that the first piece was published in, as well as the editors of the journal Jocelyn Mawdsley (Newcastle University) and Laura Chappell (University of Surrey). I would also like to give special thanks to Eva Nanopoulos (Queen Mary, University of London) for all her thoughts, our discussion of law and political economy, and her continued enthusiasm for the project.

The work around regulatory mercantilism has been shared at several conferences, workshops, and symposia, and in this context, I would like to thank in particular Andre Barrinha (University of Bath), Andrea Calderado (Cardiff University), Xuechen Chen (Northeastern University London), George Christou (Warwick University), Lizzie Coles-Kemp (Royal Holloway University), Elaine Fahey (City St George's, University of London), Xinchuchu Gao (University of Lincoln), Sebastian Heidebrecht (University of Vienna), Adam Joinson (University of Bath), Nitasha Kaul (University of Westminster), Tobias Liebetrau (University of Copenhagen), Linda Monsees (Institute of International Relations Prague), Timo Seidl (Technical University of Munich), and Tim Stevens (King's College London) for all their helpful comments, reflections, and critiques, which have helped me to develop the concept further. My thanks extend to all panellists and members of the audience who have listened to my tireless (tiresome?) explanations of regulatory mercantilism and technology policy.

I would like to thank my colleagues at Newcastle University with whom I have shared my ideas expanded upon in this book and, in particular, Michael Ashworth, Christine Beuermann, Francesco de Cecco, Zoe Gounari, Ruth Houghton, Bronwen Jones, Sylvia de Mars (even if we disagree on globalisation), Sam Ryan, Ilke Turkmendag, Hélène Tyrrell, and Neha Vyas (competitiveness not competition!). I would also like to thank Szu-Yuan Wang (Shih Hsin University), the organiser of the 2025 International Conference on New Legal Thinking in Science and Technology Development, for giving me the opportunity to provide the keynote address, which focused on the research conducted in this book. At Cambridge University Press, I would like to thank Executive Publisher Matt Gallaway for his confidence in the original monograph proposal and Jadyn Fauconier-Herry, Sharon McCann, and Gemma Smith for all their help and support in preparing the manuscript. I'd like to thank my family as well for all their love and support throughout the years.

This book owes an intellectual debt to several scholars. Even though I have never had the opportunity to meet him, Giandomenico Majone has been influential in my approach to regulation and governance. David Levi-Faur (Hebrew University of Jerusalem) and John Braithwaite (Australian National University) also inspired my interest in regulatory capitalism, from which regulatory mercantilism traces its lineage, and though our paths may not have yet crossed, I hope that this may change in the future. Finally, I extend my thanks to you, the reader. I hope that you enjoy reading this work as much as I have enjoyed writing it.

Introduction

The Geopolitical Commission and Technology Control

We have seen the birth of a geopolitical Union – supporting Ukraine, standing up to Russia's aggression, responding to an assertive China and investing in partnerships.[1]

On 13 September 2023, European Commission President Ursula von der Leyen announced the birth of the Geopolitical Union – a European Union (EU) that would no longer be naïve in its relations with the rest of the world but would instead look to protect its own interests in the face of global upheaval. Elected in 2019, President von der Leyen announced her view of world events in her political guidelines,[2] a world she described as ever more unsettled: 'Existing powers are going down new paths alone. New powers are emerging and consolidating. Changes in climate, technology, and demography are transforming our societies and way of life'.[3] The mid-2000s onwards had seen shifts that shook the European Commission's faith in the liberal international order, ranging from financial crises and contagion for the Eurozone, Russian aggression in Crimea, attacks to its legitimacy from disinformation of external origin to the United Kingdom's withdrawal from the EU. With the election of Donald Trump as US President in 2016 and the beginning of an increasingly fractious trade relationship with China, it seemed that 'Great Power' politics was back,[4] and with it, a growing sense that international cooperation was being replaced with geopolitics and geopolitical strategising.[5] Furthermore, the seeming consensus that the private sector had a valuable role to play as equal partners in networks of governance was increasingly shaken by concerns over private power and the extent to which information infrastructure owners may have interests, values, and ideologies not necessarily aligned with those of actors such as the European

---

[1] Ursula von der Leyen, '2023 State of the Union Address by President von Der Leyen: Answering the Call of History' (2023) SPEECH/23/4426 2.
[2] Ursula von der Leyen, 'A Europe That Strives for More: My Agenda for Europe' (2019).
[3] Ibid 4.
[4] Lamont Colucci, 'Great Power Conflict: Will It Return?' (2015) 177 *World Affairs* 44.
[5] Walter Russell Mead, 'The Return of Geopolitics: The Revenge of the Revisionist Powers Essay' (2014) 93 *Foreign Affairs* 69.

Commission.[6] In particular, 'Big Tech', the large technology companies responsible for some of the most significant innovations in recent history, were seen to have amassed significant economic and political power with control over infrastructure and the data that powered it. And yet, could they necessarily be trusted?[7]

Technology, where it is made, who owns it, and who uses it, have all become important geostrategic questions. In 2020, when the COVID-19 pandemic led to a global manufacturing shutdown, resulting in a decrease in the microchips available for use in a whole range of sectors, it impacted automobile manufacture first and then spread into markets for smartphones, graphics cards, and refrigerators.[8] By May 2022, exacerbated by trade conflict between the US and China, the shortage had spread to medical[9] and security[10] technologies. Access to modern technologies, previously taken as a given in the EU, was suddenly something that could not be taken for granted; Europe's dependency on technology and technology supply chains outside of its territory was no longer just part of a system of globalised trade but a vulnerability for both its economy and its security. If a natural disaster could limit Europe's access to technology, could an unfriendly state? If the liberal international economic order and its organs, such as the World Trade Organization, were losing their ability to influence and shape trade links in line with previously accepted norms and values, and if states, particularly big technology-exporting states, were in active trade conflict and increasingly protectionist regarding their critical sectors, what would this mean for the EU? How could the Commission respond in a way that could ensure its economic prosperity and guarantee its security?

The central argument made in this book is that in the face of heightened geopolitical instability and a heightened sense of its own vulnerabilities, the EU has adopted an approach to technology regulation that can be characterised as 'regulatory mercantilist' in nature. This entails a framing of regulatory intervention as a **response to geopolitical instability or perceived threat**, which necessitates a response based in **promoting sovereignty and/or reducing external dependencies**. This requires **increased regulatory control**, with an emphasis on **coordinating technology**

---

[6] Helena Carrapico and Benjamin Farrand, 'When Trust Fades, Facebook Is No Longer a Friend: Shifting Privatisation Dynamics in the Context of Cybersecurity as a Result of Disinformation, Populism and Political Uncertainty' (2021) 59 *JCMS: Journal of Common Market Studies* 1160.

[7] This in itself would not necessarily be a new or original argument, which has already been effectively explored in Marietje Schaake, *The Tech Coup: How to Save Democracy from Silicon Valley* (Princeton University Press 2024).

[8] Reuters, 'Why Is There a Global Chip Shortage and Why Should You Care?' (*Reuters*, 1 April 2021) <www.reuters.com/article/world/middle-east/why-is-there-a-global-chip-shortage-and-why-should-you-care-idUSKBN2BN30G/> accessed 16 April 2025.

[9] Franz van Houten, 'Global Chip Shortages Put Life-Saving Medical Devices at Risk' (*World Economic Forum*, 24 May 2022) <www.weforum.org/stories/2022/05/global-chip-shortages-put-life-saving-medical-devices-at-risk/> accessed 16 April 2025.

[10] Sujai Shivakumar and Charles Wessner, 'Semiconductors and National Defense: What Are the Stakes?' (*Center for Strategic & International Studies*, 6 August 2022) <www.csis.org/analysis/semiconductors-and-national-defense-what-are-stakes> accessed 16 April 2025.

industrial policy within Europe, while **promoting European rules and values as global standards** outside of Europe. It represents a **reorientation of public–private relations** from a model in which both are equal partners in regulatory networks, typified by light touch or self-regulatory regimes, to one in which an element of hierarchy is restored, with co-regulation and the creation of new regulatory bodies or expansion of the powers of existing ones. Most importantly, it positions **economy** and **security** ambitions as mutually constitutive and interdependent, rather than trade-offs. Both Europe's economy and its security are equally challenged by external vulnerabilities, and reducing the dependencies that create those vulnerabilities can help to ensure that the EU's technological sovereignty is preserved and its ability to act free of the restraints placed upon it by strategic dependencies is increased. In this sense, the Commission has become the Geopolitical Commission, in which old ways of working and old rationales for regulation in the field of technology are replaced with a new geostrategic orientation, which is readily apparent in both the policy documents informing regulatory interventions and the structures for regulation provided in the resulting legal frameworks. As the penultimate chapter of this work demonstrates, the re-election of Donald Trump as President of the US and the beginning of his second administration in January 2025 have become key sources of geopolitical concern for the Commission, reinforcing the approach in von der Leyen II that was taken in von der Leyen I.

METHODOLOGY

To demonstrate this and the relevance of regulatory mercantilism in this context, I have employed grounded theory-informed thematic analysis.[11] Grounded theory[12] is a method employed in conducting inquiry for the purpose of constructing theory.[13] Grounded theory seeks to uncover the relevant conditions in which actors make decisions, how actors respond to those conditions, and the consequences of doing so.[14] It is an abductive process, combining elements of iterative and deductive analysis, in which data is used to draw initial theoretical inferences, which are then refined by returning to the data in a form of theoretical sampling in which the data helps to expand upon the theoretical categories.[15] As argued by Corbin and Strauss,

---

[11] Virginia Braun and Victoria Clarke, 'Using Thematic Analysis in Psychology' (2006) 3 *Qualitative Research in Psychology* 77.

[12] Barney Glaser and Anselm Strauss, *Discovery of Grounded Theory: Strategies for Qualitative Research* (Aldine de Gruyter 1967).

[13] Antony Bryant and others, 'Introduction: Grounded Theory Research: Methods and Practices', in Antony Bryant and Kathy Charmaz (eds), *The SAGE Handbook of Grounded Theory* (SAGE Publications Ltd 2007) 1.

[14] Juliet M Corbin and Anselm Strauss, 'Grounded Theory Research: Procedures, Canons, and Evaluative Criteria' (1990) 13 *Qualitative Sociology* 3, 5.

[15] Kathy Charmaz, 'The Power and Potential of Grounded Theory' (2012) 6 *Medical Sociology Online* 1, 11.

with theoretical sampling in grounded theory, each concept that comprises the theory is provisional but earns its way into the theory by repeatedly being visible in the collected data.[16] Initial development of the concepts has been conducted in previous research,[17] and the concepts have been further refined throughout the analysis conducted in writing this book. The analysis is thematic insofar as it identifies key themes that serve as a basis for action, rationales for acting, and then the actions pursued. This approach was used to identify patterns that could be used to determine the characteristics[18] of these contexts, rationales, and outcomes, and whether they met the conditions to be considered indicative of a regulatory mercantilism approach. These themes are more fully explored in Chapter 1, which concerns the development and application of the regulatory mercantilism framework.

In terms of performing this analysis, I use the 'Context, Process, Outcome' (CPO) framework.[19] Context concerns the dynamic conditions that inform ideas and understandings of a given scenario or problem, which serve to shape responses to those conditions.[20] Process and outcome refer to the 'implementation processes […] and the intended and unintended process of change triggered […] leading to alterations in intermediary outcomes (e.g. knowledge, attitude, behavior, structures, collaborative climate), finally leading to the outcomes of interest'.[21] In studying the changed approach to the regulation of technology by the von der Leyen Commission, this entails looking at the geopolitical *context* in which discussions regarding technology are taken; identifying the *processes* by which shared meaning is made and communicated regarding perceived vulnerabilities arising from this context, and thus the rationale for regulating technologies; and the outcomes being changes in the way that these technologies are governed, namely through moving away from systems of regulation that could be understood as regulatory capitalist in nature to systems that could be considered regulatory mercantilist (as will be discussed in the next

---

[16] Corbin and Strauss (n14) 7.
[17] Benjamin Farrand and Helena Carrapico, 'Digital Sovereignty and Taking Back Control: From Regulatory Capitalism to Regulatory Mercantilism in EU Cybersecurity' (2022) 31 *European Security* 435; Benjamin Farrand, 'Regulating Misleading Political Advertising on Online Platforms: An Example of Regulatory Mercantilism in Digital Policy' (2024) 45 *Policy Studies* 730.
[18] See Greg Guest, Kathleen M MacQueen and Emily E Namey, *Applied Thematic Analysis* (SAGE Publications, Inc 2012); as well as an application of this approach in Sarah E Daly and Shon M Reed, '"I Think Most of Society Hates Us": A Qualitative Thematic Analysis of Interviews with Incels' (2022) 86 *Sex Roles* 14.
[19] Annemarie Fridrich, Gregor J Jenny and Georg F Bauer, 'The Context, Process, and Outcome Evaluation Model for Organisational Health Interventions' (2015) 2015 *BioMed Research International* 414832.
[20] Ali Intezari and David J Pauleen, 'Conceptualizing Wise Management Decision-Making: A Grounded Theory Approach' (2018) 49 *Decision Sciences* 335.
[21] Georg F Bauer and Gregor J Jenny, 'From Fidelity to Figuration: Current and Emerging Approaches to Organizational Health Intervention Research' in Georg F Bauer and Gregor J Jenny (eds), *Salutogenic Organizations and Change: The Concepts Behind Organizational Health Intervention Research* (Springer Netherlands 2013) 10.

section). This approach is suitable and appropriate for assessing changes in public policy,[22] as it allows for an understanding of how external conditions impact upon the decisions made by policy actors such as regulators or legislators (and in this case, the European Commission) and the choice of public policy intervention they adopt, such as binding regulations or voluntary compliance mechanisms.[23]

In this book, I analyse the policies and actions relevant to technology control that were pursued by the first von der Leyen Commission in the period 2019–2024, drawing first from the above-mentioned political guidelines and then using purposive sampling to collate the policy documents relevant to the key policy areas identified in these political guidelines, including 'A Europe Fit for the Digital Age', 'Promoting Our European Way of Life', and 'A New Push for European Democracy', as discussed in more detail in Chapter 4. Of relevance for technology control is the Shaping Europe's Digital Future Communication,[24] which served as the basis both for identifying the key technologies relevant for this analysis, as well as for the Commission's rationale for action and subsequent approach. In total, more than 120 documents were used in the analysis, including Commission Communications, EU State of the Union addresses and speeches by European Commissioners, publications by Commission President von der Leyen, and Proposals for Regulations and Directives. In each instance, documents were analysed for containing references to the conditions in which action was being considered (context), the rationale for action (process), and proposed actions (outcomes). In order to provide a structure for the analysis to follow, it is first necessary to provide an overview of the key theoretical contribution this work makes in the next section, namely the development of the regulatory mercantilist framework (which is expanded upon in Chapter 1), and then to consider the rationales for action adopted by the Commission in the field of technology control, namely 'digital/technological sovereignty' and 'strategic autonomy', covered in the subsequent section (expanded upon in Chapters 2 and 3, and then applied in Chapters 4–7).

REGULATORY MERCANTILISM: EUROPE'S APPROACH TO REGULATING TECHNOLOGY CONTROL

The key theoretical contribution that I present with this book is the use of regulatory mercantilism as a way of understanding how the EU is seeking to regulate technologies considered critical for Europe's economy and security. I came up with the concept for a co-authored article in which my co-author and I were seeking

---

[22] Hosein Aslipour and Mohamad Reza Zargar, 'Developing Grounded Theory Systematic Approach for Public Policy Researches' (2022) 21 *International Journal of Qualitative Methods* 16094069221090357.
[23] Ingo Peters, 'Introduction: The European Union's Foreign Policy "Actorness and Power": Foundations of and Challenges for a Comparative Research Design', in Ingo Peters (ed), *The European Union's Foreign Policy in Comparative Perspective* (Routledge 2015).
[24] European Commission, 'Shaping Europe's Digital Future' (2020).

to understand how the Commission was operationalising digital sovereignty in the context of its cybersecurity policies.[25] Regulatory mercantilism is an approach to policy formulation that is increasingly being referred to in work aiming to understand digital policymaking in the EU context.[26] As the name suggests, regulatory mercantilism is an approach that shares characteristics with mercantilism as a system of control, requiring a brief outline of that ideational framework.[27] Discussions of mercantilism often begin with a reference to Adam Smith, and in this respect, this work is no different. In Book IV of Wealth of Nations, Smith refers to the 'mercantile System',[28] which he concludes constituted a system concerned with the encouragement of exports and discouragement of imports, with its object being 'to enrich the country by an advantageous balance of trade'.[29] Whether to consider it a unified and coherent system of thought or policy, however, is a subject of considerable debate. As Helleiner noted 'no one in the pre-Smithian era described themselves as "mercantilists"'.[30] Magnusson has similarly remarked that 'it was after Smith that Mercantilism was constructed into a more or less coherent "system" […] constructed as an opposite to the "Smithian" or "free trade" system'.[31] Mercantilism as a set of diverse ideas about the economy is more complex than Adam Smith's account suggests: It was neither a unified system 'obsessed' with securing wealth in the form of coinage,[32] nor a set of concrete policies in which national power or wealth can be measured solely by the volume of gold acquired.[33] Heckscher, while a critic of mercantilism, argued that the view that mercantilists saw wealth and money as either identical or interchangeable was mistaken.[34]

Mercantilism, such as it was, constituted a form of political economy focused both on the relations between states in matters of *external* trade and the role of the

---

[25] Farrand and Carrapico (n17).
[26] Anke Sophia Obendiek and Timo Seidl, 'The (False) Promise of Solutionism: Ideational Business Power and the Construction of Epistemic Authority in Digital Security Governance' (2023) 30 *Journal of European Public Policy* 1305; Andreas Kruck and Moritz Weiss, 'The Regulatory Security State in Europe' (2023) 30 *Journal of European Public Policy* 1205; Sebastian Heidebrecht, 'From Market Liberalism to Public Intervention: Digital Sovereignty and Changing European Union Digital Single Market Governance' (2024) 62 *JCMS: Journal of Common Market Studies* 205; Bernd Hoeksema, 'Digital Sovereignty, the Private Sector, and a Social Republican Alternative' (2024) 3 *Digital Society* 51.
[27] This will be expanded upon in more detail in Chapter 1.
[28] Adam Smith, *Wealth of Nations* (Oxford University Press 2008) 276.
[29] Ibid 374.
[30] Eric Helleiner, *The Neomercantilists: A Global Intellectual History* (Cornell University Press 2021) 6.
[31] Lars Magnusson, *The Political Economy of Mercantilism* (Routledge 2018) 3.
[32] While Smith (n28) indicates throughout Book IV that accumulation of gold and silver is important in his schema of mercantilist thought, it is not necessarily its sole or even most fundamental aim, as has been argued in some economics textbooks.
[33] See, for example, Henrik Schmiegelow and Michèle Schmiegelow, 'The New Mercantilism in International Relations: The Case of France's External Monetary Policy' (1975) 29 *International Organization* 367.
[34] Eli F Heckscher, *Mercantilism* (Routledge 1994) 261.

state in matters of *internal* trade harmonisation, reducing barriers that prevented the unity of the economy within a state, and the form that relations between what would now be considered the public and private sectors should take. It was an approach that saw power as guaranteed by wealth, and that wealth could in turn guarantee power, and through that power, the security of territory. Viner describes this rationale in mercantilism as being about 'power and plenty',[35] and that both were mutually reinforcing goals in seventeenth- and eighteenth-century foreign policy. As will be discussed in Chapter 1 of this book, mercantilism was an approach to state-market relations that were largely defined by the geopolitical structures and conflicts of its time, in which the best way to secure the state from external (and in this context, military) threats was to amass wealth, minimising the import of goods and resources that would create dependencies on other states, while seeking to maximise the export of 'value-added' goods, with a positive balance of trade essential to furthering state interests. This required a form of economic state-making, reducing any barriers to a unified economy internally, and the pursuit of an active industrial policy to produce the goods that could be exported in order to generate wealth, which in turn could be used to promote the security of the state, whether in the form of armaments, the payment of armies, or the building of ships. This however required the exertion of power beyond territorial borders to gain access to more of the natural resources deemed essential for industrial policy.

Regulatory mercantilism shares certain of these characteristics, although tempered for the nature of international relations in the twenty-first century. Regulatory mercantilism is an approach to regulating sectors that is motivated by a sense of insecurity or vulnerability on the part of the studied policymakers, as will be explored further in Chapter 1. Geopolitical instability and the belief that traditional allies or partners cannot necessarily be trusted create a sense that the dependence on the resources, goods, or service provision originating in other states creates critical vulnerabilities, with resulting economic and security implications. This lack of control limits the ability of a state-like actor like the European Commission to act freely in its engagements with both the private and public sector actors in those other states, or, in the parlance of the Commission, hinders its strategic autonomy (a concept that will be expanded upon in the next section). Regulatory mercantilism is therefore contingent and a response to perceived vulnerability, with the response being framed in terms of sovereignty and strategic autonomy, with economic and security issues being interlinked and used as a basis for action. In approach, it is interventionist, introducing legal frameworks as a means of exerting increased control over a domain such as, in the case of this book, technology. Regulatory mercantilism as a result seeks to reorient state-market relations, subjecting critical areas to increased oversight by means of legally mandated co-regulation, replacing self-regulatory

---

[35] Jacob Viner, 'Power Versus Plenty as Objectives of Foreign Policy in the Seventeenth and Eighteenth Centuries' (1948) 1 *World Politics* 1.

regimes. The Commission approach emphasises industrial policy as a means of reducing external dependencies,[36] bringing production of essential technologies into its territory as far as possible and expresses preference for 'European' solutions promoted by European private sector actors over those solutions provided by private sector actors based in other states.

In the context of technology, data takes on the character of a natural resource, a building block for the types of technological innovation that the EU wishes to see. This motivates a desire to bring these forms of 'critical raw material' into the EU's geographical control where possible, but to export its norms and values to other states and regions where it is not. This forms a 'regulatory balance of trade', in which the EU seeks to minimise the import of rules or values as much as possible, while maximising the export of its regulations, ensuring that even if data, resources, or goods are not within the EU's territory, they are nevertheless handled in a way aligned with the EU's rules and values. The Commission seeks to achieve these through two means: the first is through using its economic power and the size of its market to essentially change the regulatory approach in other states by means of gravity, with private sector actors lobbying their own states to adopt similar rules as a means of reducing the compliance costs incurred by regulatory divergences. Known as the 'Brussels Effect',[37] this approach to regulatory export has been central to the Commission's approach to technology regulation in the von der Leyen Commission in the fields of data and artificial intelligence (AI). However, a softer approach to regulatory export is possible through processes of cyber-diplomacy. Cyber-diplomacy has been defined as diplomacy engaged in through multilateral forums such as the United Nations, or bilaterally between states, to secure national interests regarding cyberspace, whether in fields such as cybersecurity or internet governance.[38]

It is possible to expand this concept to incorporate securing national interests as they relate to the technologies facilitating access and use of cyberspace, be they information infrastructures or technical standards, or how it is used, including on social media platforms. These tools of cyber-diplomacy can include seeking to influence norms and policy development in international forums, uploading European rules and values to the global level, or leveraging agreements and relations with other states and regions, such as Mercosur or partners in the Africa-focused Global Gateway programmes as ways of tying investment and expertise provision around

---

[36] As has been noted in recent work such as Donato Di Carlo and Luuk Schmitz, 'Europe First? The Rise of EU Industrial Policy Promoting and Protecting the Single Market' (2023) 30 *Journal of European Public Policy* 2063; Kathleen R McNamara, 'Transforming Europe? The EU's Industrial Policy and Geopolitical Turn' (2024) 31 *Journal of European Public Policy* 2371; Marco Di Gregorio and Alberto Gherardini, 'From Market Failures to Systemic Failures: The Evolving Rationale for European Industrial Policy' (2025) *Journal of European Integration* 1.

[37] Anu Bradford, *The Brussels Effect: How the European Union Rules the World* (Oxford University Press 2021).

[38] André Barrinha and Thomas Renard, 'Cyber-Diplomacy: The Making of an International Society in the Digital Age' (2017) 3 *Global Affairs* 353.

digital issues with adherence to European principles concerning technology control. Through the combination of these twin policies of industrial policy and capacity building at home, while exporting European standards as global standards through demonstrating technological leadership, the EU seeks to provide for both its economic prosperity and its continued security, not as separate and distinct domains of activity, but as mutually reinforcing parts of the whole. The entirety of the book will expand upon this framework, identifying the geopolitical causes behind the adoption of the approach, how it applies in the given technology case studies covered in each of its chapters, how the control of technologies is problematised as having impacts upon the EU's strategic autonomy and technological sovereignty, and how the Geopolitical Commission then uses legislative interventions to reduce external dependencies and promote greater European control. Before moving on to provide an overview of the structure of the book, it is first important to expand upon two key terms that will be used throughout the monograph and are central to the analysis, namely 'digital/technological sovereignty' and 'strategic autonomy'.

DIGITAL/TECHNOLOGICAL SOVEREIGNTY AND EUROPE'S STRATEGIC AUTONOMY

Central to the analysis, insofar as they serve as rationales for action on the part of the Commission in its attempts to regulate technology, are the concepts of 'digital/technological sovereignty' and 'strategic autonomy'. Digital/technological sovereignty are terms that first started to be used by the Commission in 2019 and then became the focus of considerable academic interest for scholars working in European studies, broadly defined. As of 2025, the concept has been the subject of at least two special issues of journals, one in *European Security* published in 2022 and one in the *Journal of European Public Policy* in 2024.[39] As has been noted, the Commission has tended to use either the terms 'digital sovereignty' or 'technological sovereignty' interchangeably, with variance in different policy documents.[40] For the purposes of this work, when quoting directly from policy documents, I use the wording used by the author (e.g. 'digital sovereignty'). Digital sovereignty is a concept that has been drawn from the domestic level in countries such as France and Germany, where this sovereignty was defined in terms of autonomy from the US, particularly around 'Big Tech', and increased state control over data flows.[41] Similarly, China was a strong proponent of 'cyber sovereignty' as early as 2010, framing it in terms of respect for adherence to rules and laws for cyberspace within a state's territory being akin to

---

[39] The editorials of both special issues can be found here: Rocco Bellanova, Helena Carrapico and Denis Duez, 'Digital/Sovereignty and European Security Integration: An Introduction' (2022) 31 *European Security* 337; Gerda Falkner and others, 'Digital Sovereignty – Rhetoric and Reality' (2024) 31 *Journal of European Public Policy* 2099.
[40] As discussed in Farrand and Carrapico (n17).
[41] Georg Glasze and others, 'Contested Spatialities of Digital Sovereignty' (2023) 28 *Geopolitics* 919.

that between nations regarding physical borders.[42] For China, this entailed asserting control over national information infrastructures and data originating within the Chinese state, which China argued should be governed by Chinese law, rather than rules or values originating from the US, which it considered a digital hegemon.[43] Russia similarly took a more authoritarian position on digital sovereignty, going further than China in declaring Russian cyberspace to be a separate and distinct entity from the rest of the World Wide Web.[44] Russian efforts have gone so far in this field that experiments have been run to ensure that the 'Russian' internet can continue to function normally if disconnected from the rest of the global internet.[45]

Yet what does digital sovereignty mean at the EU level? For Bellanova et al., digital sovereignty in a European context is a *reaction* or response to several interrelated concerns, including: the EU's growing awareness of its dependence on non-EU digital infrastructures and technologies; a lack of control over these infrastructures, as well as digital services, often originating outside of the EU with a diminished capacity to enforce EU legislation over them; a loss of competitiveness with more technologically advanced and agile states, such as the US and China; an inability to promote European competitors aligned with European values to counter these non-EU tech giants; and finally, the EU's perceived vulnerability to externally originating threats.[46] Thumfart argues that digital sovereignty is a rhetorical practice, defined by the construction of frontlines in a deeply entangled world, constituting an attempt at 'rebordering' in the digital realm.[47] Floridi et al. identify four key models arising from the scholarship concerning digital sovereignty: a rights-based model, a market-oriented model, a centralisation model, and a state-based model.[48] They argue, however, that 'none of the existing models offers a desirable balance between comprehensive digital regulation and responsiveness to technological innovation and social changes'.[49] In this, I agree with the authors, and ultimately,

---

[42] Min Jiang, 'Authoritarian Informationalism: China's Approach to Internet Sovereignty' (2010) 30 *SAIS Review of International Affairs* 71.
[43] Stephane Couture and Sophie Toupin, 'What Does the Notion of "Sovereignty" Mean When Referring to the Digital?' (2019) 21 *New Media & Society* 2305.
[44] Stanislav Budnitsky and Lianrui Jia, 'Branding Internet Sovereignty: Digital Media and the Chinese–Russian Cyberalliance' (2018) 21 *European Journal of Cultural Studies* 594.
[45] Ekaterina Martynova and Andrey Shcherbovich, 'Digital Transformation in Russia: Turning from a Service Model to Ensuring Technological Sovereignty' (2024) 55 *Computer Law & Security Review* 106075.
[46] Bellanova, Carrapico and Duez (n39) 343.
[47] Johannes Thumfart, *The Liberal Internet in the Postliberal Era: Digital Sovereignty, Private Government, and Practices of Neutralization* (Palgrave Macmillan 2024) 13–14. It is worth noting that Thumfart regards these practices as a complex, if potentially futile, attempt at reversing something irreversible in the context of globalised data flows. While an interesting argument with some merit, further consideration of this feasibility dimension is ultimately outside the scope of this work.
[48] Samuele Fratini and others, 'Digital Sovereignty: A Descriptive Analysis and a Critical Evaluation of Existing Models' (2024) 3 *Digital Society* 59.
[49] Ibid 58.

this book considers that these models are not distinct and separate models of digital sovereignty but different dimensions of the same phenomenon. Instead, it is submitted that if we consider digital sovereignty not as a normative construct but in terms of how it is constructed and used as a rationale for action by the Commission, it comprises being rights-based, insofar as it seeks to reinforce and embed at the global level European values; market-oriented in its focus on issues such as industrial policy and competitiveness and the interdependence of economic and security goals; centralising through efforts aimed at exerting control with increased regulatory oversight; and state-based through efforts aimed at reconfiguring state-private sector relations, as will be explored in the three case study chapters. It is formulated as Europe's ability to choose and to set its own rules and values, reducing its dependencies on external actors.[50]

The ultimate purpose of this rationale of digital sovereignty is to achieve its other rationale for regulatory action, namely, strategic autonomy. Strategic autonomy is a concept that has its origins in external security and defence.[51] First discussed at the EU level in European Council Conclusions from 2013 in the context of defence technologies, the European Council argued that sustaining defence capabilities can enhance its strategic autonomy.[52] In 2016 the High Representative of the Union for Foreign Affairs and Security Policy at the time, Federica Mogherini, argued that strategic autonomy was essential for the EU's Common Security and Defence Policy (CDSP) as a means of defending the EU's citizens, its principles, and its values.[53] While Biscop argues that the development of the EU approach from 2013 onwards to strategic autonomy in security and defence was ultimately based in a desire to be able to act without relying extensively on the US,[54] it is interesting to note that the EU in its use of the term at this time does not come with a useful definition of the concept, only that it is essential. Instead, authors have suggested looking to the earlier French concept of strategic autonomy developed in the 1990s, which has internal dimensions of security and defence and external dimensions of projection (whether of force or values).[55] Interestingly, this is also framed in terms of Europe's ability to choose, with the concept connotating

---

[50] European Commission, 'Shaping Europe's Digital Future' (n24) 3, and as will be discussed in more detail in Chapter 4.
[51] Bjørn Olav Knutsen, 'European Defence Research in Crisis? The Way towards Strategic Autonomy' (2016) 2 *Global Affairs* 287; Niklas Helwig and Ville Sinkkonen, 'Strategic Autonomy and the EU as a Global Actor: The Evolution, Debate and Theory of a Contested Term' (2022) 27 *European Foreign Affairs Review* 1.
[52] European Council, 'Council Conclusions' (2013) EUCO 217/13, CO EUR 15, CONCL 8 7.
[53] European External Action Service, 'Shared Vision, Common Action: A Stronger Europe – A Global Strategy for the European Union's Foreign and Security Policy' (2016) 4.
[54] Sven Biscop, 'All or Nothing? The EU Global Strategy and Defence Policy after the Brexit' (2016) 37 *Contemporary Security Policy* 431.
[55] See Charlotte Beaucillon, 'Strategic Autonomy: A New Identify for the EU as a Global Actor' (2023) 8 *European Papers* 417.

'that Europe should be able to stand on its own feet rather than relying on others […] this revolves around "the ability to set one's own priorities and make one's own decisions"'.[56]

With a growing awareness of geostrategic positioning in the current global climate, strategic autonomy has spread beyond security and defence *specifically* to become a broader goal for the EU in terms of its economic prosperity and trade relations.[57] As will be discussed throughout the case study Chapters 4–6, strategic autonomy is a term that is applied to the EU's dependencies on external actors in such a way that 'economy' and 'security' become unified and mutually constitutive. Strategic autonomy, including 'open' strategic autonomy,[58] is about being able to act unhindered or limited by its strategic dependencies on other states or the private sector actors operating within those states, with these strategic dependencies defined as 'dependencies that are considered of critical importance to the EU and its Member States' strategic interests such as security, health, and the green and digital transformation'.[59] In this context, open strategic autonomy was defined by the Commission as 'the ability to shape the new system of global economic governance and develop mutually beneficial bilateral relations, while protecting the EU from unfair and abusive practices, including to diversify and solidify global supply chains to enhance resilience to future crises'.[60] As is indicated from the case studies, however, the terms 'open strategic autonomy' and 'strategic autonomy' often are used interchangeably, or more often, only 'strategic autonomy' is referred to. What is of relevance however is that the concepts of digital sovereignty and strategic autonomy are intimately connected and used in conjunction in the Commission's arguments for increased regulatory oversight or control of strategic industries in the context of technology. Both have the element of ensuring that the EU can act and respond to global situations without being limited by its external dependencies. For this reason, both digital sovereignty and strategic autonomy require actions on the part of the Commission that reduce these dependencies, particularly where they are considered strategic dependencies. As this book will demonstrate, the approach taken by the Commission in doing so is one of regulatory mercantilism.

---

[56] Dick Zandee and others, 'European Strategic Autonomy in Security and Defence: Now the Going Gets Tough, It's Time to Get Going' (Netherlands Institute of International Relations, 2020) Clingandael Report 6.

[57] Beaucillon (n55); Tobias Gehrke, 'EU Open Strategic Autonomy and the Trappings of Geoeconomics' (2022) 27 *European Foreign Affairs Review* 61.

[58] The word open was argued to have been added in order to show that despite the move to a more protectionist and geopolitical approach to trade, the EU was nevertheless open to global trade relations: see Gehrke (n57) 62.

[59] European Commission, 'Strategic Dependencies and Capacities: Accompanying the Communication Updating the 2020 New Industrial Strategy: Building a Stronger Single Market for Europe's Recovery' (2021) SWD(2021) 352 8.

[60] Ibid 7–8.

STRUCTURE OF THE BOOK

The book is divided into three parts. Part I, 'Regulatory Mercantilism and the Geopolitics of Technology Control', covers the first three chapters. Chapter 1 is the theoretical basis for the rest of the book, fully outlining the regulatory mercantilist framework, its origins, distinctions from other modes of regulatory governance, and its characteristics. This chapter considers the approach of regulatory capitalism and how it has been the Commission's approach to technology regulation until relatively recently, aligned with the idea of the regulatory state and the reliance on expert-led forms of self-regulation or regulatory networks as a means of achieving economic goals based on a logic of efficiency rather than one of security. It outlines in more detail the ideas of mercantilism and its core features, before expanding on how regulatory mercantilism draws from these principles, representing a changed paradigm in technology regulation in which the logic is one of security, with security and economy being mutually constitutive policy objectives, motivated by concerns over external dependency and guaranteeing sovereignty. It highlights the more interventionist approach to regulation that is adopted within a regulatory mercantilist approach, the renewed emphasis on industrial policy, and the regulatory export of standards as global standards. The chapter concludes by making clear how this can then be applied to the analysis of the von der Leyen Commission's actions.

Chapter 2 provides an overview of the Commission as a technology regulator, beginning with the development of the EU's technology policies and laws, from their beginnings in the late 1970s until the late 2000s. It starts with reflections on the limited interventions of the Commission during the period referred to as one of 'Eurosclerosis', where the emphasis of interventions was by way of negative integration through the Court of Justice of the European Union, before the beginnings of distinct technology policies and positive acts of integration around technology in the 1990s. It explores how during its development, EU technology policy was marked by a distinction between economically oriented developments, such as around intellectual property rights, and security-related ones, as in the case of cybercrime and cybersecurity. However, in the period of the late 2000s/early 2010s and the EU 'polycrisis' of financial crisis, legitimacy crisis and populism crisis, and concerns over the power of the private sector in technology governance, the groundwork was laid for seeing technology control in terms of interlinked economic and security goals, a growing distrust of 'Big Tech', and concerns about the need to externalise the EU's rules and values, including through the Brussels Effect.

Chapter 3 moves to the global level, exploring the history of technology control and its historical links to geopolitics. It begins by considering control of technology in the context of the Cold War and technology as being explicitly considered a security issue in terms of the conflict between the US and the Soviet Union. It covers the CoCom technology restrictions imposed by the US and Soviet Union attempts to gain access to critical technologies through Comecon before considering how the approach to technology changed substantially with the end of the Cold War, the collapse of the Soviet Union, and the belief in the triumph of the liberal international order and globalism as reflected by the World Trade Organization and 'free trade'. It then explores the multifaceted crises impacting upon this conviction in the benefits and resilience of the global trade system, the increased economic conflict between the US and China as a rising technological power, and a move from multilateralism in a 'unipolar' system to increased nationalism and protectionism in a 'multipolar' system, and what this meant for the EU's sense of insecurity and vulnerability in the context of geopolitical reordering.

Part II of the book, 'Technology Regulation in the von der Leyen Commission', comprises the next three chapters. Chapter 4 covers the policy agenda of the von der Leyen Commission as it relates to technology, identifying the concerns over ensuring digital sovereignty and maintaining strategic autonomy as central rationales for Commission action. Chapter 4 focuses on 'technological systems' in which the EU has sought to increase its control and regulatory oversight through regulatory mercantilist means. Analysing the Commission's actions in technical standards for technologies such as digital communications, life-cycle cybersecurity for internet-enabled products, and the fostering of an EU industrial policy for semiconductors and microchips, this chapter highlights how concerns over foreign manipulation and excessive strategic dependencies has resulted in the Commission proposing legislative interventions in order to guarantee sovereignty and strategic autonomy through increased Commission and regulatory body oversight, the explicit linkage of economic and security concerns, and active promotion of technology industrial policy internally, and exporting of norms and values through ensuring a positive regulatory balance of trade externally.

Chapters 5 and 6 cover the other two case studies, with Chapter 5 focusing on the regulation of social media platforms and platform architecture, with changes in EU perceptions regarding the reliability of these platforms and the values of their owners. It examines the shift from economically motivated self-regulatory regimes in these sectors based in logics of efficiency to a digital sovereignty-motivated move to a logic of security in regulation. It identifies the explicit linkage between economic and security concerns, particularly as it relates to disinformation and political advertising, with the promotion of co-regulatory regimes with significant levels of oversight provided by the Commission. Chapter 6 considers the desire to reduce critical dependencies on third-country-based data servers and computing capabilities. Starting with an overview of the EU's historic approach to data, and then personal data, it explores the Brussels Effect as a motivator for further action on exporting regulatory norms concerning the protection of personal data and non-personal data, coupled with concerns over lack of competitiveness in data-derived commercial activity, particularly in the field of AI. Concerns over competitiveness impacting Europe's security and the risks posed by unauthorised access to industrial or sensitive data from the governments in third countries, the Commission desires increased regulatory control. This is facilitated by industrial policy aimed at both promoting European data server infrastructure and encouraging switching to those Common European Data Spaces as a means of building up a European data economy, while placing strict limitations on the export of non-personal data outside of Europe's borders. The Commission combines this with an attempt to utilise the Brussels Effect to ensure that European standards concerning the safe use of AI technologies become global standards shaped by the EU and its values.

Part III of the book is 'The Future of the Geopolitical Union', which comprises Chapter 7 and the conclusion to the book. Chapter 7 considers the developments that have taken place since the beginning of the von der Leyen II Commission, identifying how there has not only been continuity in the EU's approach to technology control and its links to digital sovereignty but also an *expansion* and *reinforcement* of the approach. This is both structural, in terms of a significantly reorganised Commission, with a new Commission Vice President for Tech Sovereignty, Security and Democracy, and practical, in terms of the reinforced discourse of sovereignty and strategic autonomy. The Commission faces significantly more uncertain and chaotic geopolitics as a result of the re-election of Donald Trump as US President and his aggressive and unpredictable actions in his foreign policy; the increased blurring of state and private power as Big Tech players have moved closer to the Presidency and appear to have formed parts of his Administration; as well as heightened trade tensions with China over electric vehicles. As a result, the linkage of security and economy has become even more explicit for the von der Leyen II Commission, with the Competitiveness Compass[61] taking an approach that appears to be a more assertive form of regulatory mercantilism, in which the element of defence is specifically incorporated into the EU's rationale for action, with an expansion of technology controls including the development of an explicit push for defence technology industrial policy, the increased control over external dependencies and supply chains through its Preparedness Strategy, and an AI policy for Europe that includes significant investments for AI gigafactories.

The book concludes by bringing the different themes of this work together, considering the potential futures for the EU as the Geopolitical Union, reflecting upon how regulatory mercantilism could be a useful framework for analysis of policies beyond technology and beyond the EU, and suggesting potential future avenues for research based on these reflections.

---

[61] European Commission, 'A Competitiveness Compass for the EU' (2025) COM(2025) 30.

PART I

Regulatory Mercantilism and the Geopolitics of Technology Control

1

Regulatory Mercantilism as a Means of Understanding the Actions of the Geopolitical Union

What was a realistic counterfactual for an individual European nation state choosing to unilaterally embrace peaceful free trade? In the absence of anything resembling an effective collective security mechanism [...] military defeat and exclusion from foreign markets seems to us as plausible an answer as any.[1]

INTRODUCTION

To better understand the shift *to* regulatory mercantilism in the European Commission's policies and actions concerning the control of technology in the context of its ambitions as the representative of the Geopolitical Union, it is important to also understand what the shift is *from*. In other words, in an account of regulatory dynamics, considering the current approach and how it is changing is essential for demonstrating how regulatory mercantilism represents a change in governance approach in key sectors. Central to this exploration is the concept of the regulatory state, popularised in European studies through the work of the late Giandomenico Majone, to whom this book owes a considerable intellectual debt. The regulatory state (as will be discussed shortly) was a framework for understanding the move from the state as a planner and welfare provider to a state as a regulator and the shift from govern*ment* to govern*ance*. As this book will argue, regulatory mercantilism does not entail a shift away from the regulatory state but a transformation within it. Using the regulatory capitalism approach developed by authors such as Levi-Faur, Jordana, and Braithwaite, this chapter explores this approach to governance based on the state's cooperation in networks with regulatory agencies and private sector operators. In regulatory capitalism, the state takes a role in 'steering' the direction of regulation, while the private sector and agencies 'row', or in some limited circumstances, share the 'steering' role with privileged private sector actors. In regulatory mercantilism, however,

---

[1] Ronald Findlay and Kevin O'Rourke, *Power and Plenty: Trade, War, and the World Economy in the Second Millennium* (Princeton University Press 2009) 229.

we see a shift back to one in which the state takes a much more active 'steering' position, with regulation increasingly reliant on legislatively binding provisions, rather than more informal or voluntary mechanisms. In this sense, we can consider regulatory mercantilism as a move from the regulatory (capitalist) state to a more regulatory (mercantilist) state.

This chapter is structured as follows. The first substantive section discusses the basic approach of mercantilism and how it served as a means of bringing together the domains of 'economy' and 'security' as mutually constitutive and reinforcing in its approach to power and sovereignty. It then expands upon the notion of the regulatory state and its underlying rationale, demonstrating the ideas of efficiency and depoliticisation that are hallmarks of the approach to governance in its more 'liberal capitalist' form. It is then followed by a section on the concept of regulatory capitalism, which can be considered a way of understanding the actions and processes undertaken by the state and private actors in the regulatory state, providing a framework for considering regulatory mercantilism's core characteristics and how they differ from those of regulatory capitalism. The following three sections, respectively, consider the operative conditions, rationale, and means of regulatory mercantilism, and how they diverge from those of regulatory capitalism. In terms of conditions, the first substantive section will discuss the political context of regulatory capitalism's origins, with relative levels of stability and confidence on the part of western liberal democracies and trust in international organisations, with regulatory mercantilism becoming more prominent as a governance form in times of global political instability, where levels of trust in other states and private sector actors are decreased and the sense of state vulnerability is increased. Moving to rationale in the subsequent section, the chapter will discuss changes from decentralisation and delegation based on an understanding of efficiency and private sector expertise to recentralisation and control through bringing economy and security together and reasserting the sovereignty of the state. In regulatory capitalism, sovereignty is not a central concern or discursive tool, but in regulatory mercantilism, sovereignty is afforded considerable weight, with a move away from dealing with all private sector actors as equivalent, to being more selective in cooperation dependent upon geographical location. In terms of means, regulatory capitalism focuses on globalisation and trans-nationalisation as the basis for a diffused regulatory environment based on notions of private sector value neutrality and the promotion of self-regulation. In comparison, regulatory mercantilism instead seeks to assert 'state'-based laws that are used to provide oversight for private actors in forms of co-regulation. Internally, these laws promote state control and the encouragement of industrial policy, while externally, these laws are then exported as 'global' norms at the international level as a means of attempting a positive balance of 'regulatory trade'. Once these characteristics are fully identified, the concluding section of this chapter will expand upon how they will be used to consider the policies and actions of the Commission as a technology regulator.

A BRIEF INTRODUCTION TO MERCANTILISM AS A SYSTEM OF CONTROL

'Power' and 'plenty' are central to mercantilism as a system of control. Viner, writing shortly after the end of the Second World War, considered that not only were the consolidation of power and the securing of plenty key objectives of seventeenth- and eighteenth-century policy, they were harmonious objectives, insofar as each reinforced and promoted the other.[2] The interdependence of the goals of mercantilism can be summarised with the quote attributed to Hobbes by Viner that 'wealth is power, and power is wealth'.[3] Power was important, both to guarantee the internal stability of the state and to provide for its external security, with security providing for wealth and prosperity, and, in turn, wealth essential for guaranteeing security. Davenant, a seventeenth-century economist and politician, asked 'can a nation be safe without strength? And is power to be secured but by riches? And can a country become rich any way, but by the help of well-managed and extended traffick?'[4]. Similarly, List reflects that for states, 'the more advanced their economy, the more civilized and powerful will be the nation, the more rapidly will its civilization and power increase, and the more will its economical culture be developed'.[5] For this reason, Viner maintains that policies pursued by European nations at this time were governed 'by joint and harmonised considerations of power and economics'.[6] Neither power nor plenty alone was the sole concern of the mercantilists, but instead it was their interplay that helped to secure and guarantee the success of the nation that is central to their thinking. In essence, mercantilism appears to understand power in realist terms. If, as Morgenthau argued, states were the sole guarantors of the well-being of their citizens and excessive reliance upon others was to the detriment of their own security,[7] then this conceptualisation of power appears to be a good fit for mercantilism. Mercantilist states see themselves as being in competition with other states for securing wealth and power, with power ultimately being about control and the ability to exert it,[8] both over territory and over others.[9] Dependency rendered a state vulnerable; therefore, there was a need to ensure its independence, and sovereignty, from other nations.

During the seventeenth and eighteenth centuries, monarchs across Europe were engaged in war, and imperial and colonial expansion as means to consolidate and

---

[2] Jacob Viner, 'Power versus Plenty as Objectives of Foreign Policy in the Seventeenth and Eighteenth Centuries' (1948) 1 *World Politics* 1, 15.
[3] Ibid.
[4] Charles D'Avenant, 'An Essay on the East-India Trade' (*Made Accessible by the Yale Law School Avalon Project*, 1697) <https://avalon.law.yale.edu/17th_century/eastindi.asp> accessed 2 May 2023.
[5] Friedrich List, *The National System of Political Economy* (GA Matile tr, J. B. Lippincott 1856) 72.
[6] Viner (n1) 29.
[7] Hans J Morgenthau, *Politics among Nations: The Struggle for Power and Peace* (Alfred A. Knopf 1948).
[8] Ibid 13.
[9] Ibid.

secure their own states.¹⁰ War and trade became intermingled as forms of power, with trade serving to provide the bullion necessary for maintaining standing armies, and those standing armies being used to expand the trade areas under the control of that monarch. Trade in this understanding was zero-sum – more trade for one state meant less trade for another, and therefore the risk for a state was that by failing to expand, others may move to fill that space, resulting in them becoming bigger, wealthier, and therefore more powerful states. If smaller nations could be attacked by bigger nations, both in terms of power and plenty, to the extent that their commerce withers away, 'trade necessitated power – but at the same time power was a function of plenty and trade'.¹¹ Schmoller gave the example of the conflicts between 'Great Powers', such as England and the Netherlands, in which colonial expansion and the securing of trade routes in order to bring economic benefit was pursued through violent and military means and, in those means, was able to both gain wealth and secure it.¹² Power, in other words, was exercised within a combative and competitive system, rather than a cooperative one.¹³ While condemning their excesses, and the 'injustice and error mingled in with it',¹⁴ Schmoller nevertheless saw these expansions and conflicts as having secured the stability of those nations through the use of colonial resources to build their own domestic industries, including arms, to exercise power and defend against foreign adversaries. Colonial expansion was justified by those emerging nation-states as 'what was brutal and unjust should be lost to sight in each nation in the glow of national and economic success'.¹⁵ Ultimately, power within the mercantilist approach incorporates elements of Waltz's defensive realism,¹⁶ seeing states as willing to maintain the status quo if the state's own security can be protected,¹⁷ but expansionist and aggressive where that security appears to be threatened.¹⁸ This shall be expanded upon in the section of this chapter on the contexts in which mercantilist thinking were influential.

While central to mercantilist understandings, and framed as 'objectives', this book argues that 'power' and 'plenty' were means, rather than ends. Power and plenty were means intended to serve a purpose, namely, the drawing together of the economy and security in the name of sovereignty and state building. This will be

---

[10] See Charles Tilly, *Coercion, Capital, and European States, A.D. 990–1990* (Wiley-Blackwell 1993).
[11] Lars Magnusson, *The Political Economy of Mercantilism* (Routledge 2018) 59.
[12] Gustav Schmoller, *The Mercantile System and Its Historical Significance* (William James Ashley tr, MacMillan 1897) 69–71.
[13] On this, see Sophus A Reinert, 'Rivalry: Greatness in Early Modern Political Economy' in Philip J Stern and Carl Wennerlind (eds), *Mercantilism Reimagined: Political Economy in Early Modern Britain and Its Empire* (Oxford University Press 2013).
[14] Schmoller (n11) 72.
[15] Ibid 73.
[16] Kenneth N Waltz, *Theory of International Politics* (Longman Higher Education 1979).
[17] Fred Chernoff, *Theory and Metatheory in International Relations: Concepts and Contending Accounts* (Palgrave Macmillan 2007) 51.
[18] Hedley Bull, *The Anarchical Society: A Study of Order in World Politics* (3rd ed., Palgrave Macmillan 2002) 16–19.

explored further by considering in turn the conditions in which mercantilist policies were pursued, the objectives that mercantilism sought to achieve, and then how they were to be achieved, in comparison with regulatory capitalism and then regulatory mercantilism. To perform this analysis, however, it is first necessary to consider the rise of the regulatory state and its approach to regulation.

THE RISE OF THE REGULATORY STATE

Scholars of public policy since the 1990s have written about the rise of the 'regulatory state', coined by Majone.[19] The regulatory state concept was formulated as a means of assessing changes in the state taking place from the 1980s onwards, in which the role of the state moved 'from a producer of goods and services to that of an umpire whose function is to ensure that economic actors play by the agreed rules of the game'.[20] This occurred as a shift in the understanding of the role of the state in response to changing socio-economic conditions; whereas the post-Second World War state was concerned with reconstruction, redistribution, and macroeconomic stabilisation after the ruination of the 1930s and 1940s,[21] by the late 1970s, the significant shocks to the global economic system resulting from the collapse of Bretton Woods and the subsequent (but not *directly* related) oil crisis meant that the *dirigiste* welfare-providing state[22] was regarded as unable to address the increased rates of unemployment and inflation, bringing more Keynesian approaches to economic policy into disrepute.[23] Of particular interest to the arguments of this book is a point made almost as an aside by Majone regarding the government-controlled companies and monopolies under public ownership that significantly predated the period of increased privatisation and sectoral deregulation. On the purpose of public ownership, Majone stated that it 'was not simply to regulate prices, conditions of entry and quality of service, but also to pursue many other goals including economic development, technical innovation, employment, regional income redistribution, and national security'.[24] We shall see as this chapter, and indeed this book, expands upon its central thesis, these ideas are reappearing in certain sectors

---

[19] Giandomenico Majone, 'The Rise of the Regulatory State in Europe' (1994) 17 *West European Politics* 77.
[20] Ibid 80.
[21] Giandomenico Majone, 'From the Positive to the Regulatory State: Causes and Consequences of Changes in the Mode of Governance' (1997) 17 *Journal of Public Policy* 139, 139–141.
[22] See, for example, Vivien A Schmidt, 'Does Discourse Matter in the Politics of Welfare State Adjustment?' (2002) 35 *Comparative Political Studies* 168.
[23] Mark Blyth, *Austerity: The History of a Dangerous Idea* (Oxford University Press 2013) 40; see also Karen Yeung, 'The Regulatory State' in Robert Baldwin, Martin Cave and Martin Lodge (eds), *The Oxford Handbook of Regulation* (Oxford University Press 2010); Benjamin Farrand and Marco Rizzi, 'There Is No (Legal) Alternative: Codifying Economic Ideology into Law' in Eva Nanopoulos and Fotis Vergis (eds), *The Crisis Behind the Eurocrisis* (Cambridge University Press 2019).
[24] Majone (n18) 79.

deemed important to states, and shall be returned to frequently. At this juncture, however, the key theme to bear in mind is the move to *efficiency* as a central rationale of regulation.

Through the adoption of more liberal economic policies under leaders such as Thatcher in the UK and Reagan in the US, the idea of a smaller, leaner state was promoted,[25] under an understanding that a move to regulation as the mode of governance, and privatising industries and utilities and placing them under the control of independent regulatory agencies, would improve the efficiency of the economy.[26] Globalisation has been argued to have been a driver for the development of the regulatory state,[27] with increased connectedness, interdependence, and diffusion of sectoral expertise resulting in a world in which individual states lacked the capabilities or capacities to function as a *dirigiste* actor. In other words, the shift from *government* to *governance* was seen as being as much a technical necessity as a political priority,[28] placing those deemed best placed to (and indeed, understand how to) regulate and coordinate action in a particular sector in a position of authority to do so,[29] as well as endeavouring to depoliticise regulation more broadly through a more technocratic approach to sectoral control.[30] While the desirability of these changes related to issues of state distancing from decision-making and depoliticisation of what can be inherently and often intensely political fields has been subject to debate,[31] the existence of these changing dynamics and relations of regulation

---

[25] Covered in works such as Philip Mirowski and Dieter Plehwe (eds), *The Road from Mont Pèlerin the Making of the Neoliberal Thought Collective* (Harvard University Press 2009); Tony Judt, *Postwar: A History of Europe Since 1945* (Vintage 2010); Vivien A Schmidt and Mark Thatcher, 'Theorizing Ideational Continuity: The Resilience of Neo-Liberal Ideas in Europe' in Vivien A Schmidt and Mark Thatcher (eds), *Resilient Liberalism in Europe's Political Economy* (Cambridge University Press 2013) to name but a few.

[26] Majone (n18) 79.

[27] For a good overview, see Nicolas Jabko, 'The Political Foundations of the European Regulatory State' in Jacint Jordana and David Levi-Faur (eds), *The Politics of Regulation: Institutions and Regulatory Reforms for the Age of Governance* (Edward Elgar Publishing 2004).

[28] Majone (n20); see also David Levi-Faur, 'From "Big Government" to "Big Governance"?' in David Levi-Faur (ed), *The Oxford Handbook of Governance* (Oxford University Press 2014); Bob Jessop, 'State Theory' in Christopher Ansell and Jacob Torfing (eds), *Handbook on Theories of Governance* (2nd ed., Edward Elgar Publishing 2022).

[29] See, for example, Claudio M Radaelli, 'The Public Policy of the European Union: Whither Politics of Expertise?' (1999) 6 *Journal of European Public Policy* 757; Arndt Wonka, 'Technocratic and Independent? The Appointment of European Commissioners and Its Policy Implications' (2007) 14 *Journal of European Public Policy* 169.

[30] Miguel Angel Centeno, 'The New Leviathan: The Dynamics and Limits of Technocracy' (1993) 22 *Theory and Society* 307; Erik Bryld, 'The Technocratic Discourse: Technical Means to Political Problems' (2000) 10 *Development in Practice* 700; Nicole Scicluna and Stefan Auer, 'From the Rule of Law to the Rule of Rules: Technocracy and the Crisis of EU Governance' (2019) 42 *West European Politics* 1420.

[31] Colin Scott, 'Accountability in the Regulatory State' (2000) 27 *Journal of Law and Society* 38; Michael Moran, 'Understanding the Regulatory State' (2002) 32 *British Journal of Political Science* 391; Burkard Eberlein and Edgar Grande, 'Beyond Delegation: Transnational Regulatory Regimes and the EU

are largely uncontested.[32] One way of theorising and analysing these dynamics is through the use of the regulatory capitalism framework, which helps to place these ideas and their application in context – this shall begin in the next section of this chapter, before then being considered in the context of regulatory mercantilism and how it once again shifts these dynamics in the subsequent sections.

REGULATORY CAPITALISM: RETHINKING NEOLIBERALISM, DEREGULATION, AND REREGULATION

In the context of the twenty-first-century regulatory state, one way of understanding the approach to governance in sectors predominantly characterised by their economic role is through using the regulatory capitalism framework. Regulatory capitalism in essence considers the division of labour between the public and private sectors in regulating, distributing, and providing public services.[33] Indeed, Braithwaite argued in 2005 that given these dynamics, it made less sense to talk of the regulatory state at all, rather than the regulatory capitalism model.[34] In reaching this conclusion, Braithwaite relied upon the work of Levi-Faur, who argued that given this division of labour between public authorities and private sector service providers, 'regulation, though not necessarily in the old-fashioned form of command and control and not directly exercised by the state, seems to be the wave of the future, and the current wave of regulatory reforms constitutes a new chapter in the history of regulation'.[35] Regulatory capitalism therefore appears to represent a certain 'stepping-back' of the state, with Parker and Nielsen stating that it possesses two distinct characteristics – the first is that it 'includes the responsibilization of business to self-regulate to achieve policy goals and values, not just financial profits, and [the second is] the decentering of regulation away from the state to plural networks of regulation'.[36]

Regulatory State' (2005) 12 *Journal of European Public Policy* 89; and most recently in the context of the EU as a regulatory state, Vivien A Schmidt, *Europe's Crisis of Legitimacy: Governing by Rules and Ruling by Numbers in the Eurozone* (Oxford University Press 2020).

[32] Jonathan S Davies, *Challenging Governance Theory: From Networks to Hegemony* (1st ed., Policy Press 2011). Davies challenges governance theory and regulatory networks as a means of governing; but does not challenge that there has been a move to these forms of governance since the 1980s.

[33] John Braithwaite, 'Neoliberalism or Regulatory Capitalism' (2005) Regnet Occasional Paper 5 <http://papers.ssrn.com/abstract=875789> accessed 22 February 2016; David Levi-Faur, 'The Rise of Regulatory Capitalism: The Global Diffusion of a New Order' (2005) 598 *The ANNALS of the American Academy of Political and Social Science* 12.

[34] John Braithwaite, *Regulatory Capitalism: How It Works, Ideas for Making It Work Better* (Edward Elgar Publishing 2008) 1 – it is worth stating, however, that I do not necessarily see the two concepts as contradictory, but rather explanatory of different aspects of regulation.

[35] Levi-Faur (n32) 13.

[36] Christine Parker and Vibeke Nielsen, 'The Challenge of Empirical Research on Business Compliance in Regulatory Capitalism' (2009) 5 *Annual Review of Law and Social Science* 45, 48.

As will be discussed shortly, this self-regulatory aspect has been prominent in sectors in which high levels of technical or organisational expertise are customary.[37] With the coming of the 'information society',[38] economic value has increasingly been attached to the underlying knowledge (or 'know-how') and data that informs industrial processes, rather than the outputs themselves.[39] Raco provides the example of the provision of services in the context of the London Olympic Games and the requirement for adherence to strict and complex regulatory and contractual requirements, as the basis for private managerialism by large consultancy firms such as New World Consulting and PriceWaterhouseCoopers.[40] Similarly, the provision of critical information infrastructure protection, entailing the provision of effective cybersecurity to protect services such as banking, energy, and communications,[41] is largely dependent on the expertise of actors within those sectors on the basis of the perceived efficiency gains, as well as the fact that they own and operate the infrastructure.[42] These ownership structures and the diffusion of expertise across different actors in the sector result in regulatory networks being prevalent in regulatory capitalism.[43] Regulation becomes decentered,[44] with relations between the state and private sector forms becoming less hierarchical, and collaborative networks becoming the standard in these areas of technical complexity.[45] This could include the coordination of regulatory efforts in denationalised

---

[37] See, for example, Ronen Shamir, 'The Age of Responsibilization: On Market-Embedded Morality' (2008) 37 *Economy and Society* 1; Benjamin Farrand, 'Regulatory Capitalism, Decentred Enforcement and Its Legal Consequences for Digital Expression: The Use of Copyright Law to Restrict Freedom of Speech Online' (2013) 10 *Journal of Information Technology and Politics* 404.

[38] Manuel Castells, *The Rise of the Network Society: Economy, Society, and Culture* (Blackwell 1996); Frank Webster, *Theories of the Information Society* (4th ed., Routledge 2014).

[39] Hence the importance of intellectual property in advanced industrial economies and the lengths taken to ensure its effective protection at the international level. This is expanded upon in greater detail in Peter Drahos and John Braithwaite, *Information Feudalism: Who Owns the Knowledge Economy?* (Earthscan 2002); Robert P Merges, *Justifying Intellectual Property* (Harvard University Press 2011); Benjamin Farrand, *Networks of Power in Digital Copyright Law and Policy: Political Salience, Expertise and the Legislative Process* (Routledge 2014). However, this is not the main focus of this work, and so it shall not be explored further here.

[40] Mike Raco, 'Delivering Flagship Projects in an Era of Regulatory Capitalism: State-led Privatization and the London Olympics 2012' (2014) 38 *International Journal of Urban and Regional Research* 176.

[41] An issue that will be returned to in Chapters 2 and 4.

[42] Helena Carrapico and Benjamin Farrand, '"Dialogue, Partnership and Empowerment for Network and Information Security": The Changing Role of the Private Sector from Objects of Regulation to Regulation Shapers' (2017) 67 *Crime, Law and Social Change* 245.

[43] Fabrizio Gilard, and Jacint Jordana, 'Regulation in the Age of Globalization: The Diffusion of Regulatory Agencies across Europe and Latin America: Global Movements in Public Policy Ideas' in Graeme A Hodge (ed), *Privatization and Market Development* (Edward Elgar Publishing 2006).

[44] For an excellent and exhaustive explanation of this concept, see Julia Black, 'Decentring Regulation: Understanding the Role of Regulation and Self Regulation in a "Post-Regulatory" World' (2001) 54 *Current Legal Problems* 103.

[45] Walter W Powell, 'Neither Market nor Hierarchy: Network Forms of Organisation' in Mary Godwyn and Jody Hoffer Gittell (eds), *Sociology of Organizations: Structures and Relationships* (SAGE Publications 2011).

telecommunications networks,[46] or the establishment of European agencies such as the European Cybersecurity Agency (or ENISA, as it is also known) working with national authorities and private sector security experts to ensure effective resilience of critical information infrastructures in the EU.[47] Within these systems of networked governance, 'industry, civil society, and NGO associations are explicitly taking on regulatory roles that go beyond compliance with the law or that fill the gaps in legal regulation'.[48] This in essence reflects the approach of the regulatory state, and the idea of the move from government to governance, in a form where society is no longer exclusively controlled by central units but is distributed among a broader set of participants.[49]

Braithwaite has argued that regulatory capitalism emerged in essence as a response to writings about neoliberalism.[50] For, as Levi-Faur and Jordana argued in their foundational piece on the subject, 'neoliberalism preaches deregulation but paradoxically seems to expand and extend regulation. If we were to judge neoliberalism by the degree of "deregulation" it attained, it would be a failure. If we were to judge it by the degree of "regulation" it promoted, it would be, on its own term, a fiasco'.[51] Writers such as Harvey, it was argued, emphasised that within a neoliberal regulatory paradigm, 'sectors formerly run or regulated by the state must be turned over to the private sphere and be deregulated'.[52] The extent of this apparent contradiction can be somewhat overstated; Cahill has argued for the understanding of 'actually existing neoliberalism', which corresponds closely with neoliberal theory while recognising that the neoliberal ideal of the small state has not been eventuated.[53] Similarly, Harvey acknowledged that state action is required in order to achieve neoliberal aims, with state interventions and government by experts despite the positioning of the state as non-interventionist.[54] However, even one of the so-called founding thinkers of neoliberalism argued that Friedman supported the idea of market regulation rather than complete laissez-faire anarchy,[55] particularly in

---

[46] David Levi-Faur, 'Regulatory Capitalism: The Dynamics of Change beyond Telecoms and Electricity' (2006) 19 *Governance* 497.
[47] Carrapico and Farrand (n41); the European Cybersecurity Agency will be returned to in Chapters 2 and 4.
[48] Parker and Nielsen (n35) 49.
[49] See Patrick Kenis and Volker Schneider, 'Policy Networks and Policy Analysis: Scrutinizing a New Analytical Toolbox' in Bernd Marin and Renate Mayntz (eds), *Policy Networks: Empirical Evidence and Theoretical Considerations* (Campus 1991).
[50] Braithwaite (n33) 4.
[51] David Levi-Faur and Jacint Jordana, 'The Making of a New Regulatory Order' (2005) 598 *The ANNALS of the American Academy of Political and Social Science* 6, 7.
[52] David Harvey, *A Brief History of Neoliberalism* (OUP Oxford 2007) 65.
[53] Damien Cahill, *The End of Laissez-Faire?: On the Durability of Embedded Neoliberalism* (Edward Elgar Publishing 2015) 306–307.
[54] Harvey (n51) 69.
[55] Milton Friedman, *Capitalism and Freedom* (University of Chicago Press 1962); see also Braithwaite (n33) 28; Philip Mirowski, *Never Let a Serious Crisis Go to Waste: How Neoliberalism Survived the Financial Meltdown* (Verso Books 2014); for a comprehensive study of the development of neoliberal ideas that goes beyond what this book seeks to cover, see Mirowski and Plehwe (n24).

areas such as environmental protection.[56] Regardless, regulatory capitalism holds that there has been comparatively little deregulation when compared to the level of regulation and re-regulation in the economy and society, as will be explored further. In some respects, regulatory capitalism appears to be a better fit with ordoliberalism, with its emphasis on the state as setting the conditions and limits upon market activity through regulations.[57]

This brief overview of the central themes of regulatory capitalism has been useful, as it will serve to inform the discussion of regulatory mercantilism in the coming sections of this chapter. Each section will discuss a core aspect of regulatory capitalism, from its objectives through to its approach and finally its context, to then demonstrate how regulatory mercantilism as an approach to governance may be distinguished from the regulatory capitalism model. In particular, the role of the state (broadly conceived) as a regulatory actor will be considered, as well as its relationship with the private sector.

THE CONDITIONS FOR REGULATORY MERCANTILISM: CRISIS AND VULNERABILITY

Why would we see a move away from regulatory capitalism to a system of governance that could be typified as regulatory mercantilism? Geopolitical tension, instability, and economic shock were prominent features of European life in the late seventeenth and early eighteenth centuries, to the extent that states saw their survival as being dependent upon securing themselves against neighbouring states, laying claim to seemingly scarce resources as a means of empowering themselves while disempowering potential enemies. Mercantilism was in essence a philosophy of competition in a competitive world – as Findlay and O'Rourke stated, unilateral declarations of free trade were as likely to end in military defeat and exclusion from markets as they were in reciprocity.[58] In this section of the chapter, the conditions in which mercantilism arose as a way of approaching state-market relations and the governance of trade will be explored, before then distinguishing it from the

---

[56] Milton Friedman and Rose Friedman, *Free to Choose: A Personal Statement* (Thomson Learning 1990).

[57] See Franz Böhm, Walter Eucken and Hans Grossmann-Doerth, 'The Ordo Manifesto of 1936' in Alan Peacock and Hans Willgerodt (eds), *Germany's Social Market Economy: Origins and Evolution* (Palgrave Macmillan 1989) for an overview of the central ideas of ordoliberalism, which will be expanded upon in more detail in Chapter 2; as well as Franz Böhm, 'Rule of Law in a Market Economy' in Alan Peacock and Hans Willgerodt (eds), *Germany's Social Market Economy: Origins and Evolution* (Palgrave Macmillan UK 1989); Walter Eucken, 'What Kind of Economic and Social System?' in Alan Peacock and Hans Willgerodt (eds), *Germany's Social Market Economy: Origins and Evolution* (Palgrave Macmillan UK 1989); Wilhelm Röpke, *Economics of the Free Society* (Henry Regnery Company 1963) for further writings of ordoliberal thinkers.

[58] Ronald Findlay and Kevin O'Rourke, *Power and Plenty: Trade, War, and the World Economy in the Second Millennium* (Princeton University Press 2009) 229.

conditions of regulatory capitalism, concluding with a discussion of the contexts in which regulatory mercantilism approaches to regulation are likely to be pursued.

Mercantilism: The Place of the State in Turbulent Times

The conditions in which mercantilist policies were pursued in Europe were conditions of geopolitical instability and tension between states. Magnusson maintains that the long-term structural changes, sudden shocks, and rising international competition of the early seventeenth century were essential factors in the rise of mercantilist policies in Europe.[59] Constant war, whether motivated by territorial expansion, religious conflict, or consolidation of state power, served to influence economic thought,[60] to the extent that internal consolidation and protectionism, combined with aggressive expansion overseas in order to secure wealth for the defence of the realm, became a key driver of state policies. England at the beginning of the seventeenth century was suffering from severe economic shocks as a result of increased competition in the wool markets and the trade depression of 1621–1623.[61] Similarly, conflicts over fishing between England and the United Provinces in the North Sea led to increasingly belligerent behaviours and claims to sovereignty that spilt into open warfare.[62] Mun wrote on this topic that if England truly wished to rival what is now the Netherlands, then they should understand the importance of fishing for their overall security. Fishing was the 'cheifest trade and principal Gold Mines of the United Provinces [… and] if this foundation perish, the whole building of their wealth and strength both by Sea and Land must fall'.[63]

As Schmoller wrote, 'in such a time of harsh international and economic struggles, he who did not put himself on the defence would have been remorselessly crushed to pieces'.[64] In the seventeenth century, England was in a near-permanent state of war with the Netherlands, to the extent that the Navigation Act of 1651 (which will be discussed further later in this chapter) was largely motivated by fears of competition from Dutch shipping and a desire to surpass them in naval supremacy.[65] As a result of this geopolitical positioning, mercantilist tracts originating in England focused on the threat posed by the Netherlands during the seventeenth century and France in the eighteenth century, reflecting the specific security concerns of England at those

---

[59] Magnusson (n10) 136.
[60] Tilly (n9).
[61] William Cunningham, *The Growth of English Industry and Commerce in Modern Times: The Mercantile Era* (5th ed., Cambridge University Press 1910) 233.
[62] Gijs Rommelse, *The Second Anglo-Dutch War (1665–1667): Raison D'état, Mercantilism and Maritime Strife* (Uitgeverij Verloren 2006).
[63] Thomas Mun, *Englands Treasure by Forraign Trade, or The Ballance of Our Forraign Trade Is the Rule of Our Treasure* (JG for Thomas Clark 1664) 102–103.
[64] Schmoller (n11) 73.
[65] Cunningham (n60) 210; Charles Wilson, *Mercantilism* (Historical Association/Routledge 1958) 13–14.

points in time.[66] In the eighteenth century, mercantilist writings in Great Britain justified their position through reference to the threats posed by the French,[67] whereas French mercantilism was in part motivated by concerns over the rising power of the British.[68] In this respect, mercantilism is inherently linked to geopolitics and economic positioning vis-à-vis other states,[69] in the context of increasing international and imperial violence, threats of invasion, and a general sense of insecurity on the part of fledgling states.[70] Mercantilism was a response to political, strategic, and military concerns in which perceptions of political, economic, or politico-economic deterioration threatened the well-being of the state and its population.[71]

Schumpeter noted in his discussion of mercantilism that the political conditions of Europe at the time made mercantilist policies a natural equilibrium.[72] In times of significant uncertainty, states perceived themselves and their citizens as vulnerable, both to potential war or invasion and to blockades of goods such as foodstuffs.[73] If resources were finite, and trade a zero-sum game, then mercantilist policies aimed at securing the balance of trade, the consolidation of power and wealth, and the security of the realm then became logical responses to that uncertainty. Moving away from these policies to ones based in a liberal conception of free trade as currently understood would therefore appear to be irrational or illogical. It is perhaps telling that mercantilism in Great Britain began to be supplanted with Adam Smithesque classic liberalism and free trade as currently understood in the eighteenth and nineteenth centuries when the British Empire was in ascendance with supremacy in trade and naval military strength,[74] having resoundingly resulted in changes in attitudes towards the balance of trade and the inherent insecurity and vulnerability of the state.[75] Schmoller felt that Great Britain was in a position to be able to

---

[66] Daniel W Drezner, 'Mercantilist and Realist Perspectives on the Global Political Economy' in Robert Denemark (ed), *Oxford Research Encyclopedia of International Studies* (2010); Jacob Viner, *Studies in the Theory of International Trade* (Routledge Library Editions, Routledge 2018).

[67] See generally Drezner (n65).

[68] Jacques Fontanel, Jean-Paul Hebert and Ivan Samson, 'The Birth of the Political Economy or the Economy in the Heart of Politics: Mercantilism' (2008) 19 *Defence and Peace Economics* 331.

[69] Sanjaya Baru, 'Geo-Economics and Strategy' (2012) 54 *Survival* 47; Patrick O'Brien, 'Mercantilism and Imperialism in the Rise and Decline of the Dutch and British Economies 1585–1815' (2000) 148 *De Economist* 469; William R Allen, 'Mercantilism' in John Eatwell, Murray Milgate and Peter Newman (eds), *The World of Economics* (Palgrave Macmillan UK 1991).

[70] Patrick K O'Brien, *The Formation of a Mercantilist State and the Economic Growth of the United Kingdom 1453–1815* (World Institute for Development Economics Research 2006) 2006/75 2.

[71] RJ Barry Jones, 'Economic Realism' in RJ Barry Jones (ed), *The Worlds of Political Economy: Alternative Approaches to the Study of Contemporary Political Economy* (Pinter Publishers Ltd 1988) 145.

[72] Joseph A Schumpeter, *History of Economic Analysis* (Routledge 1997) 339.

[73] Eli F Heckscher, *Mercantilism*, vol II (Mendel Shapiro tr, George Allen & Unwin Ltd 1935) 101–102.

[74] For an excellent overview, see A González Enciso, *War, Power and the Economy: Mercantilism and State Formation in 18th-Century Europe* (Taylor & Francis 2016).

[75] On the changing ideas regarding trade, see Jonathan Barth, 'Reconstructing Mercantilism: Consensus and Conflict in British Imperial Economy in the Seventeenth and Eighteenth Centuries' (2016) 73 *The William and Mary Quarterly* 257.

abandon mercantilist policies on this basis and 'to think and act in the spirit of free trade'[76] due to the belief that its territory was consolidated, its institutions embedded, and its trade supremacy recognised.[77] States would pursue mercantilist policies when their economies and levels of industrialisation could not compete with those of the European powers, and as such felt vulnerable in the international system, until such time as development reached a certain level and then states may actively pursue liberalisation and open trade.[78] Mercantilism is therefore a philosophy that has more likelihood of being pursued in times in which a state is feeling vulnerable.

Regulatory Capitalism: Trust and Confidence in the Liberal Economic Order

In regulatory capitalism, vulnerability and threat do not feature prominently. In the late 1990s and early 2000s, with the end of the Cold War and the seeming 'victory' of capitalist liberal democracy,[79] liberal internationalism was arguably at its zenith. Writing in 2009, Hobson argues that 'underpinning liberal democracy's ideational strength has been a geopolitical environment favouring a core group of industrially advanced, established liberal democracies, with the United States as the self-appointed vanguard of this global democratic movement'.[80] The perception was of the existence of a unipolar world, with advanced economies rallying to that pole in an environment of healthy, mediated competition underscored by international cooperation.[81] At the same time, the world had seen the establishment of international organisations such as the World Trade Organization, and while at the level of individuals there may have been some resistance against globalisation,[82] at the

---

[76] Schmoller (n111) 61.
[77] Steve Pincus, 'Rethinking Mercantilism: Political Economy, the British Empire, and the Atlantic World in the Seventeenth and Eighteenth Centuries' (2012) 69 *The William and Mary Quarterly* 3, 4–6.
[78] Quddus Z Snyder, 'Integrating Rising Powers: Liberal Systemic Theory and the Mechanism of Competition' (2013) 39 *Review of International Studies* 209.
[79] Ideationally attributed to Francis Fukuyama, *The End of History and the Last Man: Francis Fukuyama* (Penguin 2012) originally published in 1992; and critiqued in Antonio Y Vázquez-Arroyo, 'Liberal Democracy and Neoliberalism: A Critical Juxtaposition' (2008) 30 *New Political Science* 127; Mariana Mazzucato, *The Entrepreneurial State: Debunking Public vs. Private Sector Myths* (Penguin 2018).
[80] Christopher Hobson, 'The Limits of Liberal-Democracy Promotion' (2009) 34 *Alternatives* 383, 383–384.
[81] See, for example, John M Owen, 'Transnational Liberalism and U.S. Primacy' (2001) 26 *International Security* 117; Thomas S Mowle and David H Sacko, 'Global NATO: Bandwagoning in a Unipolar World' (2007) 28 *Contemporary Security Policy* 597; Arnaud Brennetot, 'The Geographical and Ethical Origins of Neoliberalism: The Walter Lippmann Colloquium and the Foundations of a New Geopolitical Order' (2015) 49 *Political Geography* 30.
[82] See in particular Adam Warden, 'A Brief History of the Anti-Globalization Movement' (2004) 12 *University of Miami International & Comparative Law Review* 237; see also Ann Capling and Kim Richard Nossal, 'Death of Distance or Tyranny of Distance? The Internet, Deterritorialization, and the Anti-Globalization Movement in Australia' (2001) 14 *The Pacific Review* 443; Peter Van Aelst and Stefaan Walgrave, 'New Media, New Movements? The Role of the Internet in Shaping the

level of liberal democracies, support for international organisations was relatively strong. Stephan commented that the period from the 1980s to the early 2000s saw a proliferation of international organisations, exporting a technocratic and expert-led process of market liberalisations throughout the world, entailing privatisations in former Soviet states and the (often brutal) reforms of markets in countries in South America and Asia.[83] The basis of this liberal order was the establishment of an international order based on rules and opening up world markets, providing for public goods such as freedom of the seas.[84] According to Mahbubani, this liberal system was based on a number of pillars of convergence, including the economic and technological.[85] The economic pillar entailed the transnationalisation of the global economic system and the technological pillar, facilitating its greater interconnectedness and interdependence.

In this understanding of the liberal order, trust in the private sector as an actor within regulatory networks is seemingly high.[86] This trust, however, was what was described by Levi-Faur as the 'harnessing [of] the enlightened self-interest of individuals and corporations'.[87] In other words, the assumption was that profitability was the central concern of transnational corporate actors,[88] who would then operate in a responsible way that ensured their continued self-regulation rather than the imposition of top-down legal controls on their business activities.[89] In this way, trust in this context can be typified as strategic, based in realist assumptions about self-interest and reciprocation rather than violating commitments.[90] The proliferation of regulatory networks incorporating private sector actors resulted in the development

"Anti-Globalization" Movement' (2002) 5 *Information, Communication & Society* 465; Jeffrey M Ayres, 'Framing Collective Action Against Neoliberalism: The Case of the "Anti-Globalization" Movement' (2004) 10 *Journal of World-Systems Research* 11.

[83] Paul B Stephan, *The World Crisis and International Law: The Knowledge Economy and the Battle for the Future* (Cambridge University Press 2023) 42–62 provides an excellent overview of these processes.

[84] Described in Patrick Porter, *The False Promise of Liberal Order* (Polity 2020) in which Porter questions the extent to which this liberal order truly existed as imagined by the international policy experts that sought to facilitate this system.

[85] Kishore Mahbubani, *Great Convergence: Asia, the West, and the Logic of One World* (PublicAffairs 2014).

[86] Christine Parker, *The Open Corporation: Effective Self-Regulation and Democracy* (Cambridge University Press 2002); George Morgan and Mark Thorum, 'Determinants of Transnational Regulatory Regimes' in Linda Winkler and Harold Codrington (eds), *Global Economy in Transition: the European Union and Beyond* (Vernon Press 2017).

[87] Levi-Faur (n32) 21–22.

[88] Ian Maitland, 'The Limits of Business Self-Regulation' (1985) 27 *California Management Review* 132.

[89] Adrienne Héretier and Sandra Eckert, 'New Modes of Governance in the Shadow of Hierarchy: Self-Regulation by Industry in Europe' (2008) 28 *Journal of Public Policy* 113; see also Neil Gunningham, 'Environment, Self-Regulation, and the Chemical Industry: Assessing Responsible Care' (1995) 17 *Law & Policy* 57; Susan Margaret Hart, 'Self-Regulation, Corporate Social Responsibility, and the Business Case: Do They Work in Achieving Workplace Equality and Safety?' (2010) 92 *Journal of Business Ethics* 585 for further discussion of these assumptions, as well as criticisms of this approach from within a liberal regulatory paradigm.

[90] Eric M Uslaner, *The Moral Foundations of Trust* (Cambridge University Press 2002) 4–5.

of these special trust relationships between the state and corporations,[91] in which the state benefited from the expertise and technical capabilities of the private sector, which in turn benefited from being able to influence and direct policy, without being subject to overt state control.[92] In comparison, in the absence of this trust, Uslaner argues that relations would be characterised by continuous oversight, verification, and renegotiation as each party manoeuvres to protect its own interests.[93]

Regulatory Mercantilism: A Return to Geostrategy in the Face of External Threats

However, trust requires a willingness to be vulnerable.[94] If states believe in the strength of the liberal international order, a unipolar world, and shared values in a global economy, then cooperation and the incorporation of transnational private actors as equal partners in governance are acceptable as means of regulating. Trust in aligned values, or at least rational self-interest in an interdependent economy, therefore appears to make sense. Cooperation and trust are more likely when states feel secure. The formation and fostering of international organisations are both factors in promoting world security, as well as being a result of it.[95] As regulatory capitalism is a mode of governance that appears to flourish in conditions of peace, security, and international cooperation, regulatory mercantilism then is a mode of governance that arises when confidence in peace, security, and international cooperation appears weakened. In times of geopolitical instability, when those liberal international organisations are weakened or non-functioning, I propose that regulatory mercantilism becomes pronounced as an approach to regulation, based on perceptions of increased global vulnerability arising from competition with other states and the private sector actors based in their territories that may not share the interests or values of the regulating state. At the time of writing, the institutions of liberal internationalism appear weakened, and the 'strong' liberalism of the late 1990s to mid-2000s is increasingly riven by internal inconsistencies and external challenges.[96] As shall be expanded upon in Chapters 2 and 3, geopolitical shifts from the Global Financial Crisis to Russia's increasingly belligerent foreign policy to concerns over the role of China

---

[91] Alexander Klimburg, 'Mobilising Cyber Power' (2011) 53 *Survival* 41, 52.
[92] Helena Carrapico and Benjamin Farrand, 'When Trust Fades, Facebook Is No Longer a Friend: Shifting Privatisation Dynamics in the Context of Cybersecurity as a Result of Disinformation, Populism and Political Uncertainty' (2021) 59 *JCMS: Journal of Common Market Studies* 1160.
[93] Eric M Uslaner (ed), *The Oxford Handbook of Social and Political Trust* (OUP USA 2018) 2.
[94] Roger C Mayer, James H Davis and F David Schoorman, 'An Integrative Model of Organizational Trust' (1995) 20 *The Academy of Management Review* 709; Deborah Welch Larson, *Anatomy of Mistrust: U.S.-Soviet Relations during the Cold War* (Cornell University Press 1997).
[95] This will be discussed further in the Chapters 2 and 3.
[96] Georg Sørensen, 'Pyrrhic Victory: A World of Liberal Institutions, Teeming with Tensions' in Anders Wivel and TV Paul (eds), *International Institutions and Power Politics: Bridging the Divide* (Georgetown University Press 2019).

in the world order[97] give cause for states to feel insecure and vulnerable. COVID-19 and the social and economic shocks that followed further contribute to this increased sense of state insecurity.[98] In this environment, trust in global cooperation based on enlightened self-interest will be reduced, and as a result, so too will the willingness of states to incorporate transnational actors into regulatory networks as equal partners. This incorporation will be more conditional, dependent on the geographical location of the actor, with preference exhibited for a territory's own private actors, who will be deemed more trustworthy than those based in external states. Discourses outlining or justifying regulatory mercantilist policies will therefore make explicit reference to the 'externality' of this vulnerability and the geopolitical conditions that make reliance upon 'internal' actors in regulation preferable. Regulatory mercantilism is visible during periods of geopolitical instability and where policymakers perceive an increased vulnerability to externally situated actors.

THE RATIONALE OF REGULATORY MERCANTILISM: UNIFYING, SECURING, AND REASSERTING SOVEREIGNTY

Now that we have considered the conditions in which different approaches to regulation arise, it is now necessary to consider the rationale of regulation that results from those conditions. As with the preceding section of this chapter, I will first consider the rationale for regulation in mercantilism, before then comparing it to regulatory capitalism, and then highlighting how this logic shifts in the context of regulatory mercantilism.

Mercantilism: The Interdependence of Economic and Security Ambitions in State Formation

Mercantilism can be formulated as being about the desire for control in response to a sense of insecurity, bringing the economy to bear in service of the strengthening of the state as a sovereign entity. In this respect, 'economy', 'security', and 'sovereignty' are all interdependent and mutually reinforcing. Heckscher identified mercantilism as a project of unification, with its key objective being one of state-building. It intended for economic activity to be shaped to the will of the state and the forming of the state as a unified economic unit.[99] Schmoller, writing of the unification of the German states' economies in the sixteenth, seventeenth, and eighteenth centuries, stated that the purpose of this was economic *and* political; its objective was that

---

[97] As briefly outlined by Porter (n83) 9–10.
[98] See briefly Erin K Jenne, 'Populism, Nationalism and Revisionist Foreign Policy' (2021) 97 *International Affairs* 323; Florian Bieber, 'Global Nationalism in Times of the COVID-19 Pandemic' (2022) 50 *Nationalities Papers* 13.
[99] Eli F Heckscher, *Mercantilism* (Routledge 1994) 21–24.

'the social and economic forces of the whole territory consolidated [and] important legal and economic institutions [were] created'.[100] Mercantilism as a political-economic project waned in influence towards the end of the nineteenth century, in part because the processes of state unification and consolidation of power within the state were either complete or nearing completion. The period after the conclusion of the Napoleonic Wars and the Treaty of Paris was one of comparative peace, with the emphasis placed upon building an international system of cooperation.[101]

For Schmoller, mercantilism 'in its innermost kernel [is] nothing but state making – not state making in the narrow sense, but state making and national economy making at the same time'.[102] On this, Wilson argues that despite the disparate forms and measures adopted in different nations, at its core, the purpose of the mercantile system was to use 'all the devices, legislative, administrative and regulatory, by which societies [...] sought to transform themselves into trading and industrial societies, to equip themselves not only to be rich but to be strong, and to remain so'.[103] This entailed both the reorganisation of the economy and the exertion of political authority internally and the projection of force and expansion of control externally. In the context of this state and economy-making, strength was vital in ensuring the security of the state, both in terms of its integrity as an internal unit and its security from external threats to its stability or autonomy. During this period, that threat was most likely to originate with other states or the powerful merchants residing within them. The mercantilist rationale of sovereignty, therefore, was the preservation and strengthening of the state and the enhancement of the prince's wealth against his military and commercial rivals.[104]

Indeed, the conflicts between states in late-mediaeval Europe were all 'wars about national sovereign status [... in which] trade could be a useful diplomatic weapon'.[105] War and conflict between states became inherently linked to trade in the seventeenth century, and in these trade conflicts, sovereignty was not just an issue of land and land borders but equally one of control over the sea and shipping routes.[106] Indeed, states during the seventeenth and eighteenth centuries tended to make grand pronouncements regarding sovereign claims over the high seas.[107] Schmoller outlines how Spain and Portugal sought to secure a partition of the world's oceans from the Pope as their exclusive property,[108] with Portugal having secured rights

---

[100] Schmoller (n11) 44.
[101] David Kennedy, 'International Law and the Nineteenth Century: History of an Illusion Special Issue: New Approaches to International Law' (1996) 65 *Nordic Journal of International Law* 385.
[102] Schmoller (n11) 50.
[103] Wilson (n64) 26.
[104] David Scott, 'Colonial Governmentality' [1995] Social Text 191, 202.
[105] Diana Wood, *Medieval Economic Thought* (Cambridge University Press 2002) 123.
[106] Ibid.
[107] JC Sharman, 'Power and Profit at Sea: The Rise of the West in the Making of the International System' (2019) 43 *International Security* 163, 168.
[108] Schmoller (n11) 70.

over a significant proportion of the South Atlantic and Indian Oceans under the papal bull issued by *Nicholas v. Romanus Pontifex*.[109] Similarly, the English crown was a proponent of the *Mare Clausum* philosophy of John Selden, motivated particularly by conflict with the Dutch, arguing for sovereign rights over the *Oceanus Britannicus*.[110] Mercantilism helped to ensure this sovereignty vis-à-vis other states, as the securing of sea routes gave trade advantages; the secured wealth could be used to reinforce the military (particularly naval forces); and the reinforcement of the military permitted further expansion and colonisation abroad, while securing the state at home.[111] Here we can see the underlying rationale of bringing together the dimensions of economy, security, and sovereignty together in the service of unifying and securing the state.

But what of the relations between the state and the private sector? Within the state, the processes of unification and state-making discussed earlier required the coercion, co-option, and occasional cooperation with existing claimants to power. These could include rival nobility and landowners in England, the French *estates*, the towns, villages, and municipal authorities in Germany, and guilds of merchants throughout different European states and city-states. Coercion as a tool was used to bring rivals to heel, with threats of force or violence (often underscored by law, as discussed in the next section) ensuring compliance with the ruler's agenda, whether this constituted the ending of internal tolls or encouraging trade between towns. Co-option and cooperation were less overt means of control, albeit potentially more effective; establishing guilds and then granting them privileges in exchange for regulating the activities of craftsmen, for example, could prove both more lucrative and less disruptive.[112] Companies like the East India Corporation were akin to a corporate state, with considerable power over its employees, but also soldiers, colonists and colonised peoples alike, governing 'over markets outside the bounds of the English realm, generating policies and procedures over the commercial activity under their jurisdiction'.[113] For the East India Company, while possessing a monopoly over trade within its assigned geographical competence by the English Crown, its role was not solely for the purpose of the profit of the company, but for 'the

---

[109] SM Ghazanfar, 'Vasco Da Gama's Voyages to India: Messianism, Mercantilism, and Sacred Exploits' (2018) 13 *Journal of Global Initiatives* 15.

[110] Efthymios Papastavridis, 'The Right of Visit on the High Seas in a Theoretical Perspective: Mare Liberum versus Mare Clausum Revisited' (2011) 24 *Leiden Journal of International Law* 45, 51.

[111] On the links between military power and commerce generally, see Michael P Gerace, 'State Interests, Military Power and International Commerce: Some Cross-national Evidence' (2000) 5 *Geopolitics* 101.

[112] Clare Haru Crowston, 'Mercantilism, Corporate Organization and the Guilds in the Later Reign of Louis XIV' in Julia Prest and Guy Rowlands (eds), *The Third Reign of Louis XIV, c.1682–1715* (Routledge 2017).

[113] Philip J Stern, 'Companies: Monopoly, Sovereignty, and the East Indies' in Philip J Stern and Carl Wennerlind (eds), *Mercantilism Reimagined: Political Economy in Early Modern Britain and Its Empire* (Oxford University Press 2013) 179.

responsibility to tend to the English trade and intercourse with the East Indies'.[114] In this respect, central to the rationale of mercantilism was the linking of economic and security goals in order to secure the sovereignty of the state vis-à-vis other states and private interests.

Regulatory Capitalism versus Regulatory Mercantilism: Regulation Based in a Logic of Efficiency versus Regulation Based in a Logic of Security

After the horror, bloodshed, and economic ruination of the two World Wars in the first half of the twentieth century, renewed emphasis was placed on international cooperation, economic, social, and legal,[115] and particularly after the Oil Shocks of the 1970s, it was pursued with renewed emphasis on free and open trade, privatisation of national industries, and the expansion of financial capitalism.[116] It is in this context, and that of the regulatory state, that regulatory capitalism emerged. Not as part of a process of state making, but within the context of pre-existing states adapting to a world of increased complexity and the transnationalisation of corporate entities.[117] Or, as Braithwaite put it, 'mega-corporate capitalism creates regulatory capitalism'.[118] Levi-Faur expands upon this, arguing that the state is embedded within the economy and society, and thus any change in the state will be reflected in economic and social structures, and vice versa.[119] This is not about state-creation, but state change concerning the division of labour between the state and society. As a result, there is a certain relinquishing of control by the state, with 'an increase in delegation [and] the proliferation of mechanisms of self-regulation in the shadow of the state'.[120] Examples include an increase in the use of regulatory agencies and the agencification of private sector actors in Europe,[121] as well as the promotion of

---

[114] Ibid 182.
[115] For an excellent study of this period of economic transformation, see Eric Helleiner, *Forgotten Foundations of Bretton Woods: International Development and the Making of the Postwar Order* (Cornell University Press 2014).
[116] See in particular Quinn Slobodian, *Globalists: The End of Empire and the Birth of Neoliberalism* (Harvard University Press 2018); see also Thomas J Dillon, Jr., 'The World Trade Organization: A New Legal Order for World Trade?' (1995) 16 *Michigan Journal of International Law* 349; John Linarelli, 'How Trade Law Changed: How It Should Change Again' (2013) 65 *Mercer Law Review* 621 for the legal dynamics of these changes with the establishment of the World Trade Organization, which while interesting, are not of direct relevance to this chapter.
[117] Andrea Esser, 'The Transnationalization of European Television' (2002) 10 *Journal of European Area Studies* 13; Jean K Chalaby, 'From Internationalization to Transnationalization' (2005) 1 *Global Media and Communication* 28.
[118] Braithwaite (n33) 20.
[119] Levi-Faur (n32) 14.
[120] Ibid 13; see also Héretier and Eckert (n88).
[121] Tom Christensen and Per Lægreid, 'Agencification and Regulatory Reforms', in Tom Christensen and Per Lœgreid (eds) *Autonomy and Regulation* (Edward Elgar Publishing 2006); David Levi-Faur, 'Regulatory Networks and Regulatory Agencification: Towards a Single European Regulatory Space' in Berthold Rittberger and Arndt Wonka (eds), *Agency Governance in the EU* (Routledge 2012).

self-regulatory regimes in sectors such as banking.[122] The objective of this mode of governance is stated to be efficiency,[123] using the expertise and resources of these diverse actors to more effectively regulate, making up for the comparative lack of expertise or resources on the part of the state.[124] Regulatory mercantilism shares different objectives, more akin to those of mercantilism. It is about a reassertion of the role of the state in regulation, with actors engaging in it likely to state a desire to take back control or, at the very least, provide heightened oversight. While delegation may still exist, it operates on a more limited level than in a regulatory capitalism framework. In other words, it is an attempt to unify and strengthen the regulatory state internally in a way distinct from that of regulatory capitalism. In particular, the justification in regulatory mercantilism for that increased control is not made on efficiency grounds but on security grounds – a restructuring of state-private relations in each field or sector characterised as predominantly economic in nature, being rationalised on the basis that such a restructuring is necessary to achieve a broader security objective. It is the pursuit of 'stateness' to guarantee the protection of the state and securing of the 'national interest'.[125]

Sovereignty, then, is also of relevance to our understanding of regulatory capitalism. In regulatory capitalism, sovereignty is still of a hybrid form best encapsulated by the approach of Srivastava,[126] in which the idealised claim of indivisible state sovereignty and the divisible sovereign competences of lived sovereignty are accommodated; 'divisible public/private relations underlie sovereign power in *Lived Sovereignty*, while simultaneously the contours of who counts as sovereign authority are informed by *Idealized Sovereignty*. Crucially, both [...] forms coproduce sovereignty in world politics'.[127] In regulatory capitalism, this form of hybridity could be classified as *institutional hybridity*,[128] in which 'relations are mediated through insider rules and privileges gained through embedded networks'.[129] The promotion of 'self-governance' mechanisms through the International Chambers of Commerce, which Srivastava argues constitutes a private-sector-led initiative seeking

---

[122] Karsten Ronit, 'Self-Regulation and Public Regulation: Financial Services and the Out-of-Court Complaints Bodies' in Jean-Christophe Graz and Andreas Nölke (eds), *Transnational Private Governance and Its Limits* (Routledge 2008).

[123] Levi-Faur and Jordana (n50); John S Wright, 'Regulatory Capitalism and the UK Labour Government's Reregulation of Commissioning in the English National Health Service Law and Policy' (2011) 33 *Law & Policy* 27; Peter Drahos, '*Regulatory Capitalism, Globalization and the End of History*' (Autralian National University 2014) 2014/33; Jonathan Klaaren, 'The Emergence of Regulatory Capitalism in Africa' (2021) 50 *Economy and Society* 100.

[124] Jacob Torfing and Eva Sørensen, 'The European Debate on Governance Networks: Towards a New and Viable Paradigm?' (2014) 33 *Policy and Society* 329.

[125] Björn Hettne, 'Neo-Mercantilism: The Pursuit of Regionness' (1993) 28 *Cooperation and Conflict* 211, 213.

[126] Swati Srivastava, *Hybrid Sovereignty in World Politics* (Cambridge University Press 2022).

[127] Ibid 7.

[128] Ibid 59.

[129] Ibid.

governmental regulation for commercial interests,[130] can be seen as a form of regulated self-regulation that fits effectively within the regulatory capitalism framework.

This is a shared (i.e. hybrid) sovereignty, which Levi-Faur expands upon with the analogy of 'steering and rowing'.[131] In the traditional regulatory capitalism approach, the state steers, described as 'leading, thinking, directing, guiding',[132] while business rows, described as 'enterprise [and] service provision'.[133] However, this approach still demonstrates a certain level of hierarchy, with the state acting as captain and the private sector tasked with working the oars. However, in certain sectors, the relations are less hierarchical, with a 'networked' variation of regulatory capitalism becoming prominent in fields such as cybersecurity in the 2010s.[134] The combination of perceptions of private sector expertise surpassing that of the state and even some agencies, with the private ownership of telecommunications infrastructure and the global nature of the cybersecurity problems identified, results in a model in which businesses join the state and agencies in steering the direction of policy through the identification of standards, best practices, and threats, determining the content of regulation on the basis of this expertise.[135] 'The private sector does not only act as an adopter of regulation, but can also be actively involved in shaping policy responses and the resulting legislation'.[136] Sovereignty in this respect is shared, between the state laying out the general regulatory goals or ambitions, which are then detailed, devised, and implemented by the private sector in a hybridised institutional framework in which the state maintains its sovereignty to devise the rules but relies upon the expertise of the private sector to 'fill in the details' in a way that renders that regulatory regime workable. Because these rules are 'global', comprising transnational regulatory networks blurring public and private roles, governance at the international level has operated in the absence of a central sovereign authority and has been typified by horizontal or peer enforcement, rather than hierarchy.[137] Regulatory capitalism, then, encapsulates this networked approach, in which efficiency and collaboration are centred through regulatory decentring.

In regulatory mercantilism, however, we propose that regulatory relationships are much more selective, with the state seeking to reassert its sovereignty over regulatory design. While elements of networked governance remain, relationships are more hierarchical rather than horizontal, with territory playing a significant role in determining the extent of regulatory cooperation. Whereas within networked regulatory capitalism the public and private sectors work as something akin to 'equal partners',

---

[130] Ibid 167–172.
[131] Levi-Faur (n32) 15.
[132] Ibid.
[133] Ibid.
[134] Carrapico and Farrand (n41) 248.
[135] Ibid 254.
[136] Ibid.
[137] Gabrielle Simms, 'Regulating Sex in Peace Operations' in Peter Drahos (ed), *Regulatory Theory: Foundations and Applications* (Australian National University Press 2017) 419.

with the state and private sector both engaged in 'steering', regulatory mercantilism sees the state take a more active role in 'steering', with a more limited level of private sector involvement that is heavily based on geographical considerations, as a means of reducing dependency on foreign-based entities. 'Rowing' may be conducted by private actors either associated with that territory or based outside of it, albeit with greater oversight, and dependent on compliance with state-authored regulatory structures. In the networked governance that typifies regulatory capitalism, Torfing and Sørensen argued, 'the absence of a sovereign power capable of enforcing the emerging rules of the game and the periodic contestation and renegotiation of the form and functioning of governance networks ensures the ambiguity and openness of the institutional framework'.[138] In regulatory mercantilism, in comparison, there is an explicit attempt by a sovereign power to change or dictate those rules, requiring the acquiescence of the private actors involved in that sectoral activity. As a result, openness and ambiguity become replaced with a more closed, protectionist approach with clearly defined rules and lines of oversight. Regulatory mercantilism therefore represents an objective on the part of the state to reassert control over regulatory design, creating a unified legal approach within a territory based on an explicit security logic operating in fields normally underscored by an economic rationale, bringing together economy and security as policy fields and reinforcing their interdependence.

THE MEANS OF REGULATORY MERCANTILISM: THE REGULATORY BALANCE OF TRADE AND CHANGING RELATIONSHIP DYNAMICS

Regulatory mercantilism can be distinguished from regulatory capitalism on this point insofar as power relations between the private and public sectors are more hierarchical, particularly vis-à-vis the role of private sector operators as entities not located within the territory of the state. As with the idea of reasserting control, regulatory mercantilism also entails a return (or 'clawback') of regulatory power from private sector operators, with increased centralisation along territorial lines and a renewed emphasis on industrial policy. Power in regulatory mercantilism is understood by actors in more 'realist' terms, akin to the understanding of power in mercantilism more broadly. Furthermore, it goes beyond seeking the economic wealth necessary for the provision of security as discussed by Levi-Faur earlier, regulating the functioning of the economy and actors within it explicitly in security terms. The 'wealth' that states desire in the regulatory mercantilism model also varies from both regulatory capitalism and mercantilism, as it is concerned with a more intangible form, comprising data, knowledge, and know-how that can be used to maximise regulatory power, which forms the basis of a data-based industrial policy. As such, this control is sought on the basis of reinforcing this regulatory power and bringing

---

[138] Torfing and Sørensen (n123) 337.

it 'back' within the domain of the state, which then directs it through geopolitically motivated industrial policy.

Mercantilism: Industrial Policy and External Force in Service of the State

In 'traditional' mercantilism, power was very much (if not solely) attributable to 'plenty', or wealth.[139] Wealth could be used to invest in industries (such as shipbuilding) and to recruit and maintain armies as a means of securing the nation. By expanding power, more wealth could be secured, in turn allowing for the exercise of greater power. Wealth, power, and security were therefore inextricably intertwined. Internally, the purpose of laws for Schmoller was to unify: 'uniform measures and coinage, for a well-ordered system of currency and credit, for uniform laws and uniform administration, for freer and more active traffic within the land'.[140] This would help to bring the state together in common purpose, linking its economic prosperity to its guarantees of security, and vice versa. By way of example, Nettels argues that the use of laws 'internally' was to codify policies that 'sought to control, to regulate, to restrain, to stimulate, or to protect' in particular sectors.[141] Examples of internally focused interventions abound, such as measures introduced by Henry VIII and then expanded upon by Elizabeth I to protect domestic merchants and industries from foreign competition. Heckscher discusses the effectiveness of English monarchs in general internal economic regulation, 'one of the most remarkable results of English economic policy [...] so thorough [was the] control of the whole industry of a country'.[142] The Elizabethan Statute of Artificers was considered to have served as the basis for a whole legal framework, with regulation for labourers, wages, and apprenticeships.[143]

In France, the gradual move from municipal to national policy resulted in laws enforced and applicable to the entire country, and in particular by Colbert during the time of Louis XIV,[144] with the state introducing 'regulations for the conduct of industry and consequently all marks of local and corporative control were replaced by others of the state'.[145] Colbert, according to Wilson, sought to replace the 'largely ineffective regulations of earlier administrators [...] to rescue France from the poverty and chaos'[146] of earlier regimes. Production in this system was to 'be left to the

---

[139] See Viner (n1); Wilson (n64).
[140] Schmoller (n11) 51.
[141] Curtis P Nettels, 'British Mercantilism and the Economic Development of the Thirteen Colonies' (1952) 12 *The Journal of Economic History* 105, 108 although on this it must be asked given that panoply of purposes, how this would differ from other legal approaches, or indeed what other purposes may exist.
[142] Heckscher (n98) 226.
[143] Ibid 228–229.
[144] See, for example, Abbott Payson Usher, 'Colbert and Governmental Control of Industry in Seventeenth Century France' (1934) 16 *The Review of Economics and Statistics* 237.
[145] Heckscher (n98) 139.
[146] Wilson (n64) 22.

individual but supervised in minute detail to ensure quality [...] thus could industry, with trade, play its part'[147] in securing the state. Merchants and producers were consulted on the regulations to be applied to their sectors,[148] and a system of public inspectors for French manufacturing was established,[149] combining public power with private expertise to create, maintain, and enhance existing markets.[150] Similar examples exist in East Asia, including the 'centralising mercantilism' of the Meiji period in Japan, in which regulatory efforts were dedicated to promoting industry, importing skilled workers and technologies from other areas in Japan, and directing the workforce to increase wealth and thereby power.[151]

Law's 'external' dimension concerned the regulation of trade outside of the state. In England, the Navigation Act of 1651 was of particular importance as a means of securing mercantilist objectives through legal means. The first line of the legislation is indicative of the purpose behind its form of regulatory intervention, which states that it was intended 'for the Increases of Shipping and the Encouragement of the Navigation of this Nation, which under the good Providence and Protection of God, is so great a means of the Welfare and Safety of this Common wealth'.[152] Under this law, no goods could be imported into England from Asia, Africa, or America, except on English ships (with some small exceptions in the case of goods from Europe), with specific controls on the transport by means of import or export of salt fish, which could only take place in English vessels. Such measures were intended to cut off Dutch trade into England,[153] through means of legal impositions. Similarly, France under Colbert introduced measures for shaping rather than curtailing foreign trade,[154] focusing on promoting exports while limiting imports through legally imposed mechanisms such as tariffs, quotas, or outright prohibitions of certain goods.[155]

---

[147] Ibid 23.

[148] Heckscher (n98) 165; Usher (n143) 239.

[149] Esteban Pérez Caldentey, 'The Concept and Evolution of the Developmental State' (2008) 37 *International Journal of Political Economy* 27, 36.

[150] See David Levi-Faur, 'The Competition State as a Neomercantilist State: Understanding the Restructuring of National and Global Telecommunications' (1998) 27 *The Journal of Socio-Economics* 665.

[151] Eric Helleiner, *The Neomercantilists: A Global Intellectual History* (Cornell University Press 2021) 206–209.

[152] HM Stationery Office, 'October 1651: An Act for Increase of Shipping, and Encouragement of the Navigation of This Nation' in CH Firth and RS Rait (eds), *Acts and Ordinances of the Interregnum, 1642–1660* (1911) <www.british-history.ac.uk/no-series/acts-ordinances-interregnum/pp559-562> accessed 9 May 2023.

[153] Wilson (n64) 16; see also JE Farnell, 'The Navigation Act of 1651, the First Dutch War, and the London Merchant Community' (1964) 16 *The Economic History Review* 439.

[154] Andrew Moravcsik, 'Arms and Autarky in Modern European History' (1991) 120 *Daedalus* 23; see also Mark Thornton, 'Was Richard Cantillon a Mercantilist?' (2007) 29 *Journal of the History of Economic Thought* 417.

[155] Gijs Rommelse, 'The Role of Mercantilism in Anglo-Dutch Political Relations, 1650–74' (2010) 63 *The Economic History Review* 591.

During this period, in which conflict between large powers such as England, France, and the Netherlands often merged military and trade warfare, Europe saw 'the steady encroachment of government regulation into many, if not most, areas of external trade. New regulative and enforcement agencies proliferated'.[156] In this respect, law was the means by which controls could be introduced that aimed to unify the state and strengthen it against external threats by means of interventions promoting industrialisation at home and trade abroad. This idea of the balance of trade was reflected upon by Decker in 1739, in which he argued that 'if the Exports of Britain exceed its Import, Foreigners must pay the balance in Treasure and the Nation grows Rich. But if the Imports of Britain exceed its Exports we must pay the Balance in Treasure and the Nation grows Poor'.[157] This concept of the balance of trade was gradually built into the economic legislation of the seventeenth century,[158] such as through the earlier-mentioned Navigation Act, as the strategic management of foreign trade was perceived as best securing the state, as potentially conflicting states would be made more dependent upon the resources and war-making materials while reducing reliance upon *their* materials and resources that may be cut off in times of war.[159] This was less about bullionism and accumulating pure mineral wealth, as critics of mercantilism have decried, but a belief that 'a country should export products with as much value-added content as possible and import as little of such products as they could'.[160] Securing a positive (or 'overplus'[161]) balance of trade would therefore strengthen the exporting state, while potentially weakening others more reliant upon imports.[162] Intertwined with these concerns over the balance of trade were concerns regarding sovereignty, which in turn influenced the relations both between and within states.

Regulatory Capitalism versus Regulatory Mercantilism: Free Markets and Globalised Trade versus Technology Industrial Policy and Regulatory Balance of Trade

In regulatory capitalism, there is a certain degree of continuity regarding the interactions between wealth and power. Levi-Faur states that 'internal security (policing) and external security (military might) depend on plenty. Therefore, the economic

---

[156] Jones (n70) 144.
[157] Sir Matthew Decker, *An Essay on the Causes of the Decline of the Foreign Trade: Consequently of the Value of the Lands of Britain, and on the Means to Restore Both* (J Brotherton 1750) 2.
[158] Wilson (n64) 12.
[159] Jones (n70) 144.
[160] Magnusson (n10) 219.
[161] Mun (n62) 12.
[162] For more on this idea, as well as a critique of it, see Lars Herlitz, 'The Concept of Mercantilism' (1964) 12 *Scandinavian Economic History Review* 101.

logic of capitalism and the security logic of the state go hand-in-hand – that is, power and plenty are interdependent'.[163] Similarly, Braithwaite noted that a significant amount of privatisation occurred in the security sector, both domestically in the form of private police forces and internationally through the establishment of private military companies.[164] Power within this model is more distributed than centralised, shared between the state and private sector actors, fitting with the network governance approach apparent in regulatory capitalism.[165] This diffusion grants considerable discretionary power to private entities tasked with performing a regulatory role.[166] Relations of power in this context, between the public and private sectors specifically, as well as within a more liberal international order generally, are cooperative, rather than necessarily strictly competitive.[167] With regulatory mercantilism, these relations are more combative and competitive, and the relative value-neutral private sector operator concerned only with profit maximisation is no longer taken for granted – for this reason, they cannot be relied upon as neutral arbiters and nodes within a regulatory network but potentially as a competitor for regulatory control. Therefore, regulatory mercantilism in policy will work towards a reorientation of regulatory relationships, moving away from self-regulation to either mandated co-regulation or even top-down state regulation. The mechanism by which this can be achieved is law. Within the regulatory capitalism framework, laws are just one form of instrument that can be used to achieve desired outcomes. Indeed, regulatory capitalism works on the assumption of increased efficiency through engaging multiple stakeholders in regulatory networks, in which the state and private actors collaborate in regulatory design.[168] As Jordana argues, 'these sectoral regimes depend heavily on the use of regulatory instruments and the propagation of self-regulatory behaviour among the epistemic and professional communities within each sector'.[169] Command-and-control regulation, in the form of prescriptive legislation imposed by state legislative authorities, does not disappear, but in fields of economic regulation in particular, it is of less direct relevance as self-regulatory and regulated self-regulatory mechanisms become preferred as a means of creating responsive and

---

[163] David Levi-Faur, 'Regulatory Capitalism' in Peter Drahos (ed.), *Regulatory Theory: Foundations and Applications* (Australian National University Press 2017) 292.
[164] Braithwaite (n33) 21.
[165] Levi-Faur (n32); Parker and Nielsen (n35).
[166] Rebecca Schmidt and Colin Scott, 'Regulatory Discretion: Structuring Power in the Era of Regulatory Capitalism' (2021) 41 *Legal Studies* 454.
[167] Benjamin Farrand and Helena Carrapico, 'Blurring Public and Private: Cybersecurity in the Age of Regulatory Capitalism' in Oldrich Bures and Helena Carrapico (eds), *Security Privatization: How Non-security-related Private Businesses Shape Security Governance* (Springer International Publishing 2018).
[168] See generally John Yasuda, 'Regulatory Governance' in Christopher Ansell and Jacob Torfing (eds), *Handbook on Theories of Governance* (2nd ed., Edward Elgar Publishing 2022).
[169] Jacint Jordana, 'Globalizing Regulatory Capitalism' (2005) 598 *The ANNALS of the American Academy of Political and Social Science* 184, 185.

adaptable rules, based on an understanding of the private sector as more agile and quicker to learn than the state.[170]

For this reason, non-binding measures such as voluntary agreements and codes of conduct are often utilised as a means of incentivising regulatory cooperation in the absence of threats of sanction,[171] or informal governance mechanisms such as benchmarking, ranking, and naming-and-shaming can be used to encourage compliance with regulatory goals without imposing top-down legislation.[172] The risk, however, with reliance on the diffusion of this regulatory power and reliance on non-binding forms of governance is an increasing hollowing-out of the state,[173] 'weakening a central state's ability to coordinate policy, standardise regulation and maintain oversight of private actors'.[174] In a regulatory mercantilist model, however, I would expect to find considerably less use of informal governance mechanisms, or self-regulatory approaches to public policy issues. Instead, states would be concerned with this apparent weakening of authority and control and would seek instead to reassert themselves through a combination of binding legislative requirements and co-regulatory models with strong oversight, supplemented by a 'backstop' in cases of non-compliance with the specified regulatory requirements.[175] This would allow the state to take greater ownership over regulatory design, oversight, and enforcement, reasserting control of regulation where security interests act as a driver for intervention. Rather than leaving the development of technological sectors to the market to determine, there will be a return to dedicated industrial policies as a means of

---

[170] Philip Eijlander, 'Possibilities and Constraints in the Use of Self-Regulation and Co-Regulation in Legislative Policy: Experience in the Netherlands – Lessons to Be Learned for the EU?' (2005) 9 *European Journal of Comparative Law* 1.

[171] As discussed in Benjamin Farrand, 'The Ordoliberal Internet? Continuity and Change in the EU's Approach to the Governance of Cyberspace' (2023) 2 *European Law Open* 106; see also Susanne Lütz, Dagmar Eberle and Dorothee Lauter, 'Varieties of Private Self-Regulation in European Capitalism: Corporate Governance Codes in the UK and Germany' (2011) 9 *Socio-Economic Review* 315; Christopher Marsden, *Internet Co-Regulation: European Law, Regulatory Governance and Legitimacy in Cyberspace* (Cambridge University Press 2011).

[172] B Guy Peters, 'Forms of Informality: Identifying Informal Governance in the European Union' (2006) 7 *Perspectives on European Politics and Society* 25; Mareike Kleine, 'Informal Governance in the European Union' (2014) 21 *Journal of European Public Policy* 303; Benjamin Farrand, 'The Future of Copyright Enforcement Online: Intermediaries Caught between Formal and Informal Governance in the EU' in Irini Stamatoudi (ed), *New Developments in EU and International Copyright Law* (Kluwer Law International 2016).

[173] Discussed in the excellent work by the late Peter Mair, *Ruling the Void: The Hollowing of Western Democracy* (Verso 2013).

[174] Yasuda (n167) 475; see also Erik-Hans Klijn, 'Governing Networks in the Hollow State: Contracting out, Process Management or a Combination of the Two?' (2002) 4 *Public Management Review* 149.

[175] On the concept of backstops, which have become prominent in the context of the EU-UK Trade and Cooperation Agreement's Northern Ireland Protocol, see Paul Teague, 'Brexit, the Belfast Agreement and Northern Ireland: Imperilling a Fragile Political Bargain' (2019) 90 *The Political Quarterly* 690; Kimberly Cowell-Meyers and Carolyn Gallaher, 'Parsing the Backstop: Northern Ireland and the Good Friday Agreement in the Brexit Debates' (2021) 16 *British Politics* 219.

securing technologies that both provide for economic benefit and increasing the security of the state.

Regulatory mercantilism is analogous with mercantilism insofar as the guarantee of power and security is achieved through what I describe as the 'regulatory balance of trade'. The regulatory balance of trade refers to an approach to governance that seeks to minimise regulatory imports, thereby asserting control over regulatory design, while also seeking to promote regulatory exports.[176] In regulatory capitalism, as discussed earlier, the key objective of the governance model is efficiency, with networked systems of regulation seen as being most effective in achieving this aim. Transnational, non-state-based regulatory regimes of diverse types and structures are promulgated on this basis,[177] whether in the domain of international sport under FIFA, World Athletics, and the World Anti-Doping Agency (WADA);[178] international finance in the context of the Markets in Financial Instruments Regulation[179] that provides for increased regulatory cooperation between national authorities and private sector service providers;[180] or food safety across the global supply chain, comprising national authorities and private actors involved in food production and distribution under the EU's 'farm to fork' approach.[181]

Within these systems, regulation is polycentric,[182] and not motivated by desires or objectives of overall control. As such, concern over the regulatory balance of trade is not a prominent feature of regulatory capitalism, with the emphasis placed on the 'web' of the regulatory network, collaborative efforts in achieving regulatory goals, and promoting regulated self-regulation of market participants engaged in designated areas of activity.[183] Underlying this is an understanding that 'a post-industrial society must discover ways to decentralize not only commodity production, but also significant ways of law-making'.[184] Under this approach, the increased globalisation and interlinking of markets as a result of the liberal turn fosters an approach of international collaboration and partnership in policy execution, including the participation of civil society, non-governmental, and commercial entities.[185] To put it another

---

[176] The work of Anu Bradford, *The Brussels Effect: How the European Union Rules the World* (Oxford University Press 2021) is highly relevant on this point, and will be returned to in Chapter 2.
[177] See generally Natasha Tusikov, 'Regulatory Capitalism' in Peter Drahos (ed), *Regulatory Theory: Foundations and Applications* (Australian National University Press 2017).
[178] Eric L Windholz, 'International Sports Transnational Legal and Regulatory Oder: Quintessential Regulatory Capitalism' (2022) 1 *Sports Law and Governance Journal* 1.
[179] Regulation 600/2014 on markets in financial instruments and amending Regulation 648/2012.
[180] See Morgan and Thorum (n85).
[181] Sevasti Chatzopoulou, 'The Dynamics of the Transnational Food Chain Regulatory Governance: An Analytical Framework' (2015) 117 *British Food Journal* 2609.
[182] Toby Seddon, 'Drug Policy and Global Regulatory Capitalism: The Case of New Psychoactive Substances (NPS)' (2014) 25 *International Journal of Drug Policy* 1019.
[183] Braithwaite (n33) 58–60.
[184] Robert Cooter, 'Against Legal Centrism' (1993) 81 *California Law Review* 417, 418.
[185] Friedrich Kratochwil, *The Status of Law in World Society: Meditations on The Role and Rule of Law* (Cambridge University Press 2014) 105–108.

way, regulatory competence and action are diffused across state borders, not specifically tied to one region or territory, and instead attached more effectively to particular sectors. Examples include standardisation initiatives through the International Organisation for Standards in fields such as tourist information services,[186] and cybersecurity requirements devised by telecoms and critical information infrastructure providers.[187] In regulatory terms, 'different sectors and different countries introduced changes and transformed governance in different ways, and established institutions and policy styles interacted with these regulatory innovations'.[188]

In regulatory mercantilism, however, it is expected that policymakers will pay much more attention to the geopolitical positioning of actors that could be involved in a regulatory network, as well as the origins of the regulations being devised. In seeking control over regulatory design, policymakers will demonstrate considerable scepticism over the desirability of importing external rules or norms for the governance of a particular field of activity, with a preference being stated for their 'own' rules or norms, implemented and enforced by actors within or associated with that state or region, which may be expressed in terms of 'British', 'European', or 'Chinese' rules, respectively. Further, in order to strengthen this regulatory regime, there will be efforts made to export those norms internationally, requiring that other states or actors within those states be compliant with those rules if they wish to engage with, offer services in, or otherwise cooperate with that territory. If we recall the arguments of Decker made above regarding the balance of trade,[189] in regulatory mercantilist thinking, should a state entity export its regulatory approach to other states, then it is empowered vis-à-vis those states and their market operators; in turn, should they become policytakers in this respect, they are disempowered and 'poorer' in regulatory terms.

In the context of technology-related laws and policies, the reduction of dependency on foreign actors based in other states within regulatory mercantilism is also likely to extend to data. As discussed earlier, the objective of 'taking back control' of regulatory frameworks entails a quasi-mercantilist securing of wealth in order to promote power, which in turn secures more wealth. As with mercantilism, where wealth did not necessarily equate with bullion but could include it as well as critical natural resources, in regulatory mercantilism, the securing of wealth also concerns data wealth. In the 'information society', wealth is not tied to physical assets, but to underlying information, know-how, and data. The volume of data being created, processed, shared, and redistributed has resulted in the conception of an idea of the 'data economy',[190] in which value is grounded in the utility of this data, whether

---

[186] Jean-Christophe Graz, *The Power of Standards* (Cambridge University Press 2019) 92–93.
[187] Carrapico and Farrand (n41). This will be returned to in more detail in Chapter 4.
[188] Levi-Faur and Jordana (n50) 8.
[189] Decker (n156).
[190] Minna Lammi and Mika Pantzar, 'The Data Economy: How Technological Change Has Altered the Role of the Citizen-Consumer' (2019) 59 *Technology in Society* 101157.

for the purposes of commercial exploitation,[191] surveillance,[192] or shaping citizen sentiments.[193] The linkage of the physical location of this data to the security of the state, and the ascribing of geographical values to it, such as 'European' or 'American' data, will feature prominently in regulatory mercantilist discourses concerning governance. Furthermore, as with traditional mercantilism, there will be efforts made to relocate as much of that data as possible within the territory of the state seeking to reassert control, or alternatively, subject it to the regulatory controls of that state if such relocation is not feasible or likely, grounded in a sovereignty claim made over that data.[194] As with mercantilism, in regulatory mercantilism, the import of the 'resource' of data is encouraged, while its export is discouraged; similarly, while the export of the 'value-added' product of regulation is encouraged, its import is heavily discouraged. Through these endeavours, a positive balance of regulatory trade is more likely to be achieved. Regulatory mercantilism achieves the objective of regulatory control through ensuring a positive regulatory balance, accumulating data resources within a territory while reducing external dependencies, and reorienting both state and private sector relations with an explicit sovereignty rationale. This can be framed in terms of strategic autonomy, a term that will be returned to in more detail in Chapters 2 and 3.

CONCLUSIONS: REGULATORY MERCANTILISM AS A FRAMEWORK FOR ANALYSIS

With the move to regulatory governance, the regulatory state incorporated a diverse array of actors into its network, creating a more interdependent, transnational system of sectoral policy formulation. Regulatory capitalism is a system by which steering functions are as much a function of private sector actors based on accumulated technical know-how, expertise, and infrastructure control as they are one of state direction. Such a system of governance was largely a product of the liberalisations of the late twentieth century and the belief in a world largely moving beyond the

---

[191] Francesco Banterle, 'Data Ownership in the Data Economy: A European Dilemma' in Tatiana-Eleni Synodinou and others (eds), *EU Internet Law in the Digital Era: Regulation and Enforcement* (Springer International Publishing 2020).

[192] Candace L White and Brandon Boatwright, 'Social Media Ethics in the Data Economy: Issues of Social Responsibility for Using Facebook for Public Relations' (2020) 46 *Public Relations Review* 101980.

[193] Elinor Carmi and others, 'Data Citizenship: Rethinking Data Literacy in the Age of Disinformation, Misinformation, and Malinformation' (2020) 9 *Internet Policy Review* 1.

[194] See Benjamin Farrand and Helena Carrapico, 'Digital Sovereignty and Taking Back Control: From Regulatory Capitalism to Regulatory Mercantilism in EU Cybersecurity' (2022) 31 *European Security* 435; see also Anke Sophia Obendiek and Timo Seidl, 'The (False) Promise of Solutionism: Ideational Business Power and the Construction of Epistemic Authority in Digital Security Governance' (2023) 30 *Journal of European Public Policy* 1; Dennis Broeders, Fabio Cristiano and Monica Kaminska, 'In Search of Digital Sovereignty and Strategic Autonomy: Normative Power Europe to the Test of Its Geopolitical Ambitions' (2023) 61 *Journal of Common Market Studies* 1261.

ideological conflicts of the early twentieth century, with a unipolar world system based in liberal internationalism, the function of international organisations, and corporate actors largely acting in a way aligned with the interests of the state. To put it another way, the striving for expertise and efficiency in governance resulted in a system in which a belief in the enlightened self-interest on the part of companies served as a guarantor of their effective cooperation in regulatory networks.

However, any potential for a regulatory end of history[195] is, and arguably always was, unlikely. Regulatory structures are as much a result of historical circumstances, and the conditions that gave rise to a system that can be characterised as regulatory capitalism are significantly challenged. Such a challenge, however, does not result in the end of the regulatory state but instead its transformation/adaptation. As with mercantilism, regulatory mercantilism is argued to be a result of geopolitical conditions. We are currently undergoing a shift in world relations, where the function of liberal international organisations is increasingly hampered. Trust in a range of private sector actors is falling, whether based on concerns over their geographical location or the ideological positions of their owners, to the extent that states may increasingly see them not as relatively value-neutral parties upon which they can depend, but as potential threats and indeed opponents in regulatory control. Such concerns are likely to result in changing regulatory functions, in which states seek more assertive and active roles in governance, with a move to binding legislation and away from voluntary codes and guidelines, motivated by a desire both to (re)build the regulatory state and achieve its security. Sovereignty, it is argued, will be central to the discourses concerning these changes, as will the promotion of a positive regulatory balance of trade, as states seek to make their rules the ones that bind the international community more broadly.

Chapter 2 of this book will focus on the EU as a regulatory actor in the context of technology, identifying the shifting dynamics in how technology is used, who produces it, and where it is produced. It expands upon how the answers to these questions are problematized in Commission policymaking. It tracks the changes in rationale from one of internal market harmonisation through removing barriers to trade, to market refinement through active regulatory activity, to approaching technology in terms of the security challenges it presents, identifying the shifting discourses in how technology is regarded in the context of the von der Leyen Commission and its Geopolitical Union.

---

[195] Let alone a political end of history, as discussed in Chapter 3.

2

The EU as a Technology Regulator

America innovates, China replicates, Europe regulates.[1]

INTRODUCTION

To understand how the EU has changed as a regulator of technologies, and the move from a regulatory capitalism to a regulatory mercantilism frame for legislative initiatives in the context of the Geopolitical Union and its pursuit of digital sovereignty, it is necessary to first explore the historical approach of the EU and, particularly, the European Commission. The purpose of this chapter is to expand on this regulatory history, identifying the key drivers for action and preoccupations of the Commission in devising its agenda for new technologies, before identifying the junctures at which the Commission substantially reconceptualises and adapts its approach to technology governance.

Interestingly, while 'digital' as a discrete policy space only starts getting mentioned in textbooks on European integration in the mid-2010s,[2] the impact of new technologies upon the European economy has been a concern for the Commission since the 1970s. Yet if we consider 'coal extraction' and 'steel production' as forms of technology, then technology regulation has been at the heart of the integration project from its very beginning. This chapter begins with considering the processes of negative integration in the European Economic Community (EEC) from the 1950s to the late 1970s, identifying how technology was indirectly regulated through Court of Justice of the European Union (CJEU) efforts at bringing down barriers to trade that may have arisen from how

---

[1] Speech by Italian President Georgia Meloni, reproduced in Italian Government Presidency of the Council of Ministers, 'President Meloni Addresses Cernobbio Forum' (www.governo.it, 19 September 2024) <www.governo.it/en/articolo/president-meloni-addresses-cernobbio-forum/26590> accessed 13 March 2025.

[2] See, for example, Helen Wallace and others (eds), *Policy-Making in the European Union* (8th ed, Oxford University Press 2020) where digital policy received a dedicated chapter for the first time, with the 2015 7th edition not having such a chapter.

Member States approached regulation of technology, particularly in the context of intellectual property protections. The chapter then considers the processes of Commission-led positive integration, in which technology is framed in terms of its potential to contribute to Europe's economic development. It demonstrates that concerns over competitiveness vis-à-vis the US and other states (historically, Japan) have been consistent in the EU's rationale for lawmaking around technology, with the Commission considering its role as being to use regulation as a tool for creating the favourable market conditions required for private sector investment and service provision.

The chapter then moves on to considering the EU's contiguous development of a security framework for emerging technologies, exploring how cybersecurity moved from an area of *ad hoc* policymaking to a dedicated policy sector. However, it was an approach that was devised as market driven, incorporating partnership with the private sector to realise its security ambitions, and market protecting, demonstrating how the EU's technology security agenda was developed as a distinct yet internal market-supporting initiative. The final substantive section considers the significant paradigm shift that occurred in the period 2016–2019, in which a series of shocks to the EU resulted in the Commission adapting its approach to regulating technologies that was motivated by concerns over the reliability of the private sector as a partner in regulation, as well as external events that encouraged the EU to see itself as a regulatory power with the ability to influence other states and set world standards through 'the Brussels Effect'. It concludes by considering how this laid the ground for the EU's digital sovereignty agenda, allowing for consideration of how geopolitical shocks during this period created a sense of vulnerability on the part of the EU that will be explored further in Chapter 3.

THE EUROPEAN ECONOMIC COMMUNITY AND THE REMOVAL OF INTERNAL BARRIERS TO TRADE: NEGATIVE INTEGRATION AND THE INDIRECT REGULATION OF TECHNOLOGY

The formation of the European Coal and Steel Community (ECSC) in 1951 was the first step taken to the development of a single market in Europe, albeit in a very limited field, and concerned with ending historical enmity between France and Germany (represented in the Agreement by the Federal Republic of Germany) and promoting the development of industry for the purpose of aiding reconstruction efforts after the Second World War.[3] At its core, the ECSC was about technology – coal and steel as the raw resources for the industrial innovation European nations required, and the ECSC as a means to an end to the geopolitical manoeuvring for

---

[3] Dietmar Petzina, Wolfgang F Stolper and Michael Hudson, 'The Origin of the European Coal and Steel Community: Economic Forces and Political Interests' (1981) 137 *Zeitschrift für die gesamte Staatswissenschaft/Journal of Institutional and Theoretical Economics* 450.

access to these fundamentally important resources.[4] With the Treaty of Rome in 1957 and the establishment of the EEC, the process of integration became accelerated, and with it, the regulation of technology. The Spaak Report[5] was named after Paul-Henri Spaak, the head of the committee set up under the auspices of the High Authority of the ECSC, and it argued for the creation of a Customs Union, eliminating all customs duties between members, while implementing a common external tariff applicable to all trade with the bloc with the ultimate goal of realising a common market applicable to all economic activities.[6] It must be stated here that this approach is not dissimilar to that discussed by Schmoller and List, as discussed in Chapter 1. Schmoller analysed how the disparate German city-states and provinces were brought together, based on the understanding that 'territorial trade, the territorial industry, and the territorial market formed a united whole'.[7] Similarly, List argued that rather than a constant conflict, unification of markets in such a way could facilitate 'nations united in bonds political, legal, and administrative, in a state of perpetual peace and perfect unity of interests'.[8] This argument may be somewhat familiar to those knowledgeable of the origins of the EU, and the justifications for its existence as a means of guaranteeing peace between its Member States.[9]

The establishment of the common market and the free movement of goods and services was a process typified at first by negative rather than positive integration.[10] Negative integration refers to measures taken to remove barriers to trade such as tariffs, quantitative restrictions, or anticompetitive practices, whereas positive integration refers to reconstruction of the economic regulatory system[11] through legislative interventions.[12] The EEC during the period from the late 1960s to early 1980s was

---

[4] See, for example, Iris Glockner and Berthold Rittberger, 'The European Coal and Steel Community (ECSC) and European Defence Community (EDC) Treaties' in Finn Laursen (ed), *Designing the European Union: From Paris to Lisbon* (Palgrave Macmillan UK 2012); see also Craig Parsons, 'Showing Ideas as Causes: The Origins of the European Union' (2002) 56 *International Organization* 47.

[5] Information Service High Authority of the European Community for Coal and Steel, 'The Brussels Report on the General Common Market' (Information Service High Authority of the European Community for Coal and Steel 1956).

[6] Ibid 1.

[7] Gustav Schmoller, *The Mercantile System and Its Historical Significance* (William James Ashley tr, Macmillan 1897) 33.

[8] Friedrich List, *The National System of Political Economy* (GA Matile tr, JB Lippincott 1856) 354.

[9] The speech published by Martin Territt, '50 Years of the Treaty of Rome Special Issue Commemorating the 50th Anniversary of the Treaty of Rome: Speeches' (2008) 15 *Irish Journal of European Law* 13 serves as an excellent example, making the claim that it is the prosperity of the EU that is the greatest contributor to the peace between its members. See however the argument of Eva Polonska Kimunguyi, 'The Myth of Peace and Statehood in European Integration Theory: The Imperial Legal Order of the Rome Treaty' (2023) 28 *European Foreign Affairs Review* 185–214 that this understanding of peace only holds so long as we do not consider the impact of the Member States' colonial legacies and the violence and suppression that this entailed.

[10] Fritz Scharpf, *Governing in Europe: Effective and Democratic?* (Oxford University Press 1999).

[11] Ibid 45.

[12] See generally Martijn van den Brink, Mark Dawson and Jan Zglinski, 'Revisiting the Asymmetry Thesis: Negative and Positive Integration in the EU' (2025) 32 *Journal of European Public Policy* 209.

characterised as suffering from 'Eurosclerosis', with low levels of growth and limited competitiveness with the US and Japan.[13] There were external factors impacting upon the European economy that contributed to this, such as the collapse of Bretton Woods and the 1970s Oil Shock.[14] However, internally the EEC was struggling; De Gaulle's removal of French representatives from the Community's institutions in 1964 (known as the 'empty chair crisis') as a means of asserting national power and as a response to the souring of negotiations over the Common Agricultural Policy,[15] and the wave of scepticism toward supranationalism that followed the 1973 accession to the EEC by the UK, Denmark, and Ireland,[16] essentially placed a block on proactive, positive integration measures such as Regulations or Directives further unifying the European economy. The Commission's ability to regulate was hindered, resulting in an ineffective response to Europe's economic woes, further contributing to the 'stagflation' (comprising low growth and high inflation) experienced during this period.[17]

For this reason, the removal of internal barriers to trade to facilitate the free movement of goods, services, workers, and capital through processes of negative integration was how the EEC economy became further integrated during this period; accordingly, it was the CJEU that served as the main engine of European integration in the 1960s and 1970s.[18] As such, integration occurred through the removal of those barriers to trade arising from domestic regulatory regimes, in a form of integration through deregulation. Regarding the free movement of goods, it is perhaps the *Cassis de Dijon* case[19] that is most relevant, as it established the principle of mutual recognition, insofar as goods placed legally on the market in one Member State were to be considered as meeting legal requirements for sale in other Member States. Similarly, the *Van Binsbergen* case[20] had a similar effect for the free movement of services, with the Court determining that Articles 59 and 60 of the EEC Treaty had as their intent the elimination of 'any obstacle created by

---

[13] Herbert Giersch, 'Eurosclerosis' (Institut für Weltwirtschaft 1985) 112.
[14] Wayne Sandholtz and John Zysman, '1992: Recasting the European Bargain' (1989) 42 *World Politics* 95.
[15] N Piers Ludlow, 'Challenging French Leadership in Europe: Germany, Italy, the Netherlands and the Outbreak of the Empty Chair Crisis of 1965–1966' (1999) 8 *Contemporary European History* 231.
[16] Peter J Verovšek, *Memory and the Future of Europe: Rupture and Integration in the Wake of Total War* (Manchester University Press 2020) 86–88.
[17] Robert Owen Keohane and Stanley Hoffmann, *The New European Community: Decisionmaking and Institutional Change* (Westview Press 1991) 6–8.
[18] Giandomenico Majone, *Rethinking the Union of Europe Post-Crisis: Has Integration Gone Too Far?* (Cambridge University Press 2014) 99–100; See also Mark Thatcher, 'Supranational Neo-Liberalisation: The EU's Regulatory Model of Economic Markets' in Vivien A Schmidt and Mark Thatcher (eds), *Resilient Liberalism in Europe's Political Economy* (Cambridge University Press 2013); Susanne K Schmidt, 'The Shadow of Case Law: The Court of Justice of the European Union and the Policy Process' in Jeremy Richardson and Sonia Mazey (eds), *European Union: Power and Policy-making* (4th ed, Routledge 2015).
[19] Case 120/78 *Rewe-Zentral AG v Bundesmonopolverwaltung für Branntwein* EU:C:1979:42.
[20] Case 33/74 *Johannes Henricus Maria van Binsbergen v Bestuur van de Bedrijfsvereniging voor de Metaalnijverheid* EU:C:1974:31.

a Member State by reason solely of the fact that the activity concerned entails the crossing of frontiers'.[21] It is in this context that the regulation of technology during this early period of European integration must be considered; forays into this area of policymaking were *incidental* to the removal of internal barriers to trade generally, rather than *intentional* for the furtherance of technology regulation specifically. Attempts by the EEC to develop industrial policies around certain key technological sectors, such as in space and computers,[22] ultimately failed due to the wrangling between states and difficulties with working within the formative institutional structures of the EEC. Furthermore, before the UK's accession, Member State industries largely centred around older technologies rather than the 'high technologies' in which the UK was beginning to demonstrate significant development capacities.[23]

By way of comparison, efforts aimed at easing the movement of those technologies between Member States were more successful during this period – the most clearcut examples of this being cases concerning the protection of intellectual property, and its interaction with broader legal principles of European law. The *Consten and Grundig*[24] case heard in the 1960s concerned the application of competition law in the context of exclusivity agreements, in which the French company Consten would act as the sole representative of the German company Grundig in French territory. The parties to this exclusivity agreement argued that it was within their rights to maintain such an agreement based on the rights afforded to them under copyright, patent, and trademark laws, under which the goods in question were protected (namely, electronics produced by Grundig). The CJEU, however, was sceptical of Consten and Grundig's arguments concerning the need to protect intellectual property rights (discussed in terms of 'industrial rights' in this decision), commenting that the cartel prohibition rules in the Member States concerned did not permit the use of intellectual property rights to justify market partitioning. It argued that doing so constituted an improper use of those rights, stating that 'the rights of a party in a trade-mark registered by him do not allow him to frustrate economic legislation'.[25] In the case of *Deutsche Grammophon*,[26] the Court went further. In this case, Deutsche Grammophon sold records through license agreements with its parent company

---

[21] Ibid 1307.
[22] Arthe Van Laer, 'Developing an EC Computer Policy, 1965–1974' (2010) 32 *IEEE Annals of the History of Computing* 16.
[23] See Laurent Warlouzet, 'Towards a European Industrial Policy? The European Economic Community (EEC) Debates, 1957–1975' in Christian Grabas and Alexander Nützenadel (eds), *Industrial Policy in Europe after 1945: Wealth, Power and Economic Development in the Cold War* (Springer 2014); by way of comparison, however, aerospace cooperation around the establishment of Airbus during this period stands out as a rare success, as discussed in Wayne Sandholtz, *High-Tech Europe: The Politics of International Cooperation* (University of California Press 1992) 92–112.
[24] Joined cases 56 and 58/64 *Établissements Consten S.à.R.L. and Grundig-Verkaufs-GmbH v Commission of the European Economic Community* EU:C:1966:41.
[25] Ibid 316.
[26] Case 78/70 *Deutsche Grammophon Gesellschaft mbH v Metro-SB-Großmärkte GmbH & Co. KG.* EU:C:1971:59.

or one of its subsidiaries, in a form of vertical agreement. However, sound recordings sold in France were then purchased by a German company, Metro, and *resold* in German markets. When Deutsche Grammophon sought an injunction under German law seeking to prevent these resales, arguing that the reselling constituted an infringement of their copyright in those recordings, the CJEU took a somewhat dim view. The EEC Treaty did recognise the validity of intellectual property rights under Article 36, and that these rights could in principle justify restrictions on imports, exports, or transit of goods, but not where they amounted to arbitrary discrimination or a disguised restriction on trade between Member States. As the products were lawfully marketed in one Member State, the CJEU concluded that the exclusive distribution right in copyright could not be used as a means of preventing the lawful marketing of goods already available in another Member State,[27] as to do so 'would legitimize the isolation of national markets, [and] would be repugnant to the essential purpose of the Treaty, which is to unite national markets into a single market'.[28]

Nevertheless, it can be stated at this juncture that this period, ultimately concluding in the mid-1980s, was one in which technology regulation was an indirect byproduct of the CJEU's process of constructing a transnational framework facilitating increased levels of cross-border trade,[29] driving forwards the process of European integration.[30] Writing contemporaneously, Baldwin drew the analogy of a drained swamp, with muddy waters cleared making travel easier, but revealing 'all the snags and stumps […] that still have to be cleared away'.[31] The regulation of technology was not a focus of these efforts, and nor were they driven in any meaningful way by a sense of insecurity. Instead, through negative integration, the barriers to a unified market were gradually removed, allowing for the positive market-making efforts pursued in the mid-1980s, when a particularly active Commission seized the policy initiative.

THE INTERNAL MARKET IMPETUS FOR TECHNOLOGY RULES: MAKING THE MARKET WORK FOR EUROPE

The 1970s ended with the European Commission significantly concerned about the extent to which it saw the EEC falling behind competitors in developing new

---

[27] See also Bernadetta Ubertazzi, 'The Principle of Free Movement of Goods: Community Exhaustion and Parallel Imports' in Irini Stamatoudi and Paul Torremans (eds), *EU Copyright Law: A Commentary* (2nd ed, Edward Elgar Publishing 2021).
[28] Ibid 500.
[29] Alec Stone Sweet and James A Caporaso, 'From Free Trade to Supranational Polity: The European Court and Integration' in Wayne Sandholtz and Alec Stone Sweet (eds), *European Integration and Supranational Governance* (Oxford University Press 1998).
[30] Geoffrey Garrett, R Daniel Kelemen and Heiner Schulz, 'The European Court of Justice, National Governments, and Legal Integration in the European Union' (1998) 52 *International Organization* 149.
[31] Robert E Baldwin, *Nontariff Distortions of International Trade* (Brookings Institution 1970) 2.

technologies. During the significant shocks of the decade, the 1970s saw the decline of coal, steel, and shipbuilding as key sources of industrial growth, and in 1979, the Commission published a Communication stating that after a meeting of Heads of State and Government in Bonn in the previous year, it was agreed that Europe needed to focus more on the technologies of the future.[32] In particular, 'the dynamic complex of information industries based on the new electronic technologies'[33] offered a major economic alternative, offsetting the losses being experienced in other European industries.[34] The Commission identified computing power and satellite transmission as key dimensions of this new information economy (while also amusingly and portentously referring to the revolutions possible through artificial intelligence),[35] before lamenting that 'the present industrial scene leaves much to be desired [...] European-owned computer companies command a mere 16 percent of the world market compared with 73% for the American [sic] industry'.[36] Action began in this field through some relatively limited joint R&D programmes at the national level under the European Strategic Programme for Research and Development in Information Technology (ESPRIT) in 1980, which had funding agreed by the Council of Ministers of 11.5 million ECU in the first instance.[37] This arguably began the (now) EU's involvement in technology policy, albeit involvement that was largely industry led, and did not result in significant European competence over technology-related issues.[38]

The 1980s saw a significant change, however. With the renewed impetus given for European integration as a result of the Single European Act (SEA)[39] in 1987 and the ambitious Delors Commission Presidencies, there was a significant shift from funding for national programmes to the establishment of pan-European initiatives.[40] It is worth stating that regardless of how important research funding initiatives were at this point in time, these were not *regulatory* interventions. However, the SEA did begin the process of positive integration in the field of technology in which the Commission set down a legislative agenda. Under a new Title VII to the Treaty of Rome on Research and Technological Development, a new Article 130f(3) stated that in order to achieve its aims of improving European competitiveness in new technologies, 'special account

---

[32] European Commission, 'European Society Faced with the Challenge of New Information Technologies: A Community Response' (1979) COM(79) 650.
[33] Ibid 1.
[34] Ibid.
[35] Ibid 2.
[36] Ibid 3.
[37] David R Charles, 'The Evolution of European Science and Technology Policy and Its Links to the Cohesion Agenda' in Helen Lawton Smith (ed), *The Regulation of Science and Technology* (Palgrave Macmillan UK 2002).
[38] See generally Simon Parker, 'Esprit and Technology Corporatism' in Volker Bornschier (ed), *State-building in Europe: The Revitalization of Western European Integration* (Cambridge University Press 2000) for an excellent overview of ESPRIT's successes and failures.
[39] Single European Act [1987] OJ L169/1
[40] John Peterson, 'Technology Policy in Europe: Explaining the Framework Programme and Eureka in Theory and Practice' (1991) 29 JCMS: *Journal of Common Market Studies* 269.

will be taken of the connection between common research and technological development effort, the establishment of the internal market and the implementation of common policies, particularly as regards competition and trade'. The impetus here became one of developing a competitive information economy based around new technologies, while ensuring competition and a degree of protection for consumers from potentially harmful practices.[41] What became clear very quickly however was that this approach was one in which the role of the Commission was to set the conditions for successful market activity – in other words, the logic was not one of control, but instead one of facilitation. The Commission's 1993 Growth, Competitiveness and Employment Report[42] was published at a point in which *dirigiste* economic planning and the idea of industrial champions had largely been replaced by the approach of the regulatory state and the role of the private sector in market activity.[43] In the 1993 Report, the Commission made clear that it saw the future success of the European economy as being based on private sector investment in technology areas such as telecoms, with the EU's key role being to create the necessary legal conditions to promote the levels of investment that could achieve this.[44] This approach bears the hallmarks of regulatory capitalism discussed in Chapter 1, insofar as market efficiency was the driving rationale, and private sector rowing towards market goals was the means by which this was to be achieved.

This Report was followed by the 1994 Bangemann Group Report,[45] named after the Commissioner for the internal market and industrial affairs during the second Delors Commission. This group combined technical experts from the Commission with a range of different sectoral representatives from the private sector, and it was focused on how to create the conditions necessary for Europe to economically benefit from the emergence of new technologies, and in particular the internet.[46] Importantly, the Report reiterated that 'the market will drive, it will decide on winners and losers […] the prime task of government is to safeguard competitive forces'.[47] The role

---

[41] See generally Sandholtz (n23).
[42] European Commission, 'Growth, Competitiveness, Employment: The Challenges and Ways Forward into the 21st Century' (1993) COM(93) 700.
[43] Laurent Warlouzet, 'The EEC/EU as an Evolving Compromise between French Dirigism and German Ordoliberalism (1957–1995)' (2019) 57 *JCMS: Journal of Common Market Studies* 77; See also Bastiaan van Apeldoorn, *Transnational Capitalism and the Struggle over European Integration* (Routledge 2002) 117; Timo Seidl and Luuk Schmitz, 'Moving on to Not Fall behind? Technological Sovereignty and the "Geo-Dirigiste" Turn in EU Industrial Policy' (2023) 31 *Journal of European Public Policy* 2147.
[44] European Commission, 'Growth, Competitiveness, Employment: The Challenges and Ways Forward into the 21st Century' (n42) 112.
[45] European Commission and Bangemann Group, 'Europe and the Global Information Society: Recommendations of the High-Level Group on the Information Society to the Corfu European Council' (1994) S.2/94.
[46] Benjamin Farrand, 'The Ordoliberal Internet? Continuity and Change in the EU's Approach to the Governance of Cyberspace' (2023) 2 *European Law Open* 106, 117–118.
[47] European Commission and Bangemann Group (n45) 13.

of the Commission would be to regulate to promote economic activity by the private sector in the single market, which began a flurry of regulatory activity in the mid-to-late 1990s. In 1995, the EU implemented the Data Protection Directive,[48] which was pursued on the basis that there was a growing number of Member States with their own distinct data protection regimes, and the EU was concerned that these divergent approaches could raise 'an obstacle to the completion of the single market'.[49] The Commission considered it essential to regulate in this field, in order to ensure that data processing businesses and industries could develop, as a failure to do so could 'induce a Member State to place barriers in the way of free flow of data [and ...] could also, in certain circumstances, distort competition'.[50]

Similarly, a 1997 Communication entitled 'A European Initiative in Electronic Commerce'[51] saw the Commission seek to assert its role in promoting a European single market buoyed by what it described as the 'Internet revolution',[52] but on the basis that it was to ensure 'a stimulus to electronic commerce and to avoid a fragmentation of this promising market'.[53] The Commission's role was to create a favourable regulatory framework to create a unified internal market for digital services that would allow online service operators to flourish, promoting a favourable business environment,[54] but one that would be market driven.[55] This resulted in the creation of the E-Commerce Directive.[56] This Directive harmonised the conditions for the performance of electronic contracts while providing the self-regulatory principles for addressing illegal or infringing uses of their services by end users, a regime designed to ensure as light a touch as possible for overseeing a commercial sector the Commission sought to promote.[57] A proposal for a Directive harmonising aspects of copyright[58] was released in the same year, on the basis of an earlier Communication on copyright in the information society[59] that argued that the competitiveness of the internal market required legislating to provide firms with

---

[48] Directive 95/46/EC on the protection of individuals with regard to the processing of personal data and on the free movement of such data.
[49] European Commission, 'Communication on the Protection of Individuals in Relation to the Processing of Personal Data in the Community and Information Security' (1990) COM(90) 314 4.
[50] Ibid 16.
[51] European Commission, 'A European Initiative in Electronic Commerce' (1997) COM(97) 157.
[52] Ibid 4.
[53] Ibid.
[54] Ibid 5–6.
[55] Ibid 1.
[56] Directive 2000/31/EC on certain legal aspects of information society services, in particular electronic commerce, in the Internal Market (the Directive on electronic commerce).
[57] Helena Carrapico and Benjamin Farrand, 'Discursive Continuity and Change in the Time of Covid-19: The Case of EU Cybersecurity Policy' (2020) 42 *Journal of European Integration* 1111. This will be returned to in Chapter 5, in the context of the EU's approach to the regulation of online platforms.
[58] European Commission, 'Proposal for a Directive on the Harmonisation of Certain Aspects of Copyright and Related Rights in the Information Society' (1997) COM(97) 628.
[59] European Commission, 'Green Paper: Copyright and Related Rights in the Information Society' (European Commission 1995) COM(95) 382 final.

certainty concerning the enforceability of their intellectual property rights across borders.[60] By providing regulatory certainty and ensuring consistent protection of copyright, the Commission argued it would create the impetus to invest in new digital technologies on the part of the creative and cultural sectors, which are regarded as essential to adding value and competitiveness to the European economy.[61] By 2001, the Commission had successfully negotiated and implemented the copyright in the Information Society Directive,[62] providing a harmonised approach to the exercise of rights and enforcement of copyright across borders in the EU's internal market.

From the late 2000s to the mid-2010s, the emphasis of EU regulation relating to digital technologies was about creating the conditions necessary for realising their economic potential for the benefit of the internal market. In particular, and as a response to the economic downturn that resulted from the Global Financial Crisis,[63] Mario Monti wrote a report for the 2nd Barroso Commission arguing that Europe needed to reinforce the internal market both as a bulwark against economic crisis and to ensure Europe's economy could return to growth.[64] In the context of technologies, Monti argued that stimulating the development of a digital single market could add 4 per cent to Europe's GDP,[65] and that promoting the development of EU standards for technologies could help to facilitate the internal market as well as potentially provide leverage to shape international standards.[66] A number of Communications from the Commission quickly followed, each considering how positive integration through setting regulatory standards could contribute to boosting the European economy.[67] These measures predominantly focused on facilitating cross-border access to creative works by simplifying and harmonising copyright principles around making accessible works where the original copyright owner could not be found,[68] simplifying collective licensing,[69] and ensuring customers could legally access content purchased in their home Member State when temporarily residing

---

[60] Ibid 10.
[61] Ibid 11–12.
[62] Directive 2001/29/EC on the harmonisation of certain aspects of copyright and related rights in the information society.
[63] This will be returned to in more detail in Chapter 3 when considering the EU's perceptions of vulnerability in the face of external shocks and perceived crises.
[64] Mario Monti, 'A New Strategy for the Single Market: At the Service of Europe's Economy and Society', 9 May 2010, Ref. Ares(2016)841541.
[65] Ibid 44.
[66] Ibid 91. This will be returned to in Chapter 4 in the discussion of ETSI and EU standards.
[67] Such as European Commission, 'Green Paper: Unlocking the Potential of the Cultural and Creative Industries' (2010) COM(2010) 183; European Commission, 'Innovation Union' (2010) COM(2010) 546 final; European Commission, 'A Digital Agenda for Europe' (2010) COM(2010) 245 final/2; and European Commission, 'A Single Market for Intellectual Property Rights: – Boosting Creativity and Innovation to Provide Economic Growth, High Quality Jobs and First Class Products and Services in Europe' (2011) COM(2011) 287.
[68] Directive 2012/28/EU on certain permitted uses of orphan works.
[69] Directive 2014/26/EU on collective management of copyright and related rights and multi-territorial licensing of rights in musical works for online use in the internal market.

in another Member State.[70] This approach, in which technology was presented as a means of economic development and regulation justified on the basis of promoting greater integration of the internal market to the benefit of the European economy, arguably peaked with the Juncker Commission's 2015 Communication on the Digital Single Market Strategy.[71] Written at a point when the EU felt that it had weathered the worst of the global and Eurozone crises, the emphasis of lawmaking was on facilitating growth. In the foreword to the Communication, Juncker wrote that 'By creating a connected digital single market, we can generate up to EUR 250 billion of additional growth in Europe in the course of the mandate of the next Commission'.[72] However, as will be seen later in this chapter, the perception of facilitating business activity as a means of generating growth has become challenged by geopolitical shifts. Ultimately, from the 1980s until the mid-2010s, the regulation of technology by the Commission, and digital technologies in particular, was focused on internal market development through positive integration. Regulation of technology was not pursued for reasons of control *per se*, but for reasons of economic development, in which creating consistent internal market rules would allow for the commercial benefits of new technologies to be realised. Of relevance to this book is the fact that security was not an overriding concern in this regulatory approach, which was overwhelmingly market driven. This is not to say that security was not a feature of technology regulation *at all*; instead, it was treated as a distinct and complementary field of activity, as will be expanded upon now.

SECURITY AS DISTINCT BUT SUPPORTIVE: CYBERSECURITY AS A COMPLEMENTARY FRAMEWORK FOR PROTECTING THE INTERNAL MARKET

It must be stated at the outset that during the initial period of market integration discussed earlier, the Commission had little to no competence in security matters, and thus it had no formal powers of legislative initiative around issues of security or defence. While the TREVI group was established in 1975 to deal with issues of common security concern, such as organised crime and terrorism, it was ultimately a loose intergovernmental network outside of the institutional structures of the EEC.[73] In the 1980s, there was a growing awareness both in the EEC and internationally that the spread of new technologies also risked the spread of new forms of crime (or new methods of pursuing old crimes) that required some sort of intervention;[74] however, it was not until the 1990s that the

---

[70] Regulation 2017/1128 on cross-border portability of online content services in the internal market.
[71] European Commission, 'A Digital Single Market Strategy for Europe' (2015) COM(2015) 192.
[72] Ibid 2.
[73] Jeffrey Lewis, 'Informal Integration and the Supranational Construction of the Council' (2003) 10 *Journal of European Public Policy* 996.
[74] Helena Carrapico and Benjamin Farrand, 'Cyber Crime as a Fragmented Policy Field in the Context of the Area of Freedom, Security and Justice' in Ariadna Ripoll Servent and Florian Trauner (eds), *The Routledge Handbook of Justice and Home Affairs Research* (Routledge 2018).

Commission began to formally discuss the security implications of new technologies. The 1990 Communication on data protection and privacy explicitly considered information security as a challenge for the effective protection of user data, albeit insofar as information security was necessary to ensure the functioning of the internal market for data processing-related services.[75] Furthermore, information security was considered essential for trade and industry.[76] For this reason, the Communication included a Proposal for a Council Decision on Information Security, which ultimately entered into force in 1992.[77] This Council Decision formally framed the need for this intervention on economic grounds and the completion of the internal market, and under Article 2 requested the Commission draw up a two-year action plan with measures to include the development of a strategic framework for the security of information systems.

Nevertheless, formative cybersecurity regulation was constructed as being protective of the internal market specifically; rather than being philosophically based in a security logic akin to traditional security and defence, the logic was one of providing conditions for market development.[78] The Bangemann Report in particular highlighted that while information security was important, and a common European response was necessary, pursuing security should not be done at the risk of undermining the opportunity presented by digital technologies and services.[79] As a set of services, and eventually a sector, digital technologies garnered a further security dimension however as states and policymakers became increasingly aware of the way that these services could be misused. Initial efforts at security-related regulation focused on cybercrime as a phenomenon, with international efforts focused on approximating laws concerning cyberattacks such as unauthorised system penetration and information access, as well as computer-facilitated crimes such as identity theft and the trade in child sexual abuse materials.[80] This resulted in the implementation at the international level of the Cybercrime Convention,[81] which outlined *what* should be considered an offence in domestic law, how to investigate alleged cybercrimes, as well as conditions for mutual assistance. However, it is important to state that this was an

---

[75] European Commission, 'Communication on the Protection of Individuals in Relation to the Processing of Personal Data in the Community and Information Security' (n49) 4.
[76] Ibid 5.
[77] Council Decision 92/242/EEC in the field of security of information systems.
[78] Carrapico and Farrand, 'Discursive Continuity and Change in the Time of Covid-19' (n57).
[79] European Commission and Bangemann Group (n45); see also Tobias Liebetrau, 'Problematising EU Cybersecurity: Exploring How the Single Market Functions as a Security Practice' (2024) 62 *JCMS: Journal of Common Market Studies* 705.
[80] Fernando Mendez, 'The European Union and Cybercrime: Insights from Comparative Federalism' (2005) 12 *Journal of European Public Policy* 509; Stearns Broadhead, 'The Contemporary Cybercrime Ecosystem: A Multi-Disciplinary Overview of the State of Affairs and Developments' (2018) 34 *Computer Law & Security Review* 1180.
[81] Council of Europe, The Budapest Convention on Cybercrime (2001) CETS 185.

international rather than an EU initiative, and that the emphasis was on *ex post* investigation and prosecution of crime, rather than *ex ante* regulation intended to prevent or mitigate against such actions. With the development of the Justice and Home Affairs pillar of the EU under the Maastricht Treaty, however, and later the development of the EU's formalised Area of Freedom, Security and Justice under the Treaty of Lisbon, the EU became both more involved and more interventionist in the development of technology security regulations. Initial actions again focused on the creation of common approaches to certain forms of cybercrime, such as Attacks on Information Systems,[82] and tackling child sexual abuse facilitated through the internet.[83] Alongside these initiatives focused on criminal law measures for prosecuting the perpetrators of these offences, however, the EU was also beginning the development of a security approach placing obligations on the potential targets of cyberattacks.

Cybersecurity regulation as an *ex ante* system based on preventing as far as possible successful cyberattacks, and resilience in the face of successful ones,[84] has its origins in the EU with the establishment of the European Network and Information Security Agency (now known as ENISA, the EU Cybersecurity Agency) in 2004.[85] The proposal for the Regulation establishing ENISA linked the issue of cybersecurity strongly to that of the internal market, both in terms of protecting it[86] and arguing that divergent cybersecurity standards would hamper the development of the internal market.[87] ENISA was tasked with promoting a high level of network and information security, with Article 1(1) stating that doing so for the benefit of citizens, consumers, enterprises and public sector organisations would contribute 'to the smooth functioning of the Internal Market'. As the competences of the Commission have grown, it has expanded the remit of ENISA as well as establishing the basis for an EU cybersecurity policy.[88] While being regarded by some in the mid-2000s as something of a 'lame duck' agency fighting for its survival,[89] the Commission's reinforced focus on security issues saw it become central to the EU's cybersecurity agenda.

---

[82] Council Framework Decision 2005/222/JHA of 24 February 2005 on attacks against information systems.
[83] Council Framework Decision 2004/68/JHA of 22 December 2003 on combating the sexual exploitation of children and child pornography.
[84] For a comprehensive overview, see George Christou, *Cybersecurity in the European Union: Resilience and Adaptability in Governance Policy* (Palgrave Macmillan 2015).
[85] Regulation 460/2004 establishing the European Network and Information Security Agency.
[86] European Commission, 'Proposal for a Regulation Establishing the European Network and Information Security Agency' (2003) COM(2003) 63 2.
[87] Ibid 5.
[88] Helena Carrapico and André Barrinha, 'The EU as a Coherent (Cyber)Security Actor?' (2017) 55 *JCMS: Journal of Common Market Studies* 1254.
[89] Lorraine Mallinder, 'Enisa – An Agency Fighting for Its Survival' (*POLITICO*, 14 May 2008) <www.politico.eu/article/enisa-an-agency-fighting-for-its-survival/> accessed 13 March 2025.

The 2010 Internal Security Strategy published by the Commission continued to emphasise the importance of cybersecurity for the EU's internal market,[90] and highlighted that ENISA was best placed to facilitate the cooperation between Member States, as well as between Member States and the private sector, that would serve as the basis for improving Europe's ability to respond to cyberattacks.[91] Then, in 2013, EU cybersecurity became formalised as a distinct field of policy[92] with the publication of the Commission and High Representative of the European Union for Foreign Affairs and Security Cybersecurity Strategy,[93] which brought together the elements of cybercrime, cybersecurity, and cyberdefence as three pillars of a holistic approach to digital security issues. Measures discussed in the Strategy included the development of a common approach to critical information infrastructure protection, expanding the remit of ENISA to more effectively oversee compliance with cybersecurity provision in the EU, and stronger engagements with cybersecurity experts.[94] In terms of regulatory intervention, this resulted in the adoption of a new Regulation on ENISA in 2013[95] that provided competence for formal cooperation with Europol's Cybercrime Centre (EC3), as well as supporting the EU in developing network and information security laws and policies, promoting EU and Member State capacity building including through the CERTS (Computer Emergency Response Teams) and CSIRTs (Computer Security Incident Response Teams), supporting the development of best practices and standards around cybersecurity.[96]

What becomes clear through the analysis of the cybersecurity policies adopted during this period is that the approach to security taken is one firmly based within a regulatory capitalism framework for state-market relations. Implemented in 2016, the Network and Information Security Directive (NIS Directive)[97] established a system for critical information infrastructure protection that provided for co-regulatory cooperation between the private infrastructure providers and state actors, based on principles of dialogue, partnership, and mutual empowerment.[98] Within this system sectors designated as essential services under Annex II of the Directive, such

---

[90] European Commission, 'The EU Internal Security Strategy in Action: Five Steps towards a More Secure Europe' (2010) COM(2010) 673 final 9.
[91] Ibid 10.
[92] Carrapico and Farrand, 'Discursive Continuity and Change in the Time of Covid-19' (n57).
[93] European Commission and High Representative of the European Union for Foreign Affairs and Security Policy, 'Cybersecurity Strategy of the European Union: An Open, Safe and Secure Cyberspace' (2013) JOIN (2013) 1.
[94] Ibid 5–6.
[95] Regulation 526/2013 concerning the European Union Agency for Network and Information Security (ENISA) and repealing Regulation (EC) No 460/2004.
[96] Ibid Article 3.
[97] Directive 2016/1148 concerning measures for a high common level of security of network and information systems across the Union.
[98] Helena Carrapico and Benjamin Farrand, '"Dialogue, Partnership and Empowerment for Network and Information Security": The Changing Role of the Private Sector from Objects of Regulation to Regulation Shapers' (2017) 67 *Crime, Law and Social Change* 245.

as entities in the energy, transport, and digital infrastructure providers, are expected to adopt best practices and standards for cybersecurity, incident handling, business continuity and monitoring, auditing, and testing under Article 16(1). The recitals to the Directive however make it clear that this is intended to be a market-driven process (recital 66), and that under Article 19, Member States should encourage the use of European or internationally accepted standards.[99] ENISA, as the cybersecurity agency, was tasked with coordination and providing strategic guidance under Article 11, acting as part of a Cooperation Group with the Commission and representatives of the Member States. In this respect, ENISA was positioned as a key player in EU security policy[100] yet in a way that highlighted the role of private sector industries and experts in helping to formulate the rules by which cybersecurity regulation would apply. This was indicated by ENISA's 2016 work programme, which indicated that the standards that ENISA would develop would be determined through working with the public and private sectors to establish best practices, and how to implement them.[101]

The other key aspect of this historical overview of the development of EU cybersecurity policy is that the emphasis in the security approach is based in the logic of protection of the internal market, first and foremost. While the protection of citizens and consumers is of course a necessary component of this, it is nevertheless reiterated throughout policy documents that internal market protection, and indeed the avoidance of divergences in approaches that may distort the internal market, are the key drivers for actions in this field. As such, it is distinct from, yet supportive of, the goals of internal market harmonisation that typified the historical approach to technology regulation pursued by the Commission. What is evident from analysis of these policies and legislative initiatives is that the motivators are not those found within a regulatory mercantilism framework – private sector actors are framed as being expert partners in regulatory activity, rather than being an object of regulation in themselves, and the language of geopolitical instability, vulnerability, achieving strategic autonomy/reducing external dependencies, and Europe's digital/technological sovereignty are all absent. In other words, these policies were largely devised and implemented at a time when the EU's faith in the liberal international order, and indeed its effective functioning, were high. However, as will be discussed in the next section of this chapter, the period 2016–2019 results in some significant changes in Commission approaches to both internal market and security related issues that laid the foundations for von der Leyen's Geopolitical Commission, and the agendas it pursued under the auspices of digital sovereignty.

---

[99] The issue of European standards in the context of digital technologies, and EU concerns over geopolitical vulnerability regarding these standards, will be returned to in Chapter 4.

[100] Myriam Dunn Cavelty and Max Smeets, 'Regulatory Cybersecurity Governance in the Making: The Formation of ENISA and Its Struggle for Epistemic Authority' (2023) 30 *Journal of European Public Policy* 1330.

[101] ENISA, 'Work Programme 2016' (2015) 35.

EUROPE IN EXISTENTIAL CRISIS: VULNERABILITY AND THE CHANGING PERCEPTION OF TECHNOLOGY

2016 was not an easy year for the EU. After developing a sense that the worst of the GFC and resultant Eurozone crisis was over, 2015 was marred by significant conflicts with Greece over austerity and the response of the Syriza government to the conditions imposed upon it by the Commission, European Central Bank, and International Monetary Fund (known as the Troika).[102] The Russian invasion of Crimea in 2014 had tested the EU's ability to both respond and demonstrate internal unity,[103] and the outbreak of war in Syria, and the influx of refugees as a result was resulting in increased tensions between Member States, to the extent that Commission President Juncker commented in his 2015 State of the Union that 'it is time to speak frankly about the big issues facing Europe. Because our European Union is not in a good state. There is not enough Europe in this Union. And there is not enough Union in this Union'.[104] Furthermore, the Commission was becoming increasingly concerned about the market power of 'Big Tech',[105] and EU institutions, Member States, and individual citizens were alarmed about the revelations by Edward Snowden regarding the extent of US intelligence agency surveillance facilitated through private digital service operators.[106] 2016 was little better – a rise in anti-EU sentiment, perceptions of increased populism as the result of widespread disinformation campaigns and the withdrawal referendum in the UK sparked a sense of 'polycrisis' on the part of the EU, described by the Commission President as meaning that 'Our European Union is, at least in part, in an existential crisis'.[107] In each case technology was either directly implicated, or indirectly suspected, in the intensification of these perceived crises.[108]

This resulted in a changed understanding of the role of technology in the EU, as the remainder of this book will expand upon. Rather than being something to be harnessed for the benefit of the internal market, with security considered as a means of offsetting negative externalities from the expanding digitisation of services, technology itself could be a vector for insecurity for the EU as a whole, rather than the

---

[102] Covered in significant detail in Vivien A Schmidt, *Europe's Crisis of Legitimacy: Governing by Rules and Ruling by Numbers in the Eurozone* (Oxford University Press 2020).

[103] Niklas IM Nováky, 'Why so Soft? The European Union in Ukraine' (2015) 36 *Contemporary Security Policy* 244.

[104] Jean-Claude Juncker, 'State of the Union Address 2015: Time for Honesty, Unity and Solidarity' (2015).

[105] This will be returned to in Chapter 3, as well as Chapter 5.

[106] See Patrick F Walsh and Seumas Miller, 'Rethinking "Five Eyes" Security Intelligence Collection Policies and Practice Post Snowden' (2016) 31 *Intelligence and National Security* 345; Stefan Steiger, Wolf J Schünemann and Katharina Dimmroth, 'Outrage without Consequences? Post-Snowden Discourses and Governmental Practice in Germany' (2017) 5 *Media and Communication* 7. This issue will be returned to in Chapter 6 in the discussion of changing European approaches to data.

[107] Jean-Claude Juncker, 'State of the Union Address 2016: Towards a Better Europe' (2016) 6.

[108] As will be highlighted throughout the Chapters 3–7 of this book.

individuals or commercial actors that its traditional security focus had considered. Technologies such as social media platforms could not only be misused by nefarious state or non-state actors, but the operators of those platforms themselves could possess values not aligned with those of the EU.[109] The development of European technology standards could be co-opted by foreign-based technology firms that *could* potentially present security threats or undermine European firms.[110] Access to the technologies themselves, or the resources required to produce or operate them, could potentially be restricted, with repercussions in a range of different sectors.[111] European data, whether personal or proprietary, could potentially be accessed and misused in foreign states, rendering Europe all the more vulnerable as a result of its dependence on data servers either outside of the EU, or alternatively, provided by companies based outside of the EU.[112] If the EU was locked in an existential crisis, and technology was a source of this crisis, then technology was something that needed to be controlled in order to mitigate these threats.

A new lexicon to describe technology regulation became increasingly prevalent in Commission documents. The 2017 State of the Union discussed the need for 'enhancing Europe's strategic autonomy' in the context of the development of the Digital Single Market.[113] Cybersecurity was highlighted as a key strategic priority of the Commission,[114] as was the commercial reuse of data as a means to bolster the European economy.[115] While not yet talked about in terms of digital sovereignty, the basis for such an approach can be seen in the discussion of the economic and security dimensions in the same context for technological development, and the more assertive tone adopted with regard to regulation. The 2018 State of the Union referred to the 'hour of European sovereignty', and the need for the EU to take a more active role on the world stage, with integrated security and defence policies, global leadership in digital, and a more autonomous position.[116] With the successful

---

[109] See Helena Carrapico and Benjamin Farrand, 'When Trust Fades, Facebook Is No Longer a Friend: Shifting Privatisation Dynamics in the Context of Cybersecurity as a Result of Disinformation, Populism and Political Uncertainty' (2021) 59 *JCMS: Journal of Common Market Studies* 1160 and Chapter 5 of this book.

[110] See Henk J de Vries, 'Vulnerabilities of European Telecommunication Systems and the EU's Concerns about ETSI's Legitimacy – A Proposal for Value-Based Standardization' (2024) 37 *Innovation: The European Journal of Social Science Research* 1397 and Chapter 4 of this book.

[111] See Shawn Donnelly, 'Semiconductor and ICT Industrial Policy in the US and EU: Geopolitical Threat Responses' (2023) 11 *Politics and Governance* 129 and Chapter 4 of this book.

[112] See Julia Rone, '"The Sovereign Cloud" in Europe: Diverging Nation State Preferences and Disputed Institutional Competences in the Context of Limited Technological Capabilities' (2024) 31 *Journal of European Public Policy* 1 and Chapter 6 of this book.

[113] Jean-Claude Juncker, 'President Jean-Claude Juncker's State of the Union Address 2017 – Wind In Our Sails' (European Commission, 2017) 26.

[114] Ibid 36.

[115] Ibid.

[116] Jean-Claude Juncker, '2018 State of the Union Address – A Perpetual Responsibility' (European Commission, 2018) 5.

implementation of the General Data Protection Regulation[117] and indications that it was both shaping private market conduct beyond Europe[118] and was being increasingly used as a template for data protection in other regimes,[119] the EU became convinced of the existence of the 'Brussels Effect'.[120] This effect, according to its originator Professor Anu Bradford, is largely down to the EU's ability as a large economy to become a source of global standards, and use its institutional architecture to '[convert] its market size into a tangible regulatory influence'.[121] This has allowed it to exert regulatory influence beyond its borders, not only through exporting its standards through bilateral economic and political agreements, but also through the adoption of its standards by private sector entities wishing to trade with and within the EU.[122] This is an argument reiterated by the Commission, such as in the 2018 State of the Union when President Juncker stated that 'It is because of our single market – the largest in the world – that we can set standards for big data, artificial intelligence, and automation'.[123] Increasingly, the EU became characterised as something of a 'regulatory superpower',[124] and it is in this that we can see the formation of a regulatory mercantilism shift in approach to technology regulation in the Commission. It was in the final year of the Juncker Commission that the formulation of an assertive regulatory policy towards technology started to take shape, with the incorporation of a security discourse and logic of action into an area typified by a predominantly (even exclusively) economic focus, and references both to Europe's sovereignty and its ability to regulate beyond its borders.

When Ursula von der Leyen was nominated as a candidate for the position of Commission President, it was done so largely as a response to a political deadlock as to who should have the role.[125] The inability of the *Spitzenkandidat* Manfred Weber to secure the support needed for approval by the European Parliament or

---

[117] Regulation 2016/679 on the protection of natural persons with regard to the processing of personal data and on the free movement of such data, and repealing Directive 95/46/EC (General Data Protection Regulation)
[118] Michelle Goddard, 'The EU General Data Protection Regulation (GDPR): European Regulation That Has a Global Impact' (2017) 59 *International Journal of Market Research* 703.
[119] Giulio Vittorio Cervi, 'Why and How Does the EU Rule Global Digital Policy: An Empirical Analysis of EU Regulatory Influence in Data Protection Laws' (2022) 1 *Digital Society* 18.
[120] A term created by Anu Bradford, *The Brussels Effect: How the European Union Rules the World* (Oxford University Press 2021).
[121] Ibid 25.
[122] See Bradford (n120) and where this is discussed in detail in Chapter 6.
[123] Juncker, '2018 State of the Union Address – A Perpetual Responsibility' (n116) 5.
[124] Some examples of its framing as such include Bradford (n120) xiii; Merje Kuus, 'Regulatory Power and Region-Making in the Arctic: China and the European Union' (2020) 27 *European Urban and Regional Studies* 321; Carla Hobbs, 'The EU as a Digital Regulatory Superpower: Implications for the United States' (ECFR, 8 April 2020) <https://ecfr.eu/article/commentary_the_eu_as_a_digital_regulatory_superpower_implications_for_the_u/> accessed 14 March 2025.
[125] See the reporting by Melanie Amann and others, 'Surprise European Commission Nomination for von Der Leyen' (*Der Spiegel*, 5 July 2019) <www.spiegel.de/international/germany/surprise-european-commission-nomination-for-von-der-leyen-a-1275984.html> accessed 14 March 2025 for more on this.

European Council, combined with the indications that Frans Timmermans would also not be able to secure that support,[126] meant that a compromise was sought, and von der Leyen was approved by the European Parliament by 383 votes in support versus 327 against. Von der Leyen, who had previously served as German Federal Minister for Defence from 2013 to July 2019, announced quickly after her election that her Commission would be a 'geopolitical Commission',[127] seeking to bring closer together the internal and external dimensions of the EU while facing up to the challenges of 'big power' competition globally.[128] Publishing her political guidelines with the title 'A Europe That Strives for More',[129] candidate for President von der Leyen set the direction of her Commission with the acknowledgment that:

> Today's world feels ever more unsettled. Existing powers are going down new paths alone. New powers are emerging and consolidating. Changes in climate, technology and demography are transforming our societies and way of life. This has left a feeling of unease and anxiety in many communities across Europe.[130]

In order to respond to these challenges, von der Leyen set out her priorities, of which 'A Europe Fit for the Digital Age' is the most directly relevant. Under this heading, von der Leyen wrote that she wanted Europe to seize upon the opportunities of digital services but within safe and ethical boundaries.[131] Central to this was the argument that 'it may be too late to replicate the hyperscalers, but it is not too late to achieve technological sovereignty in some critical technology sectors'.[132] Not only would this involve promoting European standards as global standards through its regulatory leadership, but the initiative was also cross-referenced to some of the other priorities, such as 'A Stronger Europe in the World',[133] and 'A New Push for European Democracy'.[134] In the combination of these different priorities, insofar as they focus on the regulation of technology with a combined economic, security, and sovereignty-based rationale, these political guidelines mark the beginning of the Geopolitical Union's attempt to exert control. However, it is in a speech to the

---

[126] Pieter de Wilde, 'The Fall of the Spitzenkandidaten: Political Parties and Conflict in the 2019 European Elections', in Sylvia Kritzinger and others (eds), *Assessing the 2019 European Parliament Elections* (Routledge 2020); Ben Crum, 'Why the European Parliament Lost the Spitzenkandidaten-Process' (2023) 30 *Journal of European Public Policy* 193.

[127] Euractiv Network, 'Timmermans Unhappy with Dombrovskis Unexpected "Promotion"' (*Euractiv*, 11 September 2019) <www.euractiv.com/section/politics/news/timmermans-unhappy-with-dombrovskis-unexpected-promotion/> accessed 14 March 2025.

[128] For an overview and critique, see Nicole Koenig, *The 'Geopolitical' European Commission and Its Pitfalls* (Jaque Delors Centre, Hertie School of Governance 2019).

[129] Ursula von der Leyen, 'A Europe That Strives for More: My Agenda for Europe' (2019).

[130] Ibid 4.

[131] Ibid 13.

[132] Ibid.

[133] Ibid 19 where the link to hybrid threats is discussed, a reference to issues such as disinformation and informational warfare, as discussed in Chapter 5.

[134] Ibid 21 where the issue of platform governance is referred to, as will be expanded upon in Chapter 5.

European Parliament in November 2019 that the full extent of this approach is laid bare; reiterating her goal of a geopolitical Commission and talking about the need for European industrial policy around technologies and the balancing of economic needs with security, President-elect von der Leyen stated that 'we must be able to strike a smart balance where markets cannot [...] we must have mastery and ownership of key technologies in Europe'.[135] This mastery and ownership would entail boosting industrial capabilities, suitable technological infrastructure, accumulation of the 'raw material' of data that could generate economic development within the context of a European data strategy, with cybersecurity being described as the other side of the digitisation coin that would make this possible.[136] After the official commencement of her mandate, the Commission would act to realise this goal.

CONCLUSIONS

The story of technology regulation in Europe is something akin to a slow burn suddenly becoming everything, everywhere, all at once. And yet, while contemporary scholarship has seized upon the idea of a field of EU technology studies as a new development, in essence the EU has its origins in the control of technology. Even if not thought of as such, the establishment of the ECSC had at its heart the control of technologies and the resources necessary for utilising them, as part of a broader geostrategic realignment in Europe. With the formation of the EEC, technology was regulated indirectly, with the CJEU seeking to ensure that the efforts put into protecting them at the national level did not serve to create barriers to trade in those technologies in Europe. While we may not *necessarily* consider conflicts regarding how interactions between the protection of intellectual property rights and the free movement of goods on the other as a form of technology regulation, they do ultimately constitute ideational conflicts concerning how technologies are utilised, distributed, or potentially misused. As the competences of the Commission grew and with it the potential for positive integration, while the Commission may not have explicitly discussed its role as one of a technology regulator, this is nevertheless something that has had an important role in policymaking and legislative development since the 1970s, although this accelerated dramatically in the 1990s.

What becomes clear when thinking of the EU as a technology regulator is that historically, and somewhat analogously, its preoccupations have been with its competitiveness vis-à-vis other states and regions. For this reason, the question of *how* to regulate technology has centred on the EEC and then EU's desire to harness technology for the purposes of economic development. Whether in the context of

---

[135] Ursula von der Leyen, 'Speech by President-Elect von Der Leyen in the European Parliament Plenary on the Occasion of the Presentation of Her College of Commissioners and Their Programme' (European Parliament, 2019) 4.
[136] Ibid.

the opportunities presented by the adoption of the consumer internet, or in seeking new avenues for boosting growth and productivity in the face of economic crisis, the Commission has actively sought to regulate technology in line with its view of the functioning of the internal market, based in a regulatory capitalist framework in which the purpose of regulation is to create the necessary conditions for an empowered private sector to flourish. As such, it tended towards market-driven solutions, with law presented as a means to strip away barriers to those solutions being realised, or to prevent distortions that may arise in the absence of those positive measures, increasingly framed as being the promotion of the Digital Single Market. What this meant, however, is that security related to technology was something of a secondary concern, or at least ancillary to the Commission's broader economic goals. Initially, legislative focus was on the prosecution of offences arising from new uses of technology, then with providing frameworks to ensure that insufficient cybersecurity provision did not harm the internal market, or the critical information infrastructures upon which it relied. Again, this was coherent with a regulatory capitalist framework – based in logics of market efficiency, the emphasis was on partnership with private actors and expertise as a means of identifying best standards and practices for ensuring cybersecurity, facilitated through cooperation with European agencies.

However, with the shocks of the mid-2010s, and the increasing sense of crisis in Europe, the approach to technology regulation had changed. Increasingly, the language of security and defence permeated Commission policymaking in this field, and strategic autonomy and sovereignty entered discussions as rationales for action. The EU's apparent success in the promotion of the GDPR as a global standard for data protection also created the sense that the EU was a regulatory actor with the market power and institutional ability to promote its standards as global standards. These different threads, namely guaranteeing economic development, ensuring security, while promoting both sovereignty and extraterritorial influence, converged in the political guidelines of the von der Leyen Commission, which introduced the concept of technological sovereignty, and the idea of a geopolitical Commission, best placed to face the challenges of the twenty-first century. While these political guidelines and the assertive regulatory tone struck sought to demonstrate strength and confidence, it is arguable that they were in fact motivated by a deep sense of unease with the global conditions in which the EU found itself, as a perceived sense of its own vulnerability to the shocks being experienced. The next chapter of this book explores this further, by considering these global shocks in the context of historical approaches to international technology control and Europe's place in them, highlighting the distinct and myriad ways in which the EU finds itself beset by external security threats, highlighting the conditions of vulnerability in which a regulatory mercantilist approach to regulation is more likely to be present. After providing this account of the geopolitical instability and loss of faith in the liberal international order, it will be possible to more effectively understand the change in approach to technology regulation exemplified in each of the case study chapters.

3

The Geopolitics of Technology Control and the Crisis of Globalisation

Ignoring economic dependencies that had built up over the decades had become really perilous – from energy uncertainty in Europe to supply-chain vulnerabilities in medical equipment, semiconductors, and critical minerals [...] these were the kinds of dependencies that could be exploited for economic or geopolitical leverage.[1]

INTRODUCTION

Within a regulatory mercantilism framework, the condition in which policies are likely to be pursued is one in which regulatory actors perceive themselves to be working in a context of crisis and vulnerability. Insecurity is a motivator for mercantilist approaches to trade and relations with other states and actors, and claims to sovereignty appear stronger in cases where an actor does not see themselves as being in a particularly strong position. The purpose of this chapter is to explore the conditions that the EU found itself in by the election of President von der Leyen in order to better understand its changing approach to regulation in diverse technology-oriented fields and the logic of insecurity that has motivated it to act.

To do so, the chapter is structured as follows. Its analysis begins with the Cold War, which shares some (if not all) parallels with the global currents experienced by the EU in the build-up to the von der Leyen Commission in 2019. It explores how trade relations between states were bipolar, organised around the US and Soviet Union specifically, and the important role of technological controls and restrictions in world trade resulting from security concerns. It continues by considering the significant opening of the trade system after the collapse of the USSR and the strong support for international organisations in a liberal economic order in which economic growth and democratisation were believed to go hand-in-hand. It explores how US unipolarity was largely structured around international trade, and the pursuit of technology seen as a predominantly economic rather than security concern. However, as the subsequent

---

[1] US National Security Adviser Jack Sullivan, as quoted in Henry Farrell and Abraham L Newman, 'The New Economic Security State' (2023) 102 *Foreign Affairs* 106.

subsection argues, the increased interdependence that globalisation represents also meant that crisis contagion was also more likely, and the impacts of a US-based crisis turning into a Global Financial Crisis led to questions about whether the liberal international economic order was either failing or had already failed. It considers the tensions arising from China's growth as a major industrial exporter and leading nation in advanced technologies and the loss of confidence in international organisations such as the World Trade Organisation, resulting in trade wars, increased protectionism, and increased trade multipolarity. The final substantive section of the chapter focuses on the EU's role in and understanding of these issues – moving from the globalisation success story of the 1990s to a (self-stated) crisis-ridden region, facing numerous crises impacting the stability of its economy and market, the integrity of its information ecosystem, and the physical security of its neighbouring regions. Its responses to these crises and their basis in what was seen as Europe's dependence on an increasingly unstable and hostile world are analysed, reflecting on the EU's emphasis on 'strategic autonomy', the capacity to act independently free from constraints arising from external dependencies, as a means of responding to a heightened sense of vulnerability. With the bringing together of strategic autonomy as a rationale for action, and sovereignty as the aim, the chapter concludes by considering the political guidelines presented by Commission President von der Leyen when she was a candidate for the position and how they have served to shape the EU's regulatory response to a range of different technologies within a framework of regulatory mercantilism.

TRADE RELATIONS DURING THE COLD WAR: MULTIPOLARITY, BIG POWER POLITICS, AND TECHNOLOGY CONTROL

The Cold War has been chosen as a starting point for this analysis due to the analogous (albeit distinct) conditions observable in the international economic order developing since the 2010s. In particular, it focuses on the 'economic cold war' waged between the US and its allies and the Soviet Union and its allies, including China.[2] In the period following the end of the Second World War, not only was Europe divided, but so too was the world economy. While prior to this global conflict, the US had little in the way of trade with the Soviet Union, by 1953 all trade with the bloc had virtually ceased,[3] with trade embargoes against non-aligned states and economic protectionism being the norm.[4] Trade during this period was weaponised,[5]

---

[2] Shu Guang Zhang, *Economic Cold War: America's Embargo Against China and the Sino-Soviet Alliance, 1949–1963* (Stanford University Press 2001); James Libbey, 'CoCom, Comecon, and the Economic Cold War' (2010) 37 *Russian History* 133.
[3] Herbert Schiller, 'Some Effects of the Cold War on United States Foreign Trade' (1955) 37 *The Review of Economics and Statistics* 428.
[4] Thomas W Zeiler, 'Managing Protectionism: American Trade Policy in the Early Cold War' (1998) 22 *Diplomatic History* 337.
[5] See Alan P Dobson, *US Economic Statecraft for Survival, 1933–1991: Of Sanctions, Embargoes and Economic Warfare* (Routledge 2002).

with embargoes serving as a form of economic warfare intended to disrupt or debilitate the economy of rivals.[6] The international economic system was dominated by geopolitics – representing political positioning between 'Big Powers', in which 'realism and national security, not idealism and economic theory, took precedence'.[7] While beyond the scope of this book, decisions by states about which other states to support economically were largely driven by geopolitical concerns, particularly along the borders of Europe between those states that were US aligned and those within the Soviet Union's sphere of influence.[8] Trade policies such as embargoes, export controls, and financial aid were not economic endeavours (or at least, determined to be *successful* economic endeavours), but were instead a means by which the US and the Soviet Union communicated political signals to each other.[9]

During this period, trade and state relations were typified by bipolarity. In the 1950s, US economic policies increasingly became based in binaries of 'free markets vs communism',[10] whereas in the Soviet Union, this was framed in terms of 'socialism vs capitalism'.[11] The world was divided broadly into three categories; those aligned with the US, those aligned with the USSR, and the non-aligned.[12] For the aligned, this resulted in a certain convergence on trade-related matters and the development of international organisations that would foster cooperation between those states. For the US and its partners, this was the General Agreement on Tariffs and Trade (GATT), supplemented by the Committee for Multilateral Export Controls (COCOM), which shall be returned to later, whereas for the USSR and its allies, this was the Council for Mutual Economic Assistance (known by acronyms such as CMEA or Comecon).[13] GATT, which came into force in 1948, was ostensibly a mechanism by which trade conflicts could be resolved peacefully, with an emphasis

---

[6] Embargoes as a form of political-economy 'weapon' have been argued to have their origins in medieval state relations, as argued in Stefan Stantchev, 'The Medieval Origins of Embargo as a Policy Tool' (2012) 33 *History of Political Thought* 373.

[7] Thomas W Zeiler, *Free Trade, Free World: The Advent of GATT* (The University of North Carolina Press 1999) 3.

[8] For a comprehensive overview, see Geoffrey Warner, 'Geopolitics and the Cold War' in Richard H Immerman and Petra Goedde (eds), *The Oxford Handbook of the Cold War* (Oxford University Press 2013).

[9] Robert Mark Spaulding, 'Trade, Aid, and Economic Warfare' in Richard H Immerman and Petra Goedde (eds), *The Oxford Handbook of the Cold War* (Oxford University Press 2013) 406; see also Donald E deKieffer, 'Foreign Policy Export Controls: A Proposal for Reform' (1986) 11 *North Carolina Journal of International Law and Commercial Regulation* 39.

[10] Eric Helleiner, *Forgotten Foundations of Bretton Woods: International Development and the Making of the Postwar Order* (Cornell University Press 2014) 266.

[11] Mark Kramer, 'Ideology and the Cold War' (1999) 25 *Review of International Studies* 539.

[12] Constituting the origin of the term 'third-world' in geopolitical terms, which has remained a contested term both rejected and embraced by a diverse range of scholars, as discussed in Marcin Wojciech Solarz, '"Third World": The 60th Anniversary of a Concept That Changed History' (2012) 33 *Third World Quarterly* 1561.

[13] Libbey (n2).

on removing or reducing barriers to international trade.[14] However, while the purpose of GATT may have been at its foundations economic, it was not immune to the Big Power politics dimension that further developed it as a system for geopolitical alignment. While not as ambitious in scope as the proposed International Trade Organisation, which GATT was supposed to ultimately lead to,[15] the GATT system of liberal trade was seen by the US and its allies as a means of reinforcing the defence of 'Western' values and institutions through linkages of freer capitalist trade and democracy.[16] GATT worked more effectively as an exercise in great power diplomacy,[17] and as a signal of geopolitical alignment and democratic values intended to incentivise engagement with countries on the Soviet Union's periphery with the potential to break away in favour of the West such as Poland (which joined GATT in the 1960s).[18] Comecon served a similar function amongst those aligned with the USSR, such as Czechoslovakia, Poland, Hungary, Bulgaria, Romania, and Albania, in its formation in 1949, and was later joined by East Germany, Cuba, Mongolia, and Vietnam. Comecon was akin to a single market with central planning and price-fixing for the Soviet Union's allies,[19] serving the purpose of linking the trade between its members to the values of Marxism in support of communist state sovereignty[20] until its collapse with the Soviet Union in 1991.[21]

Of relevance to this book is the emphasis in both strategic alignments upon access to technology. For the US, technology control particularly through export controls was central to national security interests from the beginning of the post-war period, through the height of the Cold War, and even expanding beyond its cessation.[22]

---

[14] See, for example, Petros C Mavroidis, *The Regulation of International Trade, Volume 1: GATT* (MIT Press 2016) 21–23; Donald McRae, 'The Development of the Regulation of International Trade' in Daniel Bethlehem and others (eds), *The Oxford Handbook of International Trade Law* (2nd ed, Oxford University Press 2022) 10–12.

[15] Orfeo Fioretos and Eugénia C Heldt, 'Legacies and Innovations in Global Economic Governance since Bretton Woods' (2019) 26 *Review of International Political Economy* 1089.

[16] Francine McKenzie, *GATT and Global Order in the Postwar Era* (Cambridge University Press 2020) 63.

[17] Joanne Gowa and Soo Yeon Kim, 'An Exclusive Country Club: The Effects of the GATT on Trade, 1950–94' (2004) 57 *World Politics* 453, 478.

[18] Christina L Davis and Meredith Wilf, 'Joining the Club: Accession to the GATT/WTO' (2017) 79 *The Journal of Politics* 964; see also Charles S Maier, 'The Politics of Productivity: Foundations of American International Economic Policy after World War II' (1977) 31 *International Organization* 607 on the use of productivity and growth as mechanisms for sidestepping political conflicts between aligned states.

[19] Andrzej Korbonski, 'Theory and Practice of Regional Integration: The Case of Comecon' (1970) 24 *International Organization* 942; Libbey (n2).

[20] David D Finley, 'A Political Perspective of Economic Relations in the Communist Camp' (1964) 17 *Western Political Quarterly* 294.

[21] For more on this collapse, beyond 'just' the dissolution of the Soviet Union, see Akira Uegaki and Kazuhiro Kumo, 'The Collapse of the COMECON System and Trade in Transition Countries' in Ichiro Iwasaki (ed), *The Economics of Transition* (Routledge 2020).

[22] See Mario Daniels and John Krige, *Knowledge Regulation and National Security in Postwar America* (University of Chicago Press 2022).

According to Erickson, by the 1970s, the Cold War security environment had 'fostered an arms control culture led by the superpowers and focused on managing the risk of nuclear war'.[23] However, by extension, arms control also required controls over technologies that could *facilitate* nuclear war. COCOM was a forum formed by voluntary agreement through which the US-aligned nations could coordinate policies that would restrict USSR access to key technologies, expanding out of the US Export Control Act of 1949.[24] In the 1950s, as semiconductor manufacture technologies improved, microchips became seen as both an imminent source of threat should these components be made available to the Soviet Union, which could use them for the purposes of computer-guided missile systems, and a means of maintaining the technological supremacy of the US and its allies.[25] Computers too were included on the list of embargoed items, as they could potentially be used to guide missiles; as a result, in the 1960s, the export of fast computers to Eastern European designated countries, such as Poland, was limited to between 6 and 18 per year to reduce the risk of those computers making their way to the Soviet Union.[26] While lacking in enforcement mechanisms, COCOM was nevertheless adhered to by the US' allies in the early period of the Cold War due to the guarantee of military assistance provided by the US to its Western European partners and the implicit threat that this guarantee could be withdrawn should Western European companies export controlled technologies to the USSR.[27] Lacking the means to develop these technologies internally, the Soviet Union instead focused on legal and illegal means of obtaining those technologies from the West,[28] with varying degrees of success. Incidents occurred such as the Toshiba-Kongsberg 'scandal' involving the sale of machine tools by Japanese company Toshiba to the Soviet Union and numerical control devices by Norwegian company Kongsberg, which could be combined to allow for the advancement of the Soviet Union's submarine technologies.[29]

---

[23] Jennifer L Erickson, 'Changing History?: Innovation and Continuity in Contemporary Arms Control' in Peter J Katzenstein and Lucia A Seybert (eds), *Protean Power: Exploring the Uncertain and Unexpected in World Politics* (Cambridge University Press 2018) 231.
[24] Shahid Alam, 'Russia and Western Technology Control' (1993) 11 *International Relations* 469.
[25] See Chris Miller, *Chip War: The Fight for the World's Most Critical Technology* (Simon & Schuster 2022) – this shall be explored in much more detail in Chapter 6, when discussing contemporary EU hardware technology policies.
[26] Christopher Leslie and Patrick Gryczka, 'Ingenuity in Isolation: Poland in the International History of the Internet' in Kai Kimppa and others (eds), *ICT and Society* (Springer 2014).
[27] Joseph Edward Gregory, 'Controlling the Transfer of Militarily Significant Technology: COCOM after Toshiba Note' (1987) 11 *Fordham International Law Journal* 863, 868–870.
[28] David Holloway, 'Western Technology and Soviet Military Power', in Robbin F Laird and Erik P Hoffman (eds), *Technology Transfer and East-West Relations* (Routledge 1985); William T Warner, 'International Technology Transfer and Economic Espionage' (1994) 7 *International Journal of Intelligence and Counter Intelligence* 143.
[29] Christopher Parks, 'The Political Economy of Strategic Export Controls and the Toshiba Machine Company Affair' (1990) 4 *Paradigms* 74.

Indeed, while most US-allied states were content with the idea of freer trade between themselves, some also had historical trading links with Soviet and Eastern Bloc countries that meant that a tension continued to exist between national security aims (as pushed in particular by the US) and economic aims. Agar gives the example of the UK's long-standing trade with Russia pre-Soviet Union that continued through the twentieth century and its dependence on Soviet timber for housebuilding during its reconstruction that it hoped to secure in exchange for British machinery and commodities.[30] Dependencies increasingly served to render visible the tensions between the US and its allies; under Reagan, the US wanted to limit the USSR's access to hard currency, yet European countries found themselves in need of stable energy supplies as a result of the 1970s oil shock, and West Germany wanted to gain access to Russian gas and oil.[31] The USSR arguably saw the export of oil and gas to West Germany as a means of exerting some limited political influence, particularly if such influence served to cause internal rifts in the European Economic Community (EEC), the creation of which it viewed with intense mistrust.[32] The Soviet Union framed the EEC as being a threat to the stability of the world and during the 1950s and 1960s, saw their position as ensuring 'containment' of the EEC akin to the containment policy adopted by the US with regard to the Soviet Union.[33] By the 1980s, however, the relations between the EEC and the Soviet Union had begun to thaw, with Gorbachev officially recognising the EEC in 1988,[34] in part as the result of the increasing engagement with the Soviet Union and Eastern Bloc in the 1970s. Integration in the EEC and détente between the EEC and Soviet Union have been argued to form part of the same process,[35] with the promotion of increased trade (albeit in limited areas, and not normally those governed by COCOM) being central to this increasingly non-hostile interaction.[36] In the 1980s, the EEC and its members took a more relaxed position on trade with the East, increasingly diverging from the policy position adopted by the US.[37]

---

[30] Jon Agar, 'Swimming with the Coelacanth: The UK and Export Controls of Technology and Knowledge in the Cold War' (2024) 40 *History and Technology* 54, 56.

[31] Henry Farrell and Abraham Newman, *Underground Empire: How America Weaponized the World Economy* (Allen Lane 2023) 114.

[32] Wolfgang Mueller, 'The Soviet Union and Early West European Integration, 1947–1957: From the Brussels Treaty to the ECSC and the EEC' (2010) 15 *JEIH Journal of European Integration History* 67.

[33] David FP Forte, 'The Response of Soviet Foreign Policy to the Common Market, 1957–63' (1968) 19 *Soviet Studies* 373.

[34] Jacques Lévesque, *The Enigma of 1989: The USSR and the Liberation of Eastern Europe* (University of California Press 2021) 80.

[35] Angela Romano, 'Untying Cold War Knots: The EEC and Eastern Europe in the Long 1970s' (2014) 14 *Cold War History* 153.

[36] Ibid.

[37] Gregory (n27).

TRADE RELATIONS IN THE LIBERAL INTERNATIONAL ORDER: GLOBALISATION, TECHNOLOGY, AND THE RISE OF INTERDEPENDENCE

With the end of the Cold War and the collapse of the USSR came a certain conviction on the part of Western nations that this was both the success and proof of democracy and capitalism's superiority over communism and central planning.[38] The period immediately following the dissolution of the Soviet Union in 1991 was one in which much academic and policy focus concerned the nature of global trade in a 'post-Cold War era'. Fukuyama, for example, stated contemporaneously that: 'As mankind approaches the end of the second millennium, the twin crises of authoritarianism and socialist central planning have left only one competitor standing in the ring as an ideology of potentially universality: liberal democracy, the doctrine of individual freedom and popular sovereignty'.[39]

Fukuyama was not alone in this belief; according to Von Eschen, writings at this time were marked by a certain triumphalism, with assertions that it was President Reagan and military might that had overcome the Communist threat, with free market capitalism being decisive in that victory.[40] While some academics were much more cautious, arguing that this victory was by no means assured, as attributable, or as decisive as claimed,[41] there was nevertheless generalised agreement that a liberal economic order was establishing its dominance in the mid-1990s, and most countries were encouraged to open up their markets to international trade.[42] For Bayne, one of its immediate benefits and reasons for success was the establishment of international organisations over the period of the Cold War, such as GATT, the International Monetary Fund, and the World Bank, as well as the development of integrated regional 'free trade' areas in the wake of the Cold War, such as the establishment of ASEAN's expanded economic competences in 1992, the European Union's Single Market in 1993, and NAFTA in 1994.[43] Increasingly the term 'globalization' was being used to describe the developments post-1991, characterised by the

---

[38] Azeem Ibrahim, *Authoritarian Century: Omens of a Post-Liberal Future* (C Hurst & Co Publishers Ltd 2022) 64.

[39] Francis Fukuyama, *The End of History and the Last Man: Francis Fukuyama* (Penguin 2012) 42. It must be stated that Fukuyama is perhaps unfairly criticised for the positions taken in this work. While arguing for the triumph of liberal democracy, he also made clear that this 'victory' was not unassailable and irreversible, and that there was always the potential for populations to turn against liberal democracy, as expanded upon at pp. 330–332.

[40] Penny M Von Eschen, *Paradoxes of Nostalgia: Cold War Triumphalism and Global Disorder since 1989* (Duke University Press Books 2022) 23.

[41] See, for example, James M Goldgeier and Michael McFaul, 'A Tale of Two Worlds: Core and Periphery in the Post-Cold War Era' (1992) 46 *International Organization* 467; Nicholas Bayne, 'International Economic Relations after the Cold War' (1994) 29 *Government and Opposition* 3.

[42] Thomas J Biersteker, 'The "Triumph" of Liberal Economic Ideas in the Developing World' in Barbara Stallings (ed), *Global Change, Regional Response: The New International Context of Development* (Cambridge University Press 1995).

[43] Bayne (n41) 9.

increasing interconnectedness of states and their economies, and the rise of institutional structures shaping relations between markets and states.[44]

For the US under President Clinton, international trade was central to a renewed foreign policy no longer determined by national security concerns but wealth maximisation.[45] Cox has described this period as being marked by geo-economics rather than geopolitics, in which the Clinton administration saw promoting trade as being synonymous with foreign policy.[46] This did not mean that the US intended to pursue an agenda of complete free market competition; instead, the focus was on the support for developing the norms and principles that had been developed under the GATT system, ensuring their expansion throughout the world.[47] This process culminated in the Uruguay Round of GATT multilateral trade talks, which resulted in the creation of the World Trade Organization (WTO). Membership of the WTO was largely non-negotiable, as access to the US and EU markets depended upon it.[48] This of course led to the expansion of economic power on the part of developed countries, and in particular the US, the EU, and to a lesser extent Japan, with the imposition of requirements that all WTO members implement the Trade-Related Aspects of Intellectual Property Rights Agreement (TRIPS) into domestic legislation, making the intellectual property rights standards of the developed nations the global standards.[49] The WTO, despite operating on the basis of assumed equal sovereignty and consensus, was nevertheless based in the laws devised through the exertion of power on the part of larger blocs such as the US and EU, meaning that the liberal order was based on the principles desired by more powerful economic actors.[50] Nevertheless, within the context of a globalised economy, membership was sought by many of the states that were part of or aligned with the Soviet Union during the Cold War, with countries such as Poland and Hungary joining at its formation in 1995, Estonia joining in 1999, China in 2001, and Russia itself in 2012.[51]

---

[44] Seán Ó Riain, 'States and Markets in an Era of Globalization' (2000) 26 *Annual Review of Sociology* 187; see also Petra Vujakovic, 'How to Measure Globalization? A New Globalization Index (NGI)' (2010) 38 *Atlantic Economic Journal* 237.

[45] Foreign Policy Editors, 'Clinton's Foreign Policy' (2000) *Foreign Policy* 18.

[46] Michael Cox, *Agonies of Empire: American Power from Clinton to Biden* (Bristol University Press 2022) 8–9.

[47] To the extent that some equated globalisation with 'Americanisation', particularly in developing countries subject to external pressures to liberalise – see Jean-Marie Guéhenno, 'The Post-Cold War World: Globalization and the International System' (1999) 10 *Journal of Democracy* 22.

[48] Kyle Bagwell, Petros C Mavroidis and Robert W Staiger, 'It's A Question of Market Access' (2002) 96 *American Journal of International Law* 56; Davis and Wilf (n18).

[49] On this process, see Peter Drahos and John Braithwaite, *Information Feudalism: Who Owns the Knowledge Economy?* (Earthscan 2002).

[50] Richard H Steinberg, 'In the Shadow of Law or Power? Consensus-based Bargaining and Outcomes in the GATT/WTO' (2002) 56 *International Organization* 339.

[51] A full list of WTO members and their date of accession can be found at World Trade Organization, 'WTO Members and Observers' (*World Trade Organization*, 30 August 2024) <www.wto.org/english/thewto_e/whatis_e/tif_e/org6_e.htm> accessed 10 November 2024.

Technology control operated somewhat differently under the auspices of the liberal economic order. COCOM ceased to exist in 1994, but the principles of export control for weapons and dual-use technologies it contained were implemented in the Wassenaar Arrangement that was negotiated in 1995.[52] This non-legally binding Arrangement represented a move from containment to cooperation,[53] with members party to it agreeing on principles of transparency and responsibility regarding the export of technologies with potential military capabilities such as certain types of computers under the Dual Use List Category 4, and information security technologies such as cryptography under Category 5.[54] Unlike COCOM, however, the Wassenaar Arrangement is something of an exception to the rule of international trade, rather than the rule itself. Instead of being a set of stringent export controls placed upon non-aligned states (and indeed, states such as Russia are party to the Arrangement), the purpose of Wassenaar controls is to limit the transfer of technologies that could be used by terrorist groups[55] or by governments in perpetuating human rights abuses[56] and is predicated upon scrutiny of exports rather than prohibitions. The de facto principle under the WTO framework is the free flow of technologies between states as part of commercial trade, with controls on technology in trade being about economic protections (and hence the obligations regarding intellectual property protection under TRIPS rather than issues of national security).[57] As such, disputes around technology in the international trade system tended to be about the protection (or not) of intellectual property rights, with China increasingly the focus of concerns over IP 'theft' from companies based in other states and China's relatively lax domestic enforcement of IP laws.[58]

The period between the mid-1990s and early-to-mid-2000s was one in which globalisation as an idea was ascendant. The world's economies became increasingly interconnected, and by extension, states became increasingly interdependent. For some, this was seen as a positive outcome; for a reunified Germany, trade had the ability to change the world and influence the policies of more authoritarian nations (a concept named *Wandel durch Handel*, or transition through trade), heavily

---

[52] Wassenaar Arrangement on Export Controls for Conventional Arms and Dual-Use Goods and Technologies of 19 December 1995
[53] Kenneth A Dursht, 'From Containment to Cooperation: Collective Action and the Wassenaar Arrangement' (1997) 19 *Cardozo Law Review* 1079.
[54] Full information can be found at Wassenaar Arrangement Secretariat, 'List of Dual-Use Goods and Technologies and Munitions List' (Wassenaar Arrangement 2023) <www.wassenaar.org/app/uploads/2023/12/List-of-Dual-Use-Goods-and-Technologies-Munitions-List-2023-1.pdf> accessed 10 November 2024.
[55] Wade Boese, 'Wassenaar Endorses Steps to Deny Terrorists Arms' (2004) 34 *Arms Control Today* 41.
[56] Nina M Hart and Christopher A Casey, 'Transatlantic Leadership in an Era of Human Rights-Based Export Controls' (2024) 27 *Journal of International Economic Law* 130.
[57] Security, and the principle of the security exception in WTO Law under Article XXI of GATT, will be briefly discussed in the next section.
[58] See Miller (n25) 271–272; Keyu Jin, *The New China Playbook: Beyond Socialism and Capitalism* (Swift Press 2024) 197–198 for example.

influenced by the experiences of West Germany in the Cold War détente with the German Democratic Republic.[59] Under Chancellor Schroeder, German policy towards Russia was defined by this concept, particularly around energy and the Nordstream gas projects, with the argument being made that through engaging in this way, Russia could be 'modernised' with increased political liberalisation and respect for rule of law.[60] This interdependence was assumed to have reduced the risks of international conflict (related to the belief that increased economic liberalism also led to increased democratic liberalisation, and that democracies were unlikely to declare war on each other in this new post-Cold War context[61]), but it also appeared to reorient sovereignty relations between states and private capital, decreasing the power of the former while increasing that of the latter. As Bayne argued in 1994, 'governments' powers, however great, extend only to their borders. Multinational companies can now ignore boundaries and move wherever they find conditions of operation are best [...] economic policies have predominance. Electorates discover that here their governments cannot take independent decisions and find that deeply unsettling.'[62]

As Cohen argues, there was a sense amongst some states and commentators that the concept of sovereignty at the national level was increasingly undermined, with decisions increasingly taken by supranational organisations such as the WTO and UN without direct involvement of domestic legislators or policymakers.[63] Coinciding with moves from active regulation by the state in its capacity as a public actor to co-regulation and even self-regulation by private sector actors in areas of technical complexity,[64] significantly empowering profit-motivated multinationals in regulatory processes.[65] However, the belief was that within the international economic order, this was of lesser importance than continued prosperity – the strength of multinationals, combined with the development of international rules and norms under the auspices of the WTO, would ensure that it would be difficult for nations to 'backslide' during hard economic times, as the agreement to a set of rules regarding the conduct of trade policies would create a form of lock-in preventing unilateral actions that would undermine the international trade system and guarantee the

---

[59] Dietmar Petzina, 'The Economic Dimension of the East–West Conflict and the Role of Germany' (1994) 3 *Contemporary European History* 203.

[60] As discussed, and critiqued, in Bernhard Blumenau, 'Breaking with Convention? Zeitenwende and the Traditional Pillars of German Foreign Policy' (2022) 98 *International Affairs* 1895.

[61] Cox (n46) 26–27.

[62] Bayne (n41) 6.

[63] As discussed in Jean L Cohen, *Globalization and Sovereignty: Rethinking Legality, Legitimacy, and Constitutionalism* (Cambridge University Press 2012), where concepts such as global governance and global constitutionalism are argued to be born out of this reorientation of sovereignty relations.

[64] As discussed further in Chapter 4.

[65] Peter J Spiro, 'Constraining Global Corporate Power: A Short Introduction Symposium' (2013) 46 *Vanderbilt Journal of Transnational Law* 1101; Gus Van Harten, *The Trouble with Foreign Investor Protection* (Oxford University Press 2020).

stability of markets.[66] However, such beliefs were based in an understanding of the continuance of the liberal economic order. As the next section, 'The Crisis of the Liberal International Order' highlights, should that order be subject to increased contention, so too would the rules of international trade.

THE CRISIS OF THE LIBERAL INTERNATIONAL ORDER: THE RETURN OF GEOPOLITICS AND THE RISE OF NEW TECHNOLOGICAL SUPERPOWERS

If titles of recent publications alone are an indicative metric, then the liberal international order is in crisis. Characterised as either too flawed to survive,[67] sowing the seeds of its own destruction,[68] leaving,[69] failed,[70] or having passed on[71] (or any possible combination), there appears to be an acceptance that the belief in a globalised world of states working through international organisations based on a rule-based economic order has been largely shaken, particularly on the part of twenty-first-century states and policymakers. The period beginning in the mid-2000s has increasingly been marked by instability and a growing sense of crisis, which has allowed for questions to be raised as to the legitimacy of this system of governance, as well as providing the conditions for states to engage in conduct that institutions such as the WTO were ostensibly there to prevent. As a result, if the 1990s were marked by the move from geopolitics to geoeconomics, then the 2010s were marked by the move from geoeconomics to geopolitical economics. To understand this occurrence, it is necessary to consider some interrelated yet distinct developments.

The first was that a series of economic shocks in the late 2000s shook confidence in the international economic system. While during the time of the George W. Bush Presidency fault lines developed between states over security issues in the context of the 'War on Terror' following the 11 September 2001 terrorist attacks,[72] their faith in the international *economic* system appeared to have been maintained over this time. During the Obama Presidency, however, this changed substantially.

---

[66] As argued in John H Barton and others, *The Evolution of the Trade Regime: Politics, Law, and Economics of the GATT and the WTO* (Princeton University Press 2006) 205.

[67] Patrick Porter, *The False Promise of Liberal Order* (Polity 2020).

[68] Peter R Neumann, *The New World Disorder: How the West Is Destroying Itself* (David Shaw tr, 1st ed, Scribe UK 2023).

[69] Elisabeth Braw, *Goodbye Globalization: The Return of a Divided World* (Yale University Press 2024).

[70] Patrick J Deneen, *Why Liberalism Failed* (Yale University Press 2019).

[71] Matthew Rose, *A World after Liberalism: Five Thinkers Who Inspired the Radical Right* (Yale University Press 2021).

[72] Including accusations by the US that the EU and its Member States were not 'pulling their weight' in international conflicts, as discussed in Porter (n67) 45–46; and accusations by European countries that the US was flouting international law, as discussed in Rebecca Sanders, 'Human Rights Abuses at the Limits of the Law: Legal Instabilities and Vulnerabilities in the "Global War on Terror"' (2018) 44 *Review of International Studies* 2; with the result that the war on terror did more to divide the 'West' than unite it, as argued in Cox (n46) 97.

The US financial crisis instigated by the subprime mortgage crisis and the subsequent collapse of large banks such as Lehman Brothers, Bear Sterns, and Merrill Lynch & Co. had a contagion effect on the international financial system in the 2007–2008 crash that resulted in the period of market contraction known as the Great Recession. The Great Recession saw an international decline in asset values by more than $50 trillion and an increase in concerns about further systemic risks and geopolitical shifts such as the rising power of the G20 in comparison to the G8[73] and increasing tensions between former allies due to a sense that the US was largely to blame for the world's financial woes.[74] The decline in state spending, rises in unemployment, and subsequent loss of purchase power and quality of life on the part of populations in countries normally considered the net beneficiaries of globalisation[75] are due in no small part to the austerity policies pursued by states in response to this crisis.[76] This in turn increased the sense *in* those countries that globalisation did not work (or had never worked[77]), and significantly damaging the reputation of the US, and by extension President Obama,[78] despite the fact that the causes of this crisis preceded his administration.

These shocks, and the loss of US prestige in the international system, coincided with the increasing speed of Chinese development and trade. China is an example of a country that adopted a 'state and market' approach to economic reform that resulted in it moving from a largely impoverished agricultural economy to an upper-middle-income economy in the space of approximately thirty-five years.[79] China was seen as escaping the poverty trap, in which countries characterised by widespread poverty find that self-reinforcing structural issues prevent a country from being able to adopt policies that reduce or even eliminate that absolute poverty.[80] Particularly

---

[73] Daniel W Drezner and Kathleen R McNamara, 'International Political Economy, Global Financial Orders and the 2008 Financial Crisis' (2013) 11 *Perspectives on Politics* 155.

[74] As discussed in Andrea A Chua and Augustine Pang, 'US Government Efforts to Repair Its Image after the 2008 Financial Crisis' (2012) 38 *Public Relations Review* 150, where reference is made to then-German Chancellor Angela Merkel blaming the US for mishandling the regulation of Wall Street, as well as China and Russia criticising the US for failing to mitigate the risks and subsequent harms of what were perceived to be predatory lending practices.

[75] See, for example, Iyanatul Islam and Sher Verick, 'The Great Recession of 2008–09: Causes, Consequences and Policy Responses' in Iyanatul Islam and Sher Verick (eds), *From the Great Recession to Labour Market Recovery: Issues, Evidence and Policy Options* (Palgrave Macmillan UK 2011); Maria Sironi, 'Economic Conditions of Young Adults Before and After the Great Recession' (2018) 39 *Journal of Family and Economic Issues* 103.

[76] Mark Blyth, *Austerity: The History of a Dangerous Idea* (Oxford University Press 2013).

[77] Indeed, countries in South East Asia such as Thailand have been regarded as net 'losers' of globalisation due to impacts such as increasing levels of inequality, as discussed in KS Jomo, 'Globalisation, Liberalisation, Poverty and Income Inequality in Southeast Asia' (OECD 2001).

[78] Cox (n46) 83.

[79] John A Donaldson, 'The State, the Market, Economic Growth, and Poverty in China' (2007) 35 *Politics & Policy* 898.

[80] Covered in the excellent work by Yuen Yuen Ang, *How China Escaped the Poverty Trap* (Cornell University Press 2022).

relevant to this book is that China did so in a way that defied the conventional understanding described earlier that economic development and democratisation went hand-in-hand, with economic development *dependent* on the establishment of democratic and inclusive institutions.[81] Instead, it maintained an ostensibly authoritarian state with increased levels of privatisation, referred to as the 'bird cage economy'. This concept came from Chen Yun, Second Chairman of the Central Advisory Commission, who was a key figure in China's economic transition and hugely influential on the Chairman of the CCP, Deng Xiaoping.[82]

A proponent of market reforms in order to address the deficiencies in central planning without promoting full economic liberalisation, Yun stated that market socialism required that free enterprise be much like a bird in a cage – if the cage was too small, the bird would perish, yet if there were no cage at all, it would fly away.[83] Through small-scale, incremental reforms, the Chinese economy advanced dramatically between the late 1970s and mid-2010s, avoiding the ruptures and inequalities exacerbated by the economic shock therapies applied to Russia and other former Soviet Union states in the 1990s.[84] China industrialised rapidly, moving from the manufacture of basic industrial goods to making advances in various technologies, including cell phones and other consumer electronics, increasingly becoming a dominant market player in a number of technology sectors, intentionally replacing the 'old bird' of labour-intensive manufacturing of products such as textiles with the 'new bird' of technologically complex devices.[85] Arguably of relevance to this was the end of the COCOM restrictions – while we have already discussed their placement upon the Soviet Union and Eastern Bloc states, it is important to state that if anything, the restrictions placed on China were initially *greater* than those placed on the USSR through a system referred to as ChinCOM.[86] These controls were relaxed after the 1950s as ChinCOM was absorbed into COCOM, allowing for easier access to technologies in China.[87] Nevertheless, concerns remained about Chinese access to computers, both due to their potential security implications and

---

[81] Ibid 6–7; for more on this understanding of economic development, see Daron Acemoglu and James A Robinson, *Why Nations Fail: The Origins of Power, Peace and Prosperity* (Profile Books 2013).
[82] Ezra F Vogel, 'Chen Yun: His Life' (2005) 14 *Journal of Contemporary China* 741.
[83] As paraphrased by Sheryl Wudunn, 'Chen Yun, a Chinese Communist Patriarch Who Helped Slow Reforms, Is Dead at 89' (*The New York Times*, 11 April 1995) <www.nytimes.com/1995/04/11/obituaries/chen-yun-a-chinese-communist-patriarch-who-helped-slow-reforms-is-dead-at-89.html> accessed 20 November 2024.
[84] Jin (n58) 34–35.
[85] As explored in Ya-Wen Lei, *The Gilded Cage: Technology, Development, and State Capitalism in China* (Princeton University Press 2023) and as will be expanded upon in chapter nine, which discusses this in the context of Chinese electric vehicles.
[86] Yi Liu, 'The Icebreakers Group and COCOM Export Regulation Policy in the 1950s' in Gry Thomasen, Csaba Békés and András Rácz (eds), *The Palgrave Handbook of Non-State Actors in East-West Relations* (Springer International Publishing 2024).
[87] Jing-dong Yuan, 'The Politics of the Strategic Triangle: The U.S., COCOM, and Export Controls on China, 1979–1989' (1995) 14 *Journal of Northeast Asian Studies* 47.

the speed with which Chinese technological innovations were achieved based on Western designs.[88] With the end of COCOM, China's comparatively unrestricted access to digital technologies dramatically accelerated, particularly after its accession to the WTO in 2001. As early as 2007, there was an increased focus on the speedy transition of companies such as Huawei from small local firms to potentially dominant global operators.[89] With this increasing role in high-tech sectors, however, came realignment. By 2010, the Chinese economy was estimated as being bigger than Japan's as expressed by GDP,[90] and the Chinese response to the Global Financial Crisis was seen as both shoring up the world economy through its active promotion of imports and internal stimulus measures and also as creating the potential for a Chinese-centred hegemony in economic relations.[91]

For the United States, this presented a challenge to its position as the centre of a unipolar international system. Republicans regularly attacked President Obama on his policies towards China and the threat they presented to US economic dominance, and while Obama recognised these issues, he did not substantially change policies based in a belief that cooperation with China rather than competition was more conducive to American interests.[92] Obama's frustrations with China grew, however, with the leadership of Xi Jinping and his more aggressive foreign policy in South East Asia.[93] Domestically, the significant increase in the strength of China's exports since joining the WTO, from 2 per cent to 16 per cent of global manufacturing, occurred at the same time as decreasing wages and manufacturing employment in parts of the US. This led to an increasingly hawkish position on China's role in the world trade system and the belief that globalisation was failing the average worker, ideas that were seized upon during Donald Trump's 2016 campaign for the US Presidency to significant success.[94] When Donald Trump won, this was claimed as a victory of populism over liberalism that was variously attributed to cultural issues[95] and economic insecurity triggering mistrust of 'elites'.[96] Central to these Trump policies on trade however was an interlinking of these two issues,

---

[88] Frank Cain, 'Computers and the Cold War: United States Restrictions on the Export of Computers to the Soviet Union and Communist China' (2005) 40 *Journal of Contemporary History* 131.

[89] Brian Low, 'Huawei Technologies Corporation: From Local Dominance to Global Challenge?' (2007) 22 *Journal of Business & Industrial Marketing* 138.

[90] BBC News, 'China Overtakes Japan as World's Second-Biggest Economy' (*BBC News*, 13 February 2011) <www.bbc.com/news/business-12427321> accessed 22 November 2024.

[91] Harold James, 'International Order after the Financial Crisis' (2011) 87 *International Affairs* 525.

[92] Martin S Indyk, Kenneth G Lieberthal and Michael E O'Hanlon, *Bending History: Barack Obama's Foreign Policy* (Brookings Institution Press 2013) 28–30.

[93] Thomas J Christensen, 'Obama and Asia: Confronting the China Challenge' (2015) 94 *Foreign Affairs* 28.

[94] Cox (n46) 87.

[95] Pippa Norris and Ronald Inglehart, *Cultural Backlash: Trump, Brexit, and Authoritarian Populism* (Cambridge University Press 2019).

[96] Salvatore Babones, *The New Authoritarianism: Trump, Populism, and the Tyranny of Experts* (Polity Press 2018).

based in arguments that international organisations such as the WTO were technocratic bodies that did not serve US economic interests, and that globalisation in this form had failed, necessitating an 'America First' trade policy that involved withdrawing from multilateral negotiations for treaties such as the Trans-Pacific Partnership and blocking the appointment of new Appellate Body members for the WTO.[97] Tariffs were raised against Chinese products, resulting in reciprocal tariffs against US goods, resulting in dramatically reduced trade between these two countries.[98] Technology-related products such as cell phones and semiconductors were increasingly subject to import and export bans, with the US designating Huawei and ZTE products as constituting security threats. However, rather than ending with the Trump administration, the election of President Biden in 2020 saw an *increase* in trade restrictions by the Biden administration that saw additional Chinese technology providers restricted in 2022 and the adoption of a Secure Equipment Act that obliged the Federal Communications Commission to deny authorisation for any of the listed companies to provide telecommunications services or equipment in the US, fostering a 'technological de-coupling' between the two superpowers.[99] With the Biden administration also continuing the policy of non-appointment to the WTO Appellate Body, the crisis of globalisation did not recede with the end of the Trump Presidency, but deepened.[100] But what did this all mean for the EU?

THE EU IN A 'NEW COLD WAR'? WHEN INTERDEPENDENCE BECOMES VULNERABILITY

Europe at the beginning of the twenty-first century was considered a major success story of globalisation, with its single market acting as an example of how reduced barriers to trade and close economic cooperation could work for the international system, and successive waves of enlargement demonstrating that an increasing number of states saw the purported benefits of being part of this system. It showed that interdependence was a strength of the European Union, serving as a basis for how cooperation between states could work in the twenty-first century.[101] The Euro was argued to have been a massive financial success against the odds, becoming the second most used

---

[97] Cherie O Taylor, 'Twenty-First Century Trade Policy: What the U.S. Has Done & What It Might Do' (2019) 23 *Currents: Journal of International Economic Law* 49.
[98] Refk Selmi, Youssef Errami and Mark E Wohar, 'What Trump's China Tariffs Have Cost U.S. Companies?' (2020) 35 *Journal of Economic Integration* 282.
[99] John Bateman, 'U.S.-China Technological "Decoupling": A Strategy and Policy Framework' (Carnegie Endowment for International Peace 2022) 23.
[100] Mark A Pollack, 'International Court Curbing in Geneva: Lessons from the Paralysis of the WTO Appellate Body' (2023) 36 *Governance* 23; Lindsey Garner-Knapp, Shaina D Western and Henry Lovat, 'The US, the WTO, and the Appellate Body: From Great Expectations to Hard Times' in Jelena Bäumler and others (eds), *European Yearbook of International Economic Law 2021* (Springer International Publishing 2022).
[101] As argued in Mark Leonard, *Why Europe Will Run the 21st Century* (Fourth Estate 2005).

currency in the world, and it was argued to be trusted as a stable currency that could rival the US dollar as a currency of reserve.[102] While there were some concerns regarding Euroscepticism in the context of the failed 'European Constitution' as a result of referendums rejecting these initiatives in France and the Netherlands in 2005,[103] there was nevertheless a sense that in its successes in integration since the ruinous Second World War, Europe was in a position to present a model for the world. In the words of the late Tony Judt, the feeling at the time was that 'few would have predicted it sixty years before, but the twenty-first century might yet belong to Europe'.[104]

This optimism proved short-lived. The contagion of the Global Financial Crisis quickly spread to the EU and its financial institutions, as banks in Europe (particularly in Germany) were highly exposed to the subprime mortgage crisis as a result of their increased risk-taking through practices such as derivatives trading.[105] A cascade effect resulted in an increase in sovereign debt crises developing within the Eurozone in countries such as Greece and Spain,[106] resulting in the perception amongst European policymakers, including in the Commission and European Central Bank, of a 'Eurozone crisis'.[107] It must be stated that this crisis was not handled well[108]; in terms of response, the EU took an austerity-based approach, providing bailouts in exchange for severely curtailing state spending in impacted states such as Greece, Ireland, Portugal, and Spain.[109] Reinforcing economic levers with legal mechanisms,[110] the EU sought to stem market fears about the continued viability of the Euro, reduce public debt, and impose limits on budgetary deficits as a means of restoring confidence.[111] Austerity as a policy, however, weakened the

---

[102] Gertrude Tumpel-Gugerell, 'Six Years after the Euro: Success and Challenges' (*European Central Bank*, 5 November 2004) <www.ecb.europa.eu/press/key/date/2004/html/sp041105.en.html> accessed 22 November 2024.
[103] Nick Startin and André Krouwel, 'Euroscepticism Re-Galvanized: The Consequences of the 2005 French and Dutch Rejections of the EU Constitution' (2013) 51 *JCMS: Journal of Common Market Studies* 65.
[104] Tony Judt, *Postwar: A History of Europe Since 1945* (Vintage 2010) 800.
[105] Dermot Hodson and Lucia Quaglia, 'European Perspectives on the Global Financial Crisis: Introduction' (2009) 47 *JCMS: Journal of Common Market Studies* 939.
[106] Mario Gruppe and Carsten Lange, 'Spain and the European Sovereign Debt Crisis' (2014) 34 *European Journal of Political Economy* S3.
[107] David Marsh, *Europe's Deadlock: How the Euro Crisis Could Be Solved – And Why It Won't Happen* (Yale University Press 2013).
[108] While too large an issue and ultimately not within the scope of this book to cover comprehensively, the account by Adam Tooze, *Crashed: How a Decade of Financial Crises Changed the World* (Penguin 2019) is a key place to start in understanding the scale of the challenges facing the Eurozone as a result of the Global Financial Crisis.
[109] Wade Jacoby and Jonathan Hopkin, 'From Lever to Club? Conditionality in the European Union during the Financial Crisis' (2020) 27 *Journal of European Public Policy* 1157.
[110] Benjamin Farrand and Marco Rizzi, 'There Is No (Legal) Alternative: Codifying Economic Ideology into Law' in Eva Nanopoulos and Fotis Vergis (eds), *The Crisis Behind the Eurocrisis* (Cambridge University Press 2019).
[111] Stella Ladi and Dimitris Tsarouhas, 'The Politics of Austerity and Public Policy Reform in the EU' (2014) 12 *Political Studies Review* 171.

EU economically. While the US and China pursued stimulus packages as a way of trying to grow out of the crisis, the EU instead pursued policies resulting in fiscal retraction, reducing growth, investment, employment, and consumption,[112] exacerbating the impacts of the financial crisis.[113] Yet not only was the policy ineffective but the way that it was communicated and enacted sowed resentment in impacted Member States. Influenced by ordoliberal thinking and concerns that increased public spending could lead to inflation, the response of Germany to this crisis was to blame profligate governments and public expenditure for Europe's economic woes,[114] adopting a moralising tone in its engagement with Member States such as Greece. The result of this discourse, coupled with the austerity policies implemented by the Commission, European Central Bank, and International Monetary Fund, known as the 'Troika', sparked a wave of Euroscepticism from both the Left and Right of European politics.

As Schmidt states, 'the Eurozone crisis led to a dramatic increase in anti-EU feeling and loss of political trust in political institutions. The most striking political response to the Eurozone crisis was the increases in votes for anti-Establishment parties',[115] being particularly pronounced in the 2014 European Parliament elections. Questions over the legitimacy of the actions taken[116] became questions over the legitimacy of the EU itself. This was compounded by the sense of a growing 'polycrisis' due to the Eurozone crisis, the Russia–Ukraine crisis and the invasion of Crimea in 2014, the increase in Syrian war refugees seeking asylum in Europe being framed as a 'refugee' or 'migration' crisis in 2015, and then the shock decision of the UK to withdraw from the European Union following the 2016 referendum on membership.[117] Yet there was also an increasing belief on the part of European policymakers that there was an external dimension to these internal crises. Commission officials including President Jean-Claude Juncker increasingly referred to the corrosive effects of populism, and the belief that the rise in European populism was largely attributable to disinformation regarding the EU's actions and policies originating from outside its borders.[118] The metaphorical finger was pointed at Russia,

---

[112] Joseph Stiglitz, 'Austerity Has Been an Utter Disaster for the Eurozone' (*The Guardian*, 1 October 2014) <www.theguardian.com/business/2014/oct/01/austerity-eurozone-disaster-joseph-stiglitz> accessed 24 November 2024.

[113] Alberto Botta and Benjamin Tippet, 'Secular Stagnation and Core-Periphery Uneven Development in Post-Crisis Eurozone' (2022) 26 *Competition & Change* 3.

[114] Blyth (n76) 56–58.

[115] Vivien A Schmidt, *Europe's Crisis of Legitimacy: Governing by Rules and Ruling by Numbers in the Eurozone* (Oxford University Press 2020) 260–261.

[116] Antonia Baraggia, 'Conditionality Measures within the Euro Area Crisis: A Challenge to the Democratic Principle?' (2015) 4 *Cambridge International Law Journal* 268.

[117] Jeffrey J Anderson, 'A Series of Unfortunate Events: Crisis Response and the European Union After 2008' in Marianne Riddervold, Jarle Trondal and Akasemi Newsome (eds), *The Palgrave Handbook of EU Crises* (Springer International Publishing 2021).

[118] Helena Carrapico and Benjamin Farrand, 'When Trust Fades, Facebook Is No Longer a Friend: Shifting Privatisation Dynamics in the Context of Cybersecurity as a Result of Disinformation,

based in intelligence suggesting that disinformation through bodies such as the Internet Research Agency was first spread in Russia to consolidate President Putin's rule, and then Russia's periphery, before then being expanded to Europe during the Ukraine campaign.[119] The sense of threat grew, however, with the election of Donald Trump in November 2016. The EU increasingly came to believe that the US was not a partner that could be relied upon, first under Obama and his pivot to Asia and then reinforced under Trump with a substantial weakening of EU–US relations.[120]

For the EU these consecutive crises, both reflecting and reinforced by a growing loss of confidence in the liberal international order, constituted the basis for a complete reversal of its position in the late 1990s and early 2000s; rather than being the potential future for the world, it was instead a question of whether Europe had a future. Its strengths, based in interdependence in a globalised world system, instead appeared to be more akin to weaknesses. The US could not be relied upon to continue in support of the international organisations upon which the liberal order, and by extension the EU order, depended.[121] Similarly, China demonstrated significant trade surpluses in comparison to the EU,[122] and the EU and its Members States were increasingly dependent upon Chinese investment,[123] technology, and natural resources,[124] being described in 2019 as an 'economic competitor in the pursuit of technological leadership'.[125] Russia was engaged in armed conflicts on Europe's borders, and at the same time key EU Member States were highly dependent upon Russian natural gas.[126] This interdependence was increasingly seen as *dependence*, and this dependence was rendering Europe vulnerable, both in economic terms and conventional security ones. There was a sense of being caught between multiple powerful adversaries upon which it was dependent, particularly *vis-à-vis* technology,

---

Populism and Political Uncertainty' (2021) 59 *JCMS: Journal of Common Market Studies* 1160; there are of course also the more recent developments such as the COVID-19 pandemic and the 2022 invasion of Ukraine, but these will be discussed in Chapters 4–7.

[119] Andrew Dawson and Martin Innes, 'How Russia's Internet Research Agency Built Its Disinformation Campaign' (2019) 90 *The Political Quarterly* 245.

[120] Marianne Riddervold and Akasemi Newsome, 'Transatlantic Relations in Times of Uncertainty: Crises and EU-US Relations' (2018) 40 *Journal of European Integration* 505.

[121] Aseema Sinha, 'Understanding the "Crisis of the Institution" in the Liberal Trade Order at the WTO' (2021) 97 *International Affairs* 1521.

[122] Xuemei Jiang and others, 'Re-Estimation of China-EU Trade Balance' (2019) 54 *China Economic Review* 350.

[123] Roland Freudenstein, 'Rising to the Challenge: The EU and Chinese Strategic Investments in Europe' in Tim Wenniges and Walter Lohman (eds), *Chinese FDI in the EU and the US: Simple Rules for Turbulent Times* (Springer Nature 2019).

[124] Max J Zenglein, 'Mapping and Recalibrating Europe's Economic Interdependence with China' (Mercator Institute for China Studies 2020).

[125] European Commission and High Representative of the Union for Foreign Affairs and Security Policy, 'EU-China: A Strategic Outlook' (2019) JOIN (2019) 5 1.

[126] Tom Casier, 'The Rise of Energy to the Top of the EU-Russia Agenda: From Interdependence to Dependence?' (2011) 16 *Geopolitics* 536.

and, as Nouveau put it, 'falling behind and in between the US and China'.[127] The EU would therefore need to find a way to respond to these vulnerabilities, both with respect to its internal crises and to its external threats.

As Youngs argues, during the Eurozone crisis, the EU had turned inwards due to its own instabilities, demonstrating little evidence of broader geo-strategy, yet also becoming increasingly convinced of the world's increasing multipolarity.[128] This became magnified by the subsequent crises the EU faced, to the extent that the Commission began to rethink the EU's role in the world as well as its engagement with it. Central to this reconfiguration of relations in a more unstable, less cooperative world was the concept of 'strategic autonomy'. With its origins in the establishment of the Common Security and Defence Policy in the 1990s, strategic autonomy concerns the ability of the EU to act independently and was originally used in the context of military matters.[129] As it relates to technology, the first usage by the EU appears to be in 2013, with the European Council Conclusions on the Common Security and Defence Policy, which state that 'Europe needs a more integrated, sustainable, innovative and competitive defence technological and industrial base to develop and sustain defence capabilities. This can also enhance its strategic autonomy and its ability to act with partners'.[130]

As a broader political ambition, however, 2016 and the multiple crises of the EU saw a mainstreaming of the concept in European policy documents. The foreword to the 2016 Global Strategy saw the High Representative of the Union for Foreign Affairs and Security Policy Federica Mogherini state that 'the purpose, even the existence, of our Union is being questioned. Yet, our citizens and the world need a strong European Union like never before [...] this Strategy nurtures the ambition of strategic autonomy for the European Union'.[131] Similarly, Commission President Juncker referred to the need for Europe to protect its strategic interests in the field of trade and the economy in the 2017 State of the Union address, arguing that 'we are not naïve free traders. Europe must always defend its strategic interests [...] if a foreign, state-owned, company wants to purchase a European harbour, part of our energy infrastructure or a defence technology firm, this should only happen in transparency, with scrutiny and debate'.[132] Economic issues and security issues

---

[127] Patricia Nouveau, 'Falling behind and in between the United States and China: Can the European Union Drive Its Digital Transformation Away from Industrial Path Dependency?', in Jean-Christophe Defraigne and others (eds), *EU Industrial Policy in the Multipolar Economy* (Edward Elgar Publishing 2022).

[128] Richard Youngs, 'Reviving Global Europe' (2013) 50 *International Politics* 475.

[129] Stephan Keukeleire, 'European Foreign Affairs Review' (2001) 6 *European Foreign Affairs Review* 75, 84–85.

[130] European Council, 'Council Conclusions' (2013) EUCO 217/13, CO EUR 15, CONCL 8 7.

[131] European External Action Service, 'Shared Vision, Common Action: A Stronger Europe – A Global Strategy for the European Union's Foreign and Security Policy' (2016) 3–4.

[132] Jean-Claude Juncker, 'President Jean-Claude Juncker's State of the Union Address 2017 – Wind in Our Sails' (European Commission, 2017) 3.

were becoming intertwined in the context of the perceived breakdown of the liberal international economic order. This was the context in which Ursula von der Leyen, a candidate for European Commission President, made her pitch for the position in 2019, stating in her political guidelines that her intent was that Europe become a global leader, 'to strive for more at home in order to lead the world'.[133] This would involve harnessing the digital economy in promotion of the EU's technological sovereignty,[134] and being ambitious, strategic, and assertive in the way that the EU engaged with the rest of the world.[135] This document set the scene for the Commission's policies and actions between 2019 and 2024 and the merging of economic and security interests as interdependent and mutually constitutive in a way that sits at the heart of the digital sovereignty agenda. The remainder of this book will therefore draw from this agenda, engaging in a deeper analysis of specific technology sectors in the Chapters 4–6 of this book as a means of highlighting the regulatory mercantilist approach adopted, before its concluding Chapter 7 and Conclusions on the von der Leyen II Commission and the future of the EU's 'Geopolitical Union'.

CONCLUSIONS

Trade moves in cycles. After the end of the Second World War, the world was divided and trade largely circulated within US and Soviet spheres of influence, with limited contact between these rival superpowers. Ideas regarding how trade worked and the role of trade in a global system were heavily influenced by the belief that the US had 'won' the Cold War because of the twin characteristics of 'capitalism' and 'democracy', which had opened up markets and brought prosperity, in turn allowing for political opening and a move towards liberal democracy. This belief that trade and democratisation were linked served as the basis for post-Cold War US trade policy, in which globalisation was an inarguably positive development due to the potential for worldwide economic growth and liberalisation. International organisations such as the WTO were joined by more and more states, including those characterised as authoritarian or that had formerly been aligned to the USSR during the GATT period, including Russia and China. At the time, this was seen as indicative that the West German '*Wandel durch Handel*' hypothesis was true and that the liberal international order was the only game in town.

Trade moves in cycles. The unparalleled interconnectedness and interdependence also meant that there was unparalleled exposure to economic shocks in one region, with contagion spreading quickly. The US subprime mortgage crisis quickly became a Global Financial Crisis, spurring an EU Eurozone crisis. The impacts of these crises, combined with the changing weight of trade from the US as a unipolar

---

[133] Ursula von der Leyen, 'A Europe That Strives for More: My Agenda for Europe' (2019) 4.
[134] Ibid 13.
[135] Ibid 17.

power to the East with the rise of China as a key industrial and technological player, fostered resentment in those communities that felt that they were losing out in economic terms. Interstate trade relations became more belligerent, particularly under the Trump administration, resulting in trade wars becoming more frequent and support for organisations such as the WTO decreasing substantially.

For the EU, these crises were particularly damaging, leading to it falling further behind the US and China economically, as well as being increasingly subject to security and legitimacy concerns inside its borders as well as externally. Its response to the Eurozone crisis and then several subsequent crises increasingly gave the impression of an organisation lacking in a real sense of global strategy and a heavy dependence on other states for its economy and security, increasing perceptions of the EU's vulnerability. Technology, both access to and restrictions of, has been central to trade flows and conflicts across time. From the bipolarity of the Cold War period and the COCOM controls over explicit military security concerns, through to the free flow of technologies during the height of globalisation and then their subsequent restrictions and central focus in trade disputes, they have become increasingly central to the EU's concerns over both access and misuse, particularly where they impact upon the EU's interests. The concept of strategic autonomy, once closely linked to military security, has become mainstreamed in Brussels discourse and linked to the concept of sovereignty within the framework for action provided by Commission President von der Leyen. How this then serves to shape specific policy fields and actions is something that will be covered in the rest of this book. In Chapter 4, we will begin exploring the substantive developments during the von der Leyen Commission, allowing for the application of the regulatory mercantilism framework to the technology case studies comprising Chapters 4 – 6 of this book.

PART II

Technology Regulation in the von der Leyen Commission

4

Regulating Technological Systems

a. Do we have the technology in Europe?
b. If not, do we have several suppliers from stable reliable countries?
c. If still not, do we have unfettered guaranteed access to monopoly or oligopoly suppliers from a single country (often US or China)?[1]

INTRODUCTION

The first of this book's case studies is focused upon the ways in which the Commission seeks to regulate software and hardware standards, standards for cybersecurity, and supply chains for semiconductors, which have been broadly categorised as 'technological systems'. This term has been used as it effectively covers distinct technological issues that can nevertheless be grouped as systems in the context of regulatory interventions. In each of these case studies, we see regulatory mercantilist approaches to technology governance, insofar as regulatory interventions are based in addressing what the Commission identifies as key vulnerabilities on the part of the EU based in geopolitical instability and external threat, framed in these case studies as strategically detrimental dependencies. The rationale for action in each technological system is one of asserting Commission control as a means of ensuring its technological sovereignty and strategic autonomy, thereby reducing its dependence on third countries and the companies based in those countries. The means of achieving this technological sovereignty is through the adoption of laws, which in the context of this chapter entail the promotion of European standards and technological industrial policy while seeking to export its norms, values, and rules to third countries through direct regulatory means or through engaging in cyber-diplomacy as a means of exporting its standards as global standards.

To demonstrate how the pursuit of the Geopolitical Union in technology policy has developed, the chapter is structured as follows. The first section, Technological

---

[1] European Innovation Council, 'Statement to Accompany the Launch of the Full EIC: Annex 1. Statement on Technological Sovereignty' (2021) 6.

Systems in the Liberal International Economic Order, begins by considering the EU's approach to technological systems in the liberal international economic order, identifying how technology standards were perceived as being purely market-driven and market-facilitating, allowing for interoperability of systems in the context of the EU's internal market. Similarly, cybersecurity norms and supply chains were seen as contributing to the European economy, and even in the context of security, cybersecurity was pursued as a means of protecting the EU's economic growth and prosperity. The next section, Concerns Over System Vulnerability, considers the vulnerabilities identified by the Commission in the context of its 2019 political guidelines and resulting digital and security policies, highlighting how even technological standards became increasingly politicised and viewed in terms of geopolitical tensions, and that in the context of geopolitical instability, access to goods in the context of semiconductor production slowdowns became framed in security terms. The third substantive section, Built European to European Standards, focuses on the rationale for action identified by the Commission, which identified the intersection of security and economic goals, with regulation necessary to ensure that the EU could secure its digital/technological sovereignty through adopting rules that sought to strengthen its strategic autonomy through boosting its own competitiveness and reducing external dependencies. The final substantive section, Law's Role in Securing Europe's Strategic Autonomy and Reducing Dependencies, considers the specific legal instruments adopted, identifying the trends of regulatory mercantilism that can be seen in the increase in regulatory oversight and Commission control in place of voluntary mechanisms, the emphasis on technological industrial policy, and the promotion of European standards as international standards and regulatory exports to third countries.

TECHNOLOGICAL SYSTEMS IN THE LIBERAL INTERNATIONAL ECONOMIC ORDER: A QUESTION OF ECONOMY RATHER THAN SECURITY

Commission activity in fields associated with technological systems is not new; indeed, it has a long history in seeking to develop 'European' standards in a range of different fields, including protective equipment for potentially explosive atmospheres,[2] personal watercraft,[3] and, of more direct relevance to this chapter, technical regulations and rules for information society services.[4] Similarly, the EU has been active in the development of cybersecurity frameworks and standards as discussed in Chapter 2, including in the context of critical information infrastructure

---

[2] Directive 2014/34/EU on the harmonisation of the laws of the Member States relating to equipment and protective systems intended for use in potentially explosive atmospheres (recast).
[3] Directive 2013/53/EU on recreational craft and personal watercraft and repealing Directive 94/25/EC.
[4] Directive 2015/1535 laying down a procedure for the provision of information in the field of technical regulations and of rules on Information Society services, replacing Directive 98/34/EC.

protection under the NIS1 Directive.[5] What is evident, however, is that these have been historically treated as separate technical domains. The Directive on technical regulations states clearly its focus is on ensuring effective functioning of the internal market (recital 2) and that barriers to trade should only be permitted when the technical regulation is essential to achieving a public interest requirement (recital 5), but it is not specified what this may entail. Article 1(a) makes clear that the Directive applies to any manufactured industrial products, which would include hardware, and Article 1(b) that it covers services normally provided for remuneration, at a distance, by electronic means, and at the individual request of a recipient of services. Article 1(f) makes clear that it covers technical regulations, including laws, voluntary agreements, or technical specifications, which under Article 1(c) constitute 'characteristics required of a product such as levels of quality, performance, safety or dimensions'. It is worth noting that security is not listed as an explicit goal of this Directive at any point, nor is it a feature of the Regulation on European standardisation of 2012.[6] This Regulation establishes the functioning of the European standardisation organisations (ESOs), such as the European Committee for Standardisation (CEN) and the European Telecommunications Standards Institute (ETSI). CEN was established in the 1960s as a means of both ensuring internal market functioning through working to common European standards for goods and services, promoting the competitiveness of European industry, and increasing product safety.[7]

The Commission's historical approach to standards is that they are essential to the functioning of the internal market, and ostensibly technocratic and non-political in nature.[8] While many firms involved in the setting or adoption of those standards saw them as constituting a set of self-regulatory principles, the Court of Justice of the European Union (CJEU)[9] has clarified that they are in essence to be treated as forming part of EU law with legal effect.[10] The motivator for the 2012 Regulation was indirectly related to the Eurozone crisis but directly related to internal market motivators; the Europe 2020 Strategy Communication[11] argued that effective rules

---

[5] Directive 2016/1148 concerning measures for a high common level of security of network and information systems across the Union.
[6] Regulation 1025/2012 on European standardisation, amending Council Directives 89/686/EEC and 93/15/EEC and Directives 94/9/EC, 94/25/EC, 95/16/EC, 97/23/EC, 98/34/EC, 2004/22/EC, 2007/23/EC, 2009/23/EC, and 2009/105/EC of the European Parliament and of the Council and repealing Council Decision 87/95/EEC and Decision No 1673/2006/EC of the European Parliament and of the Council
[7] See, for example, Gérard Rivière, 'European and International Standardisation Progress in the Field of Engineered Nanoparticles' (2009) 21 *Inhalation Toxicology* 2.
[8] See Harm Schepel, *The Constitution of Private Governance: Product Standards in the Regulation of Integrating Markets* (Hart Pub 2005) 65–67.
[9] In case C-613/14 *James Elliott Construction Limited v Irish Asphalt Limited* EU:C:2016:821.
[10] See Arnaud van Waeyenberge and David Restrepo Amariles, 'James Elliot Construction: A "New(Ish) Approach" to Judicial Review of Standardisation' (2017) 42 *European Law Review* 882.
[11] European Commission, 'Europe 2020: A Strategy for Smart, Sustainable and Inclusive Growth' (2010) COM(2010) 2020.

for standard setting could form part of an 'industrial policy for the globalisation era'[12] and promote Europe's competitiveness through international standard setting in the wake of the economic crisis, including in the context of an increasingly international value chain for goods and services.[13] The Proposal for the 2012 Regulation therefore highlighted three core aims for the legislative intervention; firstly, to ensure the smooth functioning of the internal market, particularly as it related to standards for digital services,[14] secondly, improving the participation of SMEs in standardisation processes,[15] and thirdly, responding to the issues that many of the information and communication technology (ICT) standards were not devised in Europe, hindering interoperability.[16] Once again, security was not expressly identified as a concern in the development of these standards or the tasks of the ESOs.

In terms of trade in technological goods, the focus was also on the economic dimension. In terms of trade in technology, the EU was predominantly concerned with ensuring that its intellectual property rights (IPRs) were respected, particularly vis-à-vis China. Under Article 207 TFEU establishing the Common Commercial Policy, the Commission was empowered to conclude agreements relating to trade in goods and services, including those relating to the commercial dimension of IPRs. For the Commission, this meant ensuring that the European economy and European consumers were protected from the sale of illicit counterfeit goods, with the vast majority of goods seized at European borders originating in China.[17] These measures were predominantly framed in terms of protections for the internal market and economic actors, as well as the safety of individuals, rather than in terms of broader security concerns.[18] In 2014, the Commission reported that effective IPR enforcement was essential to supporting the European economy after the financial crisis and that piracy and counterfeiting were costing the EU €8 million per year,[19] and that, as well as ensuring better coordination and cooperation internally and amongst stakeholders,[20] a robust enforcement system required better engagement

---

[12] Ibid 16.
[13] Ibid.
[14] European Commission, 'Proposal for a Regulation on European Standardisation' (2011) COM(2011) 315 2.
[15] Ibid.
[16] Ibid 2–3.
[17] See, for example, OECD/EUIPO, 'Dangerous Fakes: Trade in Counterfeit Goods That Pose Health, Safety and Environmental Risks' (OECD Paris 2022); Anita Lavorgna, 'The Online Trade in Counterfeit Pharmaceuticals: New Criminal Opportunities, Trends and Challenges' (2015) 12 *European Journal of Criminology* 226; Benjamin Farrand, '"Alone We Can Do So Little; Together We Can Do So Much": The Essential Role of EU Agencies in Combatting the Sale of Counterfeit Goods' (2019) 28 *European Security* 22.
[18] Regulation 608/2013 concerning customs enforcement of intellectual property rights and repealing Council Regulation (EC) No 1383/2003 discusses health and safety at recital (2) for example, but does not discuss European security.
[19] European Commission, 'Trade, Growth and Intellectual Property – Strategy for the Protection and Enforcement of Intellectual Property Rights in Third Countries' (2014) COM(2014) 389 2.
[20] Ibid 11–14.

with third countries, both in terms of making formal agreements and in terms of working to promote European standards for protection and technical assistance in combating IPR infringements in third-country markets.[21] Again, however, this was framed in terms of economic concerns, rather than European security, indicating that even until the late 2010s, issues of trade in technology were not being inherently linked to Europe's vulnerabilities or dependencies and were not framed in terms of strategic autonomy.

The EU was, however, expressing concerns regarding the international trade system as distinct from technology and IPRs, particularly due to the US's increased reluctance to engage with the World Trade Organisation (WTO) or its procedures. Even during the Obama Administration, there was a growing consensus that US trade policy had become increasingly aggressive and protectionist,[22] culminating in the refusal to allow the appointment of a member to the WTO Appellate Body in a politicisation of the process based in concerns that the Body was not considered sufficiently sensitive to US concerns over Chinese trade policies.[23] Under the first Trump Presidency, these policies became even more assertive, with then-President Trump maintaining the US's policy of non-appointment to the WTO Appellate Body and making clear the position that the US was not interested in multilateralism in the trade system, only a transactional bilateralism in pursuit of US interests.[24] Rejecting this approach, President Juncker in his 2018 State of the Union address referred obliquely to the Trump Administration when he argued in favour of a Europe that aimed to achieve peace, trade agreements, and stable currency relations, 'even as others become rather too prone to trade and currency wars [...] I will always champion multilateralism'.[25]

Within this argument there was an implicit understanding of the increasingly geopolitical dimension of trade, and the crisis being experienced in globalisation. It is worth noting that while maintaining its commitment to the WTO and multilateralism, the EU and its Member States were nevertheless concerned and scathing regarding what it saw as unfair competition from Chinese industry, including tech, as a result of their significant dependence on state subsidies, restricted internal competition and openness to European companies, and economies of scale that made it

---

[21] Ibid 14–17.
[22] With these hostilities being identified as early as former President Obama's election campaign, as discussed in Jeffrey J Schott, 'Trade Policy and the Obama Administration' (2009) 44 *Business Economics* 150; Edward Ashbee and Alex Waddan, 'The Obama Administration and United States Trade Policy' (2010) 81 *The Political Quarterly* 253.
[23] See, for example, Robert Howse, 'The World Trade Organization 20 Years On: Global Governance by Judiciary' (2016) 27 *European Journal of International Law* 9.
[24] Daniel CK Chow, 'U.S. Trade Infallibility and the Crisis of the World Trade Organization' (2020) 2020 *Michigan State Law Review* 599; Kristen Hopewell, 'Trump & Trade: The Crisis in the Multilateral Trading System' (2021) 26 *New Political Economy* 271.
[25] Jean-Claude Juncker, '2018 State of the Union Address – A Perpetual Responsibility' (European Commission, 2018) 3.

a trade power rivalled only by the US.[26] While the EU was a major trading power, it was one increasingly subject to the whims of other powerful states. It was only during the opening months of the von der Leyen Commission, however, that the extent of this crisis became clear, as well as the EU's critical dependencies.

CONCERNS OVER SYSTEM VULNERABILITY: FROM STANDARDS TO CRITICAL SUPPLY CHAINS

When the von der Leyen Commission began its activities in December 2019, a series of critical vulnerabilities in the context of geopolitical instability became increasingly apparent. Whereas the Commission under President Juncker had identified geostrategic risks arising from the increased foreign ownership of physical infrastructure such as ports,[27] as well as the volume of foreign direct investment coming from China,[28] technology standards also became seen as a source of potential insecurity. Whereas the emphasis of the EU's ESOs had been upon effective market governance in the context of the liberal international economic order, and as such designed with no underlying security dimension, in the geopolitical context of the late 2010s, technology standardisation became an instrument of power. As one interviewee quoted in a 2020 report stated, 'The time when we [in China] naively believed in globalisation is over [...] The central government rightly believes that standardisation is one of the most important factors for the economic future of China and our standing in the world'.[29] China had become increasingly influential in the International Telecommunication Union (ITU), the UN agency responsible for international internet technical standards, with companies such as Huawei, ZTE, and China Telecom actively driving ITU standardisation in areas such as transport, networks, and cloud service provision.[30]

For the EU, this is an issue that has clear economic consequences, insofar as control over standards leads to increased global influence and revenues from IPRs and the determination of which technologies to adopt.[31] Yet it also presents

---

[26] For more comprehensive coverage, see Keyu Jin, *The New China Playbook: Beyond Socialism and Capitalism* (Swift Press 2024) 240–245.

[27] Isaac B Kardon and Wendy Leutert, 'Pier Competitor: China's Power Position in Global Ports' (2022) 46 *International Security* 9; Tero Poutala, Elina Sinkkonen and Mikael Mattlin, 'EU Strategic Autonomy and the Perceived Challenge of China: Can Critical Hubs Be De-Weaponised?' (2022) 27 *European Foreign Affairs Review* 79.

[28] Haiyan Zhang and Daniel Van Den Bulcke, 'China's Direct Investment in the European Union: A New Regulatory Challenge?' (2014) 12 *Asia Europe Journal* 159; Marc Bungenberg and Angshuman Hazarika, 'Chinese Foreign Investments in the European Union Energy Sector: The Regulation of Security Concerns' (2019) 20 *The Journal of World Investment & Trade* 375.

[29] Tim Nicholas Rühlig, 'Technical Standardisation, China and the Future International Order: A European Perspective' (Heinrich Böll Stiftung 2020) 6.

[30] See Sebastian Klotz, 'Who Drives the International Standardisation of Telecommunication and Digitalisation? Introducing a New Data Set' (2023) 14 *Global Policy* 558.

[31] Simon Curtis and Ian Klaus, *The Belt and Road City: Geopolitics, Urbanization, and China's Search for a New International Order* (Yale University Press 2024) 164.

a security issue if trust in standard-setting companies is low.[32] Companies such as Huawei experienced something akin to exponential growth in global markets, and according to Statista had a 20 per cent market share for smartphones in Europe in 2020.[33] As well as influencing international standards through the ITU, Chinese firms were increasingly influential in the setting of European standards through ETSI[34] – for the EU, this presented a significant concern, as the increasing number of Chinese (and to a lesser extent US) firms involved in the standardisation voting process 'allow an uneven voting power to certain corporate interests: some multinationals have acquired more votes than the bodies that represent the entire stakeholder community'.[35] ETSI developed at a time of regulatory capitalism, in which its open membership system was considered a benefit, as all companies could contribute as value-neutral actors to the development of European standards.[36] However, the Commission argued, 'many third party countries are taking an assertive stance to standardisation, providing their companies with a competitive edge in terms of market access and technology roll-out'.[37] In other words, the EU saw itself as having a competitive disadvantage in standard-setting, risking no longer being a driver of international standards but a recipient of standards already agreed upon. This was of particular concern in areas impacting upon security; 'standards for cybersecurity or the resilience of critical infrastructure carry a strategic dimension'.[38]

Standards and security, and indeed the interlinking of the economic and security policy arenas, also featured prominently in the concerns regarding the vulnerability of network and information systems. Published in July 2020, the Communication on the Union Security Strategy[39] was heavily influenced by the COVID-19 pandemic, and a sense of crisis runs through the document. The Security Strategy brings together explicitly the economic and traditional security dimensions of EU policy, and in its opening paragraph states that 'security [...] also protects fundamental rights and provides foundations for confidence

---

[32] For an excellent account of Huawei's rise and fall, see Eva Dou, *House of Huawei: Inside the Secret World of China's Most Powerful Company* (Abacus 2025).
[33] Statista, 'Europe: Smartphone Market Share by Vendor 2015–2024' (*Statista*, 2024) <www.statista.com/statistics/632599/smartphone-market-share-by-vendor-in-europe/> accessed 17 March 2025.
[34] Stephanie Bijlmakers and others, 'The Historical Evolution of the European Telecommunications Standards Institute (ETSI): Legitimacy Strategies and Dynamics' (2024) 37 *Innovation: The European Journal of Social Science Research* 1265.
[35] European Commission, 'An EU Strategy on Standardisation: Setting Global Standards in Support of a Resilient, Green and Digital EU Single Market' (2022) COM(2022) 31 4.
[36] See generally Panagiotis Delimatsis and Zuno Verghese, '"To Antipolis, My Sisters!": ETSI as a Forum of Contestation, Collaboration and Orchestration' (2024) 37 *Innovation: The European Journal of Social Science Research* 1305.
[37] European Commission, 'An EU Strategy on Standardisation: Setting Global Standards in Support of a Resilient, Green and Digital EU Single Market' (n35) 1.
[38] Ibid 4.
[39] European Commission, 'Communication on the EU Security Union Strategy' (2020) COM(2020) 605.

and dynamism in our economy, our society and our democracy'.[40] Cybersecurity and critical information infrastructure protection were identified as of key importance, particularly as a result of increased dependence in the context of the COVID-19 pandemic and global lockdowns, in which digital connectivity became one of the key ways in which people engaged in work and personal communications. Yet during this time, Europol identified a considerable increase in malicious cyberattacks occurring in the EU, both against individuals and against state and public institutions and organisations, including a dramatic increase in the number of ransomware attacks.[41] For the Commission, the cybersecurity of technologies was therefore an issue of strategic importance, with the global environment and geopolitical instability accentuating the threats identified, and state and non-state actors using a combination of cyberattacks, damage to critical infrastructure, disinformation, and radicalisation of political messages as a means of exposing EU vulnerabilities.[42]

Highlighting the need to ensure better standards of critical information infrastructure resilience, as well as improved standards and certifications for cybersecurity,[43] the Commission and High Representative for Foreign Affairs and Security Policy subsequently published a Cybersecurity Strategy in December 2020,[44] which was again framed in terms of the EU's vulnerability in the context of geopolitical tensions, in this case 'over the global and open Internet and over control of technologies across the entire supply chain'.[45] These threats were not only to international security but also economic confidence on the part of consumers and domestic physical security through malicious attacks on information infrastructure,[46] again highlighting the intersection of economic and security concerns. These concerns were heightened dramatically by the Russian invasion of Ukraine in 2023, which the EU Strategic Compass for Security and Defence described as representing 'a tectonic in European history. Overall, the Compass describes a European global security landscape that is more volatile, complex and fragmented than ever due to multi-layered threats'.[47] Internal security, external defence, and economic prosperity were becoming increasingly enmeshed and mutually constitutive, yet equally

---

[40] Ibid 1.
[41] Europol, 'The Internet Organised Crime Threat Assessment (iOCTA)' (Europol 2020) 6–7; Europol, 'The Internet Organised Crime Threat Assessment (iOCTA)' (Europol 2021) 20–22.
[42] European Commission, 'Communication on the EU Security Union Strategy' (n39) 3–4. This will be returned to in Chapter 5, in which disinformation as a form of hybrid threat is discussed in more detail in the context of platform regulation.
[43] Ibid 6–8.
[44] European Commission and High Representative of the Union for Foreign Affairs and Security Policy, 'The EU's Cybersecurity Strategy for the Digital Decade' (2020) JOIN (2020) 18.
[45] Ibid 1. This will be returned to in the context of semiconductor supply chains shortly.
[46] Ibid 2–3.
[47] High Representative of the European Union for Foreign Affairs and Security Policy, 'Strategic Compass for Security and Defence' (2023) 7371/22 1.

interdependent in their vulnerabilities. As such, the Seventh Report on Hybrid Threats reported that the trend of state and non-state actors involved in hybrid acts against the EU, including disinformation campaigns and attacks on critical information infrastructure, was 'exacerbated in 2022 and 2023 by Russia's ongoing war of aggression against Ukraine'.[48]

Returning to the issues of supply chains, a new critical vulnerability for the EU was identified in the context of the COVID-19 crisis. With global lockdowns came global shutdowns to prevent the spread of the coronavirus infection between workers. Factories and production lines ceased activity, with hugely significant economic impacts.[49] Where the Commission felt this hit particularly hard was in the context of its access to microprocessors, a form of microchip (colloquially referred to as 'chips'). Microchips are constructed using naturally occurring minerals known as semiconductors (such as silicon), which are highly useful as they conduct electricity more effectively at higher heats, rather than becoming less effective as with normal metal conductors.[50] These devices power all modern electronics, and, as will be discussed in Chapter 6, the most high-value chips are regarded as essential for the powering of powerful new generative AI systems. Access to these chips had become increasingly politicised in the context of the US–China trade war, with the Trump Administration placing tariffs of 25 per cent on semiconductors imported from China in 2018, which were duly reciprocated, and then further export controls in 2019 aimed specifically at Huawei over alleged concerns regarding its threats to critical network infrastructure.[51] However, with the pandemic came slowdowns in the production and distribution of chips generally, and with the shutdown of Taiwanese producer TSMC (the Taiwanese Semiconductor Manufacturing Company), this was exacerbated. As of 2023, TSMC was responsible for almost 60 per cent of microchip production, rising to 90 per cent for advanced chips,[52] and in 2020 this shutdown resulted in a 'semiconductor supply shock', in which advanced electronics suddenly became much harder to purchase. For the Commission, this revealed a significant dependency that placed the EU at a distinct economic and security

---

[48] European Commission and High Representative of the Union for Foreign Affairs and Security Policy, 'Seventh Progress Report on the Implementation of the 2016 Joint Framework on Countering Hybrid Threats and the 2018 Joint Communication on Increasing Resilience and Bolstering Capabilities to Address Hybrid Threats' (2023) SWD (2023) 315 1.

[49] See Adam Tooze, *Shutdown: How Covid Shook the World's Economy* (Penguin UK 2021).

[50] BG Yacobi, *Semiconductor Materials: An Introduction to Basic Principles* (Kluwer 2003) 2–3; see also Benjamin Farrand, 'The Economy–Security Nexus: Risk, Strategic Autonomy and the Regulation of the Semiconductor Supply Chain' (2024) *European Journal of Risk Regulation* 1; and for a very accessible overview of how these devices function, see John W Orton, *Semiconductors and the Information Revolution: Magic Crystals That Made IT Happen* (Academic Press 2009).

[51] Chad P Bown, 'How the United States Marched the Semiconductor Industry into Its Trade War with China' (2021) 24 *East Asian Economic Review* 349, 350–351.

[52] Mateus Lee, Ming-Hung Weng and Show-Ling Jang, 'The Competitiveness and Future Challenge of the Taiwan Semiconductors Industry' in Peter C.Y. Chow (ed), *Technology Rivalry Between the USA and China* (Springer Nature Switzerland 2024).

disadvantage. After all, as von der Leyen pronounced, 'We all realised what Europe still lacks when it comes to one of the most crucial assets for the digital transition. Because there is no digital without chips'.[53]

This 'lack' on the part of the EU in the field of semiconductors is substantial. In terms of the raw materials required to produce semiconductors, more than 97 per cent of the magnesium relied upon by the EU is found in China, and while 63 per cent of the world's cobalt resource is mined in the Democratic Republic of Congo, 60 per cent of that supply is then refined in China.[54] For semiconductor production, 71 per cent of the silicon, 80 per cent of the germanium, and 98 per cent of the gallium required for manufacture are produced or processed in China.[55] As with other dimensions of security, the Ukraine conflict also exacerbated these supply issues, as Russia is a key source of palladium, and Ukraine the neon used for semiconductor manufacturing.[56] For production, the EU is also heavily dependent on the rest of the world, rendering it particularly susceptible to supply shocks. The EU does not possess any advanced 'fabs', the production facilities used to produce cutting-edge microchips, with the majority of its production being for microchips increasingly regarded as 'mature' bordering on 'antique' and has the smallest amount of production capacity compared to other players in this market, such as China, Japan, South Korea, and the US.[57] In terms of global revenues, EU production accounted for less than 10 per cent.[58] For the Commission, this presents a significant vulnerability to the EU, as the issues of semiconductor access are not only economic but also security-influencing and strategic, with the Commission explicitly framing its concerns about its external dependencies in geopolitical terms; 'Europe has an overall global semiconductors market share of only 10% and largely relies on third-country suppliers [...] semiconductors are at the centre of strong geostrategic interests, and of the global technological race'.[59] For this reason, the Commission concluded that decisive action was required, on chips, on cybersecurity, and on standardisation, in order to address these dependencies and vulnerabilities.

---

[53] Ursula von der Leyen, 'President's Speech at the "Masters of Digital 2022" Event' (*European Commission*, 3 February 2022) <https://ec.europa.eu/commission/presscorner/detail/en/speech_22_746> accessed 18 March 2025.

[54] European Commission, 'Proposal for a Regulation Establishing a Framework for Ensuring a Secure and Sustainable Supply of Critical Raw Materials' (2023) COM(2023) 160 1.

[55] Council of the European Union, 'The Semiconductor Ecosystem- Global Features and Europe's Position' <www.consilium.europa.eu/media/58112/220712-the-semiconductor-ecosystem-global-features-and-europe-s-position.pdf> accessed 31 October 2023.

[56] Lin Jones and others, 'US Exposure to the Taiwanese Semiconductor Industry' (US International Trade Commission 2023) Working Paper 2023-11-A 3.

[57] Jan-Peter Kleinhans, 'The Lack of Semiconductor Manufacturing in Europe' (Stiftung Neue Verantwortung 2021) 12–13.

[58] European Commission, 'A Chips Act for Europe' (2022) COM(2022) 45 8.

[59] Ibid 2.

BUILT EUROPEAN TO EUROPEAN STANDARDS: DIGITAL SOVEREIGNTY AND TECH INDUSTRIAL POLICY

The Commission's interventions into technology regulation around standards, information infrastructure, and semiconductor supply chains are key examples of regulatory mercantilist policymaking. The 'A Europe Fit For the Digital Age' political priority highlighted in Chapter 2 centred its actions around promoting the EU's digital/technological sovereignty as a rationale for a more interventionist and assertive regulatory approach. The first major Communication on the topic was 'Shaping Europe's Digital Future' (SEDF),[60] which outlined a significant range of different interventions the Commission intended to pursue around digital technologies. However, and indicative of the bringing together of economy and security ambitions underscored by a sovereignty discourse, the actions in SEDF intersected with other key areas of activity under the 'A Stronger Europe in the World' and 'A New Push for European Democracy' priorities. SEDF clearly outlines the EU understanding of digital/technological sovereignty, stating that it:

> starts from ensuring the integrity and resilience of our data infrastructure, networks and communications. It requires creating the right conditions for Europe to develop and deploy its own key capacities, thereby reducing our dependency on other parts of the globe for our most crucial technologies. Europe's right to define its own rules and values in the digital age will be reinforced by such capacities. European technological sovereignty is not defined against anyone else, but by focusing on the needs of Europeans and of the European social model. The EU will remain open to anyone willing to play by European rules and meet European standards, regardless of where they are based.[61]

This entire statement is worth reproducing in full, as it demonstrates the different characteristics of regulatory mercantilism in its definition of the term. It has the element of mutually constitutive economic and security goals and the desire to reduce dependencies on other states and regions (or the companies/materials based in them), with the desire to both regulate on the basis of its own rules and values while seeking to export those rules and values to the broader world, indicating a perception of regulatory sovereignty that extends beyond Europe's borders. In the fields of standardisation, infrastructure, and supply chains, as discussed earlier, the EU sees itself as particularly vulnerable. Central then to the Commission's arguments for increased regulatory control of technological systems is technological sovereignty based in concerns over strategic autonomy and an EU heavily dependent on technologies developed outside of its borders. For this reason, a regulatory

---

[60] European Commission, 'Shaping Europe's Digital Future' (2020).
[61] Ibid 3.

mercantilist approach to interventions becomes readily apparent due to the impact of these dependencies on the EU's strategic autonomy.

On the issue of standardisation, SEDF states under the heading of 'Europe as a global player' that 'in geopolitical terms, the EU should leverage its regulatory power, reinforced industrial and technological capabilities, domestic strengths and external financial instruments to advance the European approach and shape global interactions'.[62] It then moves on to state that many states have followed European standards, and that the EU should move to solidify this position as a global leader, with the publication of a standardisation strategy being identified as one of the key actions.[63] Prior to the publication of this strategy, the EU published an Industrial Strategy[64] in which it stated that a core aim of its approach to standard setting would be to ensure global leadership, based in strong internal market provisions, in order to ensure the EU's competitiveness and resilience. This would help to support 'a more assertive stance on European interests in standardisation'.[65] The Strategy on Standardisation was published in early 2022, in which it was stated that the ability to set standards at the international level was essential in order to secure Europe's competitiveness, technological sovereignty, ability to reduce dependencies, and protection of EU values, and that 'while European standardisation has been such a success story for the establishment of the EU's single market, the strategic importance of standards has not been adequately recognised at the cost of EU leadership in standard-setting. This must change.'[66] As will be discussed at the end of this part of the chapter, the rationale for action provided in the field of standards is clearly regulatory mercantilist in nature and strongly influenced by geopolitical concerns.

Similar rationales can be identified in the development of the von der Leyen Commission's cybersecurity initiatives. While the Cybersecurity Act introduced in 2019[67] expanded the competences of ENISA (discussed in Chapter 2) and introduced a voluntary cybersecurity certification regime, it did not represent a significant shift in regulatory approach for the EU and fit comfortably within a regulatory capitalism model of governance.[68] However, with the geopolitical instabilities and vulnerabilities identified by the Commission at the beginning of its mandate, cybersecurity was reframed in geostrategic terms. SEDF announced the publication of the

---

[62] Ibid 7.
[63] Ibid.
[64] European Commission, 'Updating the 2020 New Industrial Strategy: Building a Stronger Single Market for Europe's Recovery' (2021) COM(2021) 350.
[65] Ibid 15.
[66] European Commission, 'An EU Strategy on Standardisation: Setting Global Standards in Support of a Resilient, Green and Digital EU Single Market' (n35).
[67] Regulation 2019/881 on ENISA (the European Union Agency for Cybersecurity) and on information and communications technology cybersecurity certification and repealing Regulation (EU) No 526/2013 (Cybersecurity Act)
[68] See Helena Carrapico and Benjamin Farrand, 'Discursive Continuity and Change in the Time of Covid-19: The Case of EU Cybersecurity Policy' (2020) 42 *Journal of European Integration* 1111.

earlier-discussed Cybersecurity Strategy,[69] which made clear that cybersecurity was part of an approach on the part of the Commission that sought to promote its technological sovereignty, resilience, and leadership.[70] Measures that the Commission identified as essential to achieve this included increased regulatory activity in order to strengthen critical information infrastructure resilience, which was framed both in terms of strategic control (reflecting the dimension of increased control in regulatory mercantilism) and upholding the EU's values as it related to promoting the resilience of democratic processes and institutions.[71] Other measures proposed to ensure resilience and reduce external dependencies included implementing a 'European cyber shield' based in a joined-up cybersecurity threat response programme based in mutual assistance, with proposed investments in order to create such a European system;[72] reduction of dependencies and strategic vulnerabilities by implementing regulation around the security of digitally connected devices;[73] and promotion of European interests in technology supply chains as part of a technological industrial strategy, 'building capacity [...] and reducing dependence on other parts of the globe for the most crucial technologies'.[74] On this basis, President von der Leyen was explicit in the 2021 State of the Union address, arguing that 'it should be here in Europe where cyber defence tools are developed. This is why we need a European Cyber Defence Policy, including legislation on common standards under a new Cyber Resilience Act.'[75] These initiatives would be promoted internationally, with the intent that the EU's cybersecurity rules would serve as the basis for alignment or convergence with EU regulatory norms and standards.[76] Here we again see hallmarks of regulatory mercantilism – motivated by a sense of vulnerability, highlighted in terms of defence, the Commission seeks to introduce an industrial policy of developing defence tools in Europe, regulating to provide greater oversight while seeking to promote a positive balance of regulatory trade by exporting EU standards as world standards.

However, it is in its approach and rationale for regulating the semiconductor supply chain that a regulatory mercantilism approach is the most pronounced. If the 2021 State of the Union was clear on the need for cyber defence policy, it was even more clear on the Commission's perceived need for increased control over technology supply chains. Stating that Europe needed strong financial investment in

---

[69] European Commission, 'Shaping Europe's Digital Future' (n60) 4.
[70] European Commission and High Representative of the Union for Foreign Affairs and Security Policy (n44) 4.
[71] Ibid 5–6.
[72] Ibid 6–7.
[73] Ibid 9–10.
[74] Ibid 11.
[75] Ursula von der Leyen, '2021 State of the Union Address by President von Der Leyen: Strengthening the Soul of Our Union' (European Commission 2021) SPEECH/21/4701 8.
[76] European Commission, '2030 Digital Compass: The European Way for the Digital Decade' (2021) COM(2021) 118 final/2 19.

its technological sovereignty, von der Leyen outlined a 'chips' policy emphasising vulnerability. While global demand had grown, the share of European manufacturing had shrunk, with the EU dependent on semiconductors produced in Asia.[77] This dependency is, according to von der Leyen, 'not just a matter of our competitiveness. This is a matter of tech sovereignty [...] The aim is to jointly create a state-of-the-art European chip ecosystem, including production. That ensures our security of supply and will develop new markets for ground-breaking European tech.'[78] In a report on the EU's strategic dependencies, the lack of strong production of leading-edge chips was identified as a key concern, along with China's demand (comprising approximately 50 per cent of global sales) and the significant state subsidies provided to chip manufacturers, including by the US.[79] The report therefore recommended joint action in the EU, with significant investment coupled with regulation intended to boost European competitiveness while protecting the Union's interests.[80] By early 2022, the Commission had published its strategy for semiconductors, framed as 'A Chips Act for Europe'.[81] Concluding that reinforcing leadership in semiconductors was essential for competitiveness, technological sovereignty, and security (the three interconnected constructs in regulatory mercantilism),[82] the Chips Act for Europe argued that it needed to both invest in European production and its own security of supply in the global arena, as 'the only way for Europe to have the means to achieve the leverage required in times of crisis'.[83] The establishment of a semiconductor industrial policy would be facilitated through a Regulation intended to ensure European supply chain resilience, providing the conditions for the investment necessary and strengthening Europe's technological leadership.[84]

As indicated in the previous section of this chapter, the war in Ukraine exacerbated the concerns over security of supply, as did increased controls over semiconductors as President Biden demonstrated continuity with the Trump Administration as it concerned trade (war) with China and its own increasingly protectionist approaches even towards its allies.[85] In the 2023 State of the Union, President von

---

[77] von der Leyen, '2021 State of the Union Address by President von Der Leyen: Strengthening the Soul of Our Union' (n75) 4.

[78] Ibid.

[79] European Commission, 'Strategic Dependencies and Capacities: Accompanying the Communication Updating the 2020 New Industrial Strategy: Building a Stronger Single Market for Europe's Recovery' (2021) SWD (2021) 352 83.

[80] Ibid 89.

[81] European Commission, 'A Chips Act for Europe' (n58); See also Benjamin Farrand, Helena Carrapico and Aleksei Turobov, 'The New Geopolitics of EU Cybersecurity: Security, Economy and Sovereignty' (2024) 100 *International Affairs* 2379.

[82] European Commission, 'A Chips Act for Europe' (n58) 22.

[83] Ibid 2.

[84] Ibid 4.

[85] See, for example, Thomas J Schoenbaum, 'The Biden Administration's Trade Policy: Promise and Reality' (2023) 24 *German Law Journal* 102.

der Leyen referenced China's restrictions on gallium and germanium,[86] and the need to work with like-minded partners in securing natural resources important for technologies like semiconductors.[87] This would be pursued through a proposed Critical Raw Materials Act,[88] with a Communication preceding the publication of a Proposal indicating that 'Russia's illegal aggression against Ukraine showcased how untrustworthy suppliers can exploit and weaponize such dependencies to their advantage'.[89] This Communication framed the proposed Regulation in terms of strategic autonomy and reducing dependencies on highly concentrated supplies,[90] promoting both investment in increased exploration for these resources in Europe and seeking as far as possible to lead globally on supply chain security, through exporting its norms and values as the basis for global standards around the extraction and exploitation of critical raw materials, through bilateral partnerships and engagement with international organisations.[91] In the Proposal for the Regulation, we once again see a regulatory mercantilist rationale for action made clear, insofar as the Commission seeks to exert greater control over these supply chains, using law as the means to do so; 'non-regulatory actions have not been enough to ensure the EU's access to a secure and sustainable supply of critical raw materials.'[92] Achieving this security of supply is argued to be essential for the EU's strategic autonomy and its sovereignty – for this reason, proactive regulation is necessary to achieve this, as part of its renewed industrial strategy.[93] In the next section of this chapter, the operationalisation of these proposals for regulation will be further scrutinised, highlighting the regulatory mercantilist aspects enacted as part of the Commission's pursuit of its ambitions for the Geopolitical Union.

LAW'S ROLE IN SECURING EUROPE'S STRATEGIC AUTONOMY AND REDUCING DEPENDENCIES

Now that the conditions in which these legal interventions were devised and the underlying rationale for action have both been identified, it is possible to determine the extent to which the legislation adopted can be inferred to possess regulatory

---

[86] Ursula von der Leyen, '2023 State of the Union Address by President von Der Leyen: Answering the Call of History' (2023) SPEECH/23/4426 8.
[87] Framed as a 'Critical Raw Materials Club' ibid.
[88] Ibid 3.
[89] European Commission, 'A Secure and Sustainable Supply of Critical Raw Materials in Support of the Twin Transition' (2023) COM(2023) 165 1.
[90] Ibid 2.
[91] See ibid 10–12; Farrand, Carrapico and Turobov (n81); Linda Monsees, 'The Paradox of Semiconductors – EU Governance between Sovereignty and Interdependence' (2025) 38 *Cambridge Review of International Affairs* 3.
[92] European Commission, 'Proposal for a Regulation Establishing a Framework for Ensuring a Secure and Sustainable Supply of Critical Raw Materials' (n54) 2.
[93] Ibid 3.

mercantilist characteristics. The first key characteristic is a move to a more hierarchical form of intervention based on exerting public control rather than allowing for a more voluntary approach to governance, in this instance, working to develop European technological industrial policy. The second is a move to ensure a positive regulatory balance of trade, through minimising regulatory import and pursuing means of exporting European standards as global standards. While each area of legislative development, namely around standards, infrastructure resilience, and supply chain security, differs, commonalities between the areas exist as will be explored later.

Regulation and Industrial Policy at Home

If we take standards first, the first Regulation adopted by the Commission was the Regulation amending the 2012 Standardisation Regulation.[94] It is a relatively short one, but its recitals are revealing. Recital (4) obliquely refers to the concerns of the Commission regarding the impact of non-EU states and companies influencing European standards, stating that when ESOs execute standardisation requests in support of Union legislation and policies, 'it is essential that their internal decisions take into account the interests, policy objectives and values of the Union'. Recital (6) states that national standardisation bodies acting in the European standardisation bodies are the best ones to ensure this. Article 1(1) requires that a paragraph is replaced in the 2012 Regulation, replacing Article 10(1) with text requiring that 'European standards and European standardisation deliverables shall be market-driven, take into account the public interest as well as the policy objectives clearly stated in the Commission's request and be based on consensus'. Furthermore, Article 1(2) inserts a paragraph 2a into Article 10, which states that decisions on the acceptance or rejection of standardisation requests, new work items relating to standardisation, and decisions on the adoption, amendment, or withdrawal of standards are to be taken *exclusively* by the representatives of the national standardisation bodies, in essence excluding private stakeholders from the process. Ultimately, as de Vries argues, this is intended to drive ETSI to be 'more European'.[95]

This increased regulatory oversight of standards becomes even clearer when looking at the adoption of cybersecurity standards during the von der Leyen Commission. The first set are those relevant to network and information security, implemented through the NIS2 Directive.[96] The Proposal clearly framed the implementation of

---

[94] Regulation 2022/2480 amending Regulation 1025/2012 as regards decisions of ESOs concerning European standards and European standardisation deliverables, which is admittedly not the snappiest title a piece of legislation has ever received.

[95] Henk J de Vries, 'Vulnerabilities of European Telecommunication Systems and the EU's Concerns about ETSI's Legitimacy – A Proposal for Value-Based Standardization' (2024) 37 *Innovation: The European Journal of Social Science Research* 1397, 1404.

[96] Directive 2022/2555 on measures for a high common level of cybersecurity across the Union, amending Regulation (EU) No 910/2014 and Directive (EU) 2018/1972, and repealing Directive (EU) 2016/1148 (NIS 2 Directive).

the Directive in terms of maintaining the EU's strategic autonomy and improving and expanding the remit from the NIS1 Directive in light of the evolving threat landscape,[97] referring to the Cybersecurity Strategy regarding the nature of these threats. Recital (4) of the Directive makes clear the links between the functioning of the economy and internal market on the one hand and a robust cybersecurity framework on the other, as well as the need to ensure that in an evolving threat landscape, there is a unified approach with an avoidance of divergences between Member States under Recital (5). In terms of more effective oversight, Recital (38) states that Member States should be able to appoint one or more national bodies with the competence to provide supervision over cybersecurity provision. Article 1 does not fundamentally change the nature of regulation from the NIS1 Directive (although it changes the terminology from a high level of network and information security to a high level of cybersecurity), which is maintained as obligations on Member States to establish national cybersecurity policies and ensure cybersecurity risk management and incident reporting obligations for critical information infrastructure providers; however, it is in the application of these measures that we see increased oversight and establishment of clearer regulatory hierarchies.[98]

In particular, the expansion of the number of entities to which the Directive applies is substantial, moving them out of the realm of self-regulation to one of active regulation on the part of national cybersecurity authorities, as indicated by the Annexes. Annex I covers essential industries (sectors of high criticality), which now includes a wider range of energy providers (including hydrogen), an increased number of digital infrastructure providers including cloud computing and data storage providers, and new categories including wastewater management, ICT service management, public administration, and space-based services. Annex II (other critical sectors) is entirely new, expanding the scope to cover sectors such as postal services and digital providers such as social media platforms, search, and marketplaces.[99] Furthermore, the *level* of oversight has been increased, with Article 7 providing increased levels of prescriptiveness concerning the content of national cybersecurity strategies, a requirement that these strategies are communicated to the Commission within three months of adoption, and a requirement for updates every five years. The other key expansion of regulatory oversight is under Article 32, which allows for audits of companies to ensure compliance with their cybersecurity plans,

---

[97] Council of the European Union, 'Proposal for a Regulation of the European Parliament and of the Council Laying down Measures for a High Common Level of Cybersecurity at the Institutions, Bodies, Offices and Agencies of the Union – General Approach' 1 <https://eur-lex.europa.eu/legal-content/EN/TXT/PDF/?uri=CONSIL:ST_14128_2022_INIT> accessed 10 June 2024.

[98] See, for example, Niels Vandezande, 'Cybersecurity in the EU: How the NIS2-Directive Stacks up against Its Predecessor' (2024) 52 *Computer Law & Security Review* 105890.

[99] See Charanjit Singh, 'The European Approach to Cybersecurity in 2023: A Review of the Changes Brought in by the Network and Information Security 2 (NIS2) Directive 2022/2555' (2023) 34 *International Company and Commercial Law Review* 251 for a comprehensive overview.

as well as providing for significantly greater powers of enforcement on the part of national cybersecurity authorities.[100]

The NIS2 Directive was followed by a series of additional cybersecurity laws that represent a desire on the part of the Commission to have protection of technological systems; the first is the Cyber Resilience Act,[101] and the second is the Cyber Solidarity Act.[102] The Cyber Resilience Act represents an explicit linkage of economic and security concerns, providing a set of standards and frameworks for hardware and software devices aiming to ensure that products made available in the Single Market are cyber-secure.[103] The Cyber Resilience Act provides for greater state control of digitally enabled technologies, providing for: rules for making products available; essential cybersecurity requirements for those products; requirements regarding vulnerability handling processes; and rules on market surveillance, including monitoring and enforcement under Article 1. Article 13 provides a significant list of obligations concerning cybersecurity for devices, with Article 14 outlining reporting obligations for manufacturers regarding exploited vulnerabilities, which are to be communicated to the Computer Security Incident Response Teams (CSIRTS) and ENISA, along with obligations for importers under Article 19 and distributors under Article 20. Should products conform to the requirements they are entitled to EU declarations of conformity under Article 28, but should they fail to do so, the market enforcement mechanisms under Chapter V apply. This is where we see the Commission attempt to exercise greater control, providing for a system of market surveillance under Article 52, where market surveillance authorities and CSIRTs can investigate non-compliant firms. Under Article 55, products considered as posing cybersecurity risks can be withdrawn from the EU market, and the ability to impose fines of up to €15 million or 2.5 per cent of worldwide annual turnover, whichever is higher. Ultimately, the Cyber Resilience Act represents a move from voluntary compliance codes in this field, with greater regulatory oversight based on a security logic.[104]

The Cyber Solidarity Act represents a form of cybersecurity industrial policy on the part of the Commission, explicitly established in order to guarantee the EU's

---

[100] For more, see Vandezande (n98).

[101] Regulation 2024/2847 on horizontal cybersecurity requirements for products with digital elements and amending Regulations (EU) No 168/2013 and (EU) 2019/1020 and Directive (EU) 2020/1828 (Cyber Resilience Act).

[102] Regulation 2025/38 laying down measures to strengthen solidarity and capacities in the Union to detect, prepare for, and respond to cyber threats and incidents and amending Regulation (EU) 2021/694 (Cyber Solidarity Act).

[103] See generally Helena Carrapico and Benjamin Farrand, 'Cybersecurity Trends in the European Union: Regulatory Mercantilism and the Digitalisation of Geopolitics' (2024) 62 *JCMS: Journal of Common Market Studies* 147; see also European Commission, 'Proposal for a Regulation on Horizontal Cybersecurity Requirements for Products with Digital Elements and Amending Regulation 2019/1020' (2022) COM(2022) 454.

[104] Mohammed Raiz Shaffique, 'Cyber Resilience Act 2022: A Silver Bullet for Cybersecurity of IoT Devices or a Shot in the Dark?' (2024) 54 *Computer Law & Security Review* 106009.

technological sovereignty and ensure Union-wide resilience to cyberattacks.[105] The Regulation explicitly discusses external vulnerabilities including to Russian attacks under Recital (2), and the need to increase the competitiveness of EU industry in cybersecurity under Recital (3), with Cross-Border Cyber Hubs being described as a means of pooling data and exploiting its value as a means of ensuring sovereignty, strategic autonomy, competitiveness, and resilience under Recital (18), all characteristics of regulatory mercantilism. This is reinforced as a binding obligation under Article 1(1), where it states the objectives of creating a European Cybersecurity Alert System, Cybersecurity Emergency Mechanism, and European Cybersecurity Incident Review Mechanism, with Article 1(2) reinforcing the goals of increased industry competitiveness, resilience, sovereignty, and strategic autonomy through boosting European innovation. Interestingly, Article 9 concerns the funding of the European Cybersecurity Alert System, stating that all Member States participating in the system will be expected to contribute to the funding of tools, infrastructure, or services required to set up the National Cyber Hubs established under Article 4, with an element of cybersecurity industrial policy indicated at Article 9(4), where it is stated that in mapping the tools, infrastructures, and services necessary to set up the Cyber Hubs, attention will be paid to 'their availability, including from legal entities established or deemed to be established in Member States and controlled by Member States or by nationals of Member States', indicating a preference for EU-based providers, as a means of reducing external dependencies and promoting strategic autonomy.

Finally, there is the establishment of a technology industrial policy under the Chips Act.[106] The Proposal for the Regulation framed the need for regulatory intervention in terms of reducing external dependencies, using Article 173 TFEU, which concerns actions to boost the competitiveness of European industry for pillar 1 of its actions, which concerns creating innovation capacity, and Article 114 TFEU for pillars 2 and 3 on investment and market monitoring and crisis response specifically. Article 1 of the Chips Act makes clear the regulatory mercantilist dimension to the policies pursued. The first is a 'Chips for Europe' initiative, the second is the creation of the conditions for EU foundries for semiconductor production, and the third is setting up the conditions for Member State and Commission cooperation for monitoring the EU semiconductor sector and identifying potential vulnerabilities or crises in supply. The obligations under Article 4 constitute highly ambitious goals for 'domestic' EU production as a means of reducing dependencies on external suppliers, with Article 5 providing for measures to achieve those goals.

---

[105] European Commission, 'Proposal for a Regulation Laying down Measures to Strengthen Solidarity and Capacities in the Union to Detect, Prepare for and Respond to Cybersecurity Threats and Incidents' (2023) COM(2023) 209 2–3.
[106] Regulation 2023/1781 establishing a framework of measures for strengthening Europe's semiconductor ecosystem and amending Regulation 2021/694 (Chips Act).

The Commission is afforded considerable competence to foster these developments, including the ability under Article 12 to adopt delegated acts to give effect to Article 4's development goals, with Articles 13 and 14 seeking to ensure resilience through facilitating integrated production facilities and 'Open EU foundries', respectively. Guidance, recommendations, and oversight are provided by a newly constituted European Semiconductor Board (ESB) under Article 28, which is to have representatives from each Member State and be chaired by a representative of the Commission under Article 29. Overall, the Chips Act is an ambitious attempt at technological industrial policy,[107] aimed at ensuring the EU's strategic autonomy and using heightened regulatory control as its means of achieving it. This was complemented by the STEP Regulation,[108] which established a platform for identifying critical technologies in fields such as digital under Article 1, with the aim under Article 2 of ensuring the EU's strategic autonomy and sovereignty through investing in those critical technologies, with financial support under Article 3 being issues to STEP of €1.5 billion to invest in those technologies.[109] In this respect, these regulatory interventions, pursued in the name of sovereignty and strategic autonomy by way of reducing external dependencies, are clear examples of regulatory mercantilism, reflecting a desire to bring as much of EU semiconductor and critical technology development within Europe's geographical territory as possible for explicitly geopolitical reasons.[110]

Global Leadership and European Standards Abroad

Implementing these standards and technological industrial policy at home was coupled with engaging in cyber-diplomacy abroad[111] as a means of exporting European rules, norms, and values as international standards, or as a means of achieving compliance in other states. As part of the move to 're-Europeanise' ETSI as a standardisation organisation, the EU aimed to promote ETSI standards as global standards. As well as creating an EU excellence hub on standards tasked with both developing

---

[107] Bob Hancké and Angela Garcia Calvo, 'Mister Chips Goes to Brussels: On the Pros and Cons of a Semiconductor Policy in the EU' (2022) 13 *Global Policy* 585; Louise Viktoria Axelina Winstrup and Gustav Anders Blomqvist, 'The Global Race for Microchips: A Study of the EU Chips Act as a Reshoring Incentive', *Business and Policy Challenges of Global Uncertainty* (World Scientific (Europe) 2024).

[108] Regulation 2024/795 establishing the Strategic Technologies for Europe Platform (STEP), and amending Directive 2003/87/EC and Regulations 2021/1058, 2021/1056, 2021/1057, 1303/2013, 223/2014, 2021/1060, 2021/523, 2021/695, 2021/697, and 2021/241.

[109] Daniel Lambach and Linda Monsees, 'Beyond Sovereignty as Authority: The Multiplicity of European Approaches to Digital Sovereignty' (2025) 4 *Global Political Economy* 71.

[110] Farrand (n50); Lambach and Monsees (n109).

[111] As outlined in the Introduction and Chapter 1 of this book, based on the work of André Barrinha and Thomas Renard, 'Cyber-Diplomacy: The Making of an International Society in the Digital Age' (2017) 3 *Global Affairs* 353.

EU-based expertise and monitoring international standards developments,[112] the Standardisation Strategy argued for a more strategic approach to the EU and Member States' engagements with the ITU and other international standardisation bodies as a means of advancing European standards in order to achieve global leadership in defence of competitiveness, strategic autonomy, and the promotion of EU values.[113] These standards would then be promoted through bodies such as the EU-US Trade and Technology Council (TTC), encourage the adoption of European standards in bilateral agreements, through its Global Europe initiative, and develop standards with countries in Africa through the Global Gateway.[114] Examples of the EU's exporting of global standards include the establishment of the technology standards working group at the TTC,[115] and the EU's promotion of its technology standards around e-Identity and providing assistance with the development of standards that promote both economic development and security in the context of privacy, AI, and data sharing in the context of its partnership with Sub-Saharan Africa.[116]

In terms of cybersecurity and resilience, the norm-exporting measures adopted by the EU combine cyber-diplomacy with binding legal obligations. While the EU had a 'cyber-diplomacy toolbox' for cybersecurity since 2017,[117] an expansion of this toolbox with the von der Leyen Commission saw standards for resilience such as in the NIS2 Directive promoted as international standards, with the Council of the European Union arguing in 2022 that the Commission and High Representative for Foreign Policy and Security should actively pursue the adoption of EU cybersecurity standards in international forums and in its bilateral agreements.[118] Active promotion of these standards has been pursued through actions such as engaging in cyber-dialogues, as well as providing expertise and cyber-capacity building, with third countries[119] such as in Latin America and the Caribbean,[120] and through concerted action against private sector actors deemed as presenting potential cybersecurity

---

[112] European Commission, 'An EU Strategy on Standardisation: Setting Global Standards in Support of a Resilient, Green and Digital EU Single Market' (n35) 2.
[113] Ibid 5–6.
[114] Ibid 7.
[115] European Commission, 'EU and US Take Stock of Trade and Technology Cooperation' (*European Commission*, 30 January 2024) <https://ec.europa.eu/commission/presscorner/detail/en/ip_24_575> accessed 23 March 2025.
[116] AU-EU Digital Economy Taskforce, 'New Africa-Europe Digital Economy Partnership – Accelerating the Achievement of the Sustainable Development Goals' (2021).
[117] Hanna Smith, 'The Geopolitics of Cyberspace and the European Union's Changing Identity' (2023) 45 *Journal of European Integration* 1219.
[118] Council of the European Council, 'Council Conclusions on the Development of the European Union's Cyber Posture' (2022) 9362/22 5, 14–16.
[119] Dimitrios Anagnostakis, 'The External Face of the EU's Cybersecurity Policies: Promoting Good Cybersecurity Governance Abroad?' in Digdem Soyaltin-Colella (ed), *EU Good Governance Promotion in the Age of Democratic Decline* (Springer International Publishing 2022).
[120] Carrapico and Farrand (n103).

threats such as Huawei in the context of the EU's actions around the 5G toolbox and exclusion of Huawei from provision of critical technologies.[121]

In terms of legal obligations, the Cyber Resilience Act has a key focus on norm and rule-exporting, particularly as it relates to the obligations imposed on manufacturers of technologies under Article 13. The recitals of the Regulation make clear the application to manufacturers regardless of physical location, with frequent references to third countries and manufacturers based in third countries, with Recital (52) in particular stating that the Regulation should be read in line with the NIS2 Directive Article 22 as regards undue interference by a third country. Similarly, Recital (58) states that when considering cybersecurity risks in products with digital elements, 'risks may be linked, but not limited, to the jurisdiction applicable to the manufacturer, the characteristics of its corporate ownership and the links of control to a third-country government where it is established'. Therefore, to be able to make products available in the internal market, third-country manufacturers are required to comply with the EU's cybersecurity standards for these products or risk not only fines but also loss of market access as discussed earlier. In the context of the Cyber Solidarity Act, Digital Europe Programme (DEP)[122] associated countries may benefit from the technical expertise, cyber-incident management capacities, and even funding available under the Regulation, so long as certain conditions are met under Article 19. The first is that they complete an agreement with the EU under the DEP programme that provides for access to the Cyber Reserve, compliance with the cyber-risk assessment and national strategy obligations as laid down in the Cyber Solidarity Act based on the definitions in the NIS2 Directive, and where it is consistent with Union security policy. In this respect, this is a clear exporting of EU rules and norms concerning cybersecurity, using the leverage provided by access to the EU's capabilities and finances as a way of ensuring effective compliance. At the time of writing, there are no DEP agreements that currently cover specific objective 3, concerning cybersecurity, with the exception of the EFTA countries; nevertheless, should states wish to expand agreements to cover cybersecurity, this would be a key means of the EU exporting its regulations in this area.

Finally, due to the nature of semiconductor supply chains, externalisation of the EU regulatory approach is a key ambition. The Chips Act, as discussed earlier, places considerable efforts in the development of an EU-based industrial policy. Yet the EU acknowledges that even as an ambitious target, by 2030 it may be able to secure 20 per cent of the world production of cutting-edge semiconductors.[123] Furthermore, as discussed in the Communication on Critical Raw Materials, the EU is likely to remain heavily dependent on other parts of the world for access to

---

[121] For more on this, see Berna Akcali Gur, 'Cybersecurity, European Digital Sovereignty and the 5G Rollout Crisis' (2022) 46 *Computer Law & Security Review* 105736.

[122] Regulation 2021/694 establishing the Digital Europe Programme.

[123] European Commission, '2030 Digital Compass: The European Way for the Digital Decade' (n76) 6; European Commission, 'A Chips Act for Europe' (n58) 9.

materials necessary for semiconductor development – its ambition for 2030 here is that it secures 10 per cent of strategic materials extracted in Europe, 40 per cent of processing and refining, and 15 per cent of recycling in terms of the global value, with a hope that it would not be reliant for more than 65 per cent of its annual consumption of each raw material from one third country.[124] Therefore, influence on the international level is essential for ensuring strategic autonomy, in the eyes of the Commission. In the Chips Act, the attempt to achieve this is through third-country monitoring; Recital (8) states that cooperation with third countries is essential for monitoring vulnerabilities in the semiconductor supply chain, and that the ESB should advise the Commission on strategic relations with third countries to guarantee supply, as well as ensure resilience to third-country restrictions placed on exports through international strategic partnerships under Recital (9), given legal effect under Article 28(3). Article 19 requires the Commission and ESB to monitor vulnerabilities, including dependencies on third countries, and to take preventative action in the event of disruptions to the supply chain under Article 22, which can include 'entering into consultations or cooperation with relevant third countries with a view to seeking cooperative solutions to address supply-chain disruptions'. An example of this is the EU-Singapore Digital Partnership, with s.52 outlining enhanced cooperation on semiconductor supply chain resilience, 'taking advantage of Singapore's position as a logistics hub'.[125]

The Critical Raw Materials Act[126] seeks to further set European standards as global standards, with many of the Recitals making clear the EU's vulnerability to potential restrictions on supply by third countries. It creates obligations concerning strategic and critical raw materials under Articles 3 and 4, respectively, which are listed in Annexes I and II, with the strategic raw materials list including those that are required for semiconductor manufacture, such as germanium, gallium, and silicon. Article 5 provides benchmarks, including obligations to meet the standards for extraction, processing, and recycling that were discussed in the Critical Raw Materials Communication, and under Article 6, empowers the Commission to recognise strategic projects intended to secure the supply of raw materials, which under Article 6(1)(e) can include projects in third countries, where 'the project would be mutually beneficial for the Union and the third country concerned by adding value in that third country'. Article 35 sets up a European Critical Raw Materials Board (ECRMB), chaired by the Commission under Article 36, with the Board empowered under Article 37 to work with the Commission to develop avenues for international cooperation and Strategic Partnerships with third countries to secure

---

[124] European Commission, 'A Secure and Sustainable Supply of Critical Raw Materials in Support of the Twin Transition' (n89) 3.
[125] European Commission and Ministry of Trade and Industry Singapore, 'EU-Singapore Digital Partnership' (2023) 8.
[126] Regulation 2024/1252 establishing a framework for ensuring a secure and sustainable supply of critical raw materials and amending Regulations 168/2013, 2018/858, 2018/1724, and 2019/1020.

the supply of raw materials, including with Global Gateway countries in Africa, so long as this is done in a way consistent with the EU's values and norms, including around labour standards.[127] The EU has concluded a number of agreements on raw materials with partner countries such as Ukraine, Canada, Namibia, Argentina, Chile, the Democratic Republic of Congo, and others,[128] in a form of externalisation of the EU's strategic autonomy goals to secure access to raw materials necessary for semiconductor production, while working in international forums to promote the adoption of international standards concerning extraction, supply, and resilience.[129]

CONCLUSIONS

As a region that has increasingly become a net importer rather than exporter of advanced technologies, the EU has found itself vulnerable to the dependencies that have been created as a result. Powerful (and arguably state-affiliated) companies have the power to dictate the terms of technological standardisation. Security vulnerabilities are present in the software and hardware that can be used in the context of critical information infrastructures or by end-user European consumers. Even the components that allow these technologies to function are a vulnerability – the dependence on chips produced outside the EU, using raw materials outside of European control, became an example of the EU's reliance on third countries and foreign companies, underscored by an understanding that global crises, whether in the form of pandemic or war, could render Europe even more vulnerable.

How did the Geopolitical Commission respond? Through its various policy documents, whether they were written in the context of its digital, security, or democracy portfolios, the Commission maintained a consistent line: Europe's strategic autonomy, and by extension, its digital sovereignty, could only be ensured through increasing its regulatory control over technological systems. In the field of technology standardisation, it meant increased European control over standard setting in ETSI and limiting the ability of non-European companies to intervene in devising those standards. In the context of critical information infrastructure resilience, it entailed expanding the scope of cybersecurity policies and the number of sectors captured by its requirements. The proliferation of cybersecurity-related Regulations adopted by the EU emphasised the need for European industrial policy in the context of developing tools, standards, and rules, including over how digitally enabled products could circulate in the internal market, as well as how a unified state and

---

[127] For more on this, see Article 37(1)(c) and Alessandra Hool, Christoph Helbig and Gijsbert Wierink, 'Challenges and Opportunities of the European Critical Raw Materials Act' (2024) 37 *Mineral Economics* 661.

[128] John Seaman, 'Critical Raw Materials, Economic Statecraft and Europe's Dependence on China' *The International Spectator* 1.

[129] European Commission, 'A Secure and Sustainable Supply of Critical Raw Materials in Support of the Twin Transition' (n89) 15.

market approach could help to ensure resilience through pan-European solidarity in the face of cyberattacks. In the field of microchip development, it was reflected in the most ambitious form of industrial strategy the Commission has pursued, with the establishment of funding for building domestic production capacity and financing innovation in this field through open foundries. In each of these cases, the Commission took an active steering role, providing oversight in the context of the ESB and ECRMB.

We also have seen the promotion of European standards as global standards as a means of giving effect to a positive regulatory balance of trade; minimising the risk of foreign influence of standards in ETSI, coupled with active measures to advance ETSI standards both in international forums such as the ITU and in agreements and relations with other countries, including by seeking to rival Chinese influence by promoting European standards in the context of the EU's Global Gateway partnerships. Cyber-diplomacy has also been pursued in the context of Strategic Partnerships build around ensuring semiconductor supply chain security and raw material access, coupled with explicit regulatory extraterritoriality through the Cyber Resilience Act to ensure third-country-based manufacturers abide by European cybersecurity standards, and exporting the principles of cybersecurity in the NIS2 Directive by attaching them to capacity building, technical assistance, and financial support in the context of the Cyber Solidarity Act and the DEP. In these ways, not only does the EU exert greater control over markets for security purposes *in* Europe, but it also exports these regulatory provisions to the rest of the world. For these reasons, these case studies serve as excellent examples of regulatory mercantilist policymaking on the part of the Commission. In Chapter 5, we will see how this works in a different sector of activity by exploring how concerns over the economy, security, and democracy have influenced the Commission's approach to platform governance, both in terms of market structure and in terms of content regulation, which has been framed in terms of securing digital sovereignty.

5

Regulating Platform Content and Architecture

By passing the Digital Services Act and the Digital Markets Act into law in record time, the EU has become the first jurisdiction in the world where online platforms no longer set their own rules. They are now regulated entities in the same way financial institutions are.[1]

INTRODUCTION

While Chapter 4 has discussed hardware, software, and standards (as technological systems) and how the geopolitics of technology control have impacted the EU's approach to a number of issues in a way that can be categorised as regulatory mercantilist in nature, this chapter focuses on 'platforms', the online service providers such as Meta's Facebook and Elon Musk's X, and the obligations that the Commission has imposed upon them in light of economic and security concerns. Social media in particular has been a key cause for concern for countries, regulators, and academics throughout the world due to the combination of their economic power, potential political influence, and involvement in the spread of radicalising content such as disinformation.[2] The Digital Services Act (DSA),[3] the Digital Markets Act (DMA),[4] and the Political Advertising Regulation (PRA)[5] are all legislative initiatives concluded by the von der Leyen Commission, in which we

---

[1] Thierry Breton, 'Digital Platforms as Regulated Entities: Our Single Market, Our Rules' (*European Commission*, 17 March 2023) <https://ec.europa.eu/commission/presscorner/detail/en/SPEECH_23_1761> accessed 22 April 2025.

[2] See, for example, Siva Vaidhyanathan, *Antisocial Media: How Facebook Disconnects Us and Undermines Democracy* (Oxford University Press 2018); Terry Flew, *Regulating Platforms* (Polity 2021); Jillian C York, *Silicon Values: The Future of Free Speech Under Surveillance Capitalism* (Verso 2022); Benjamin Farrand, '"Is This a Hate Speech?" The Difficulty in Combating Radicalisation in Coded Communications on Social Media Platforms' (2023) 29 *European Journal on Criminal Policy and Research* 477.

[3] Regulation 2022/2065 on a Single Market for Digital Services and Amending Directive 2000/31/EC (Digital Services Act).

[4] Regulation 2022/1925 on contestable and fair markets in the digital sector and amending Directives 2019/1937 and 2020/1828 (Digital Markets Act).

[5] Regulation 2024/900 on the transparency and targeting of political advertising.

have seen a move from light-touch self-regulation to binding frameworks with strict regulatory oversight in the name of preserving the EU's digital sovereignty. While the General Data Protection Regulation (GDPR)[6] does deal with digital power and is of relevance to the arguments in this book, it is covered explicitly and in much more detail in Chapter 6, which concerns data governance specifically.

The structure of this chapter is as follows. It begins in 'Online Platforms and Market Power' with an overview of the pre-established self-regulatory regime relevant to online platforms that pre-dated the von der Leyen Commission and its links to a regulatory capitalist form of governance. It highlights the growing concerns over platforms and their economic power and the increased perception on the part of policymakers that some form of intervention may be necessary. The subsequent section, 'Caught Between "Big States" and "Big Tech"', identifies the growing concerns over disinformation in particular being spread through these platforms and the position of the von der Leyen Commission on the significant economic and security threats posed by significant market operators, predominantly based outside the EU, and used by foreign states to attempt to destabilise the EU, providing evidence of the geopolitical context in which regulatory mercantilist approaches can be adopted. The chapter then moves to the regulatory mercantilist rationale in 'Reining in Platform Power', highlighting the Commission's explicit linkage of security and economy as interdependent policy fields, underscored by a desire to reassert control over policymaking for the internet, reorienting sovereignty relations with the private sector and third-country states through the adoption of these policies within a digital sovereignty discourse. It then identifies the regulatory mercantilist means by which these goals were given effect, namely through moving from voluntary codes to binding regulations, replacing light-touch requirements regarding standards with prescriptive requirements concerning risk assessment, threat mitigation, transparency, and accountability, and providing formalised state-based oversight mechanisms through national coordinators working in conjunction with the Commission itself. Finally, in 'International Players Bound by EU Rules', it identifies the concerns over the balance of regulatory trade, with the EU seeking to export these standards as the 'gold standard' of internet regulation, as well as minimising the risk that Europe's rules would be dictated by either Silicon Valley or Shenzhen.

ONLINE PLATFORMS AND MARKET POWER: WITH GREAT (PRIVATE) POWER COMES GREAT (PUBLIC) RESPONSIBILITY?

The EU concern with control over online platforms and the rules that govern them predates the von der Leyen Commission and the digital sovereignty agenda. The

---

[6] Regulation 2016/679 on the protection of natural persons with regard to the processing of personal data and on the free movement of such data, and repealing Directive 95/46/EC (General Data Protection Regulation).

regulation of content, particularly illegal content, constituted one of the first legal initiatives on cyberspace pursued by the EU along with the rules governing the conclusion of contracts concluded online, which were enshrined in the E-Commerce Directive.[7] As was discussed in Chapter 5, however, this content regulation can be best understood as responding to a discrete set of quasi-security concerns recognised in explicitly economically focused legislation. The explicit intention of this legislation was to set the conditions in which service providers would operate in new and emerging forms of digital market activity, along broadly ordoliberal lines.[8] The E-Commerce Directive did not reflect a regulatory mercantilist preoccupation with indivisible economic and security goals, nor an explicit consideration of either sovereignty or the balance of regulatory trade. It was instead far more reflective of a regulatory capitalist approach, in which the private sector was determined as best placed to regulate its own activities in a form of light-touch regulated self-regulation working within market-making and shaping frameworks provided by the European Commission.

With the maturation of digital markets, however, there has been a consolidation of power on the part of certain market participants. Known variously as 'Big Tech', 'US Tech Giants', or 'GAMAM (an acronym of Google, Amazon, Meta, Apple, and Microsoft)', the paradoxical power of these market players in which increasingly dominant positions at once potentially harm market entrants while providing increased convenience and affordability for consumers has been the subject of academic interest.[9] Their potentially market-distorting effects *vis-à-vis* their competitors have been of concern for the EU for some time. One example is the competition case brought by the Commission against Microsoft in the late 2000s for the abuse of a dominant position involved in the 'tying' or 'bundling' of software such as the Internet Explorer web browser, a decision largely upheld by the Court of First Instance in 2007,[10] and then by the General Court in 2012.[11] In 2008, Apple was subject to a Statement of Objections over potential market partitioning and differential pricing for music made available through the Apple iTunes store in different Member States. This was directed to both Apple and major record labels concerning potential anticompetitive practices under Article 101 TFEU (then Article 81 EC), concerning territorial restrictions upon consumers, consequently determining

---

[7] Directive 2000/31/EC on certain legal aspects of information society services, in particular electronic commerce, in the Internal Market.
[8] Benjamin Farrand, 'The Ordoliberal Internet? Continuity and Change in the EU's Approach to the Governance of Cyberspace' (2023) 2 *European Law Open* 106.
[9] Including in Lina M Khan, 'Amazon's Antitrust Paradox' (2017) 126 *The Yale Law Journal* 710, which refers to GAFAM rather than GAMAM, the previous acronym used before Facebook changed its name to Meta; and Manuel Wörsdörfer, 'Apple's Antitrust Paradox' (2023) Online first doi:10.1080/17 441056.2023.2262870 European Competition Journal 1, which has applied Khan's approach to Apple specifically.
[10] Case T-201/04 *Microsoft v Commission* EU:T:2007:289.
[11] Case T-167/08 *Microsoft v Commission* EU:T:2012:323.

'what music is available, and at what price'.[12] This did not focus, however, on potential abuse of a dominant position by Apple, and upon notification that the differential pricing and territorial restrictions were not the result of any agreement between the labels and Apple but on copyright licensing requirements, the investigation was closed.[13]

The potential for 'Big Tech' to potentially distort markets through their significant gatekeeping roles in the online environment was being discussed at the level of the European Commission from the late 2000s onwards. In the Digital Agenda for Europe, published in 2010 by the Barroso Commission, the Commission discussed the role of platforms in comparatively neutral terms. It spoke of the need for 'open platforms',[14] the risks posed to consumers by territorial fragmentation of music platforms,[15] and the need for competitive platforms that would improve consumer choice, yet argued that legislation may not be necessary, instead relying on platforms to develop innovative business models and engage in voluntary agreements intended to facilitate competition.[16] The focus upon platforms was very much upon their role in fostering economic growth in the context of the 'digital' single market, perhaps influenced by the global financial crisis' impact upon the Eurozone, and the perception that deeper market integration would help to ensure private growth while reducing public spending.[17] Power in this context was discussed in terms of market power, with market effects. Security threats as posed by these platforms were not yet on the agenda – instead, platforms were considered as partners in the tackling of online threats from activities such as phishing or online identity theft through to the distribution of child sexual abuse material (CSAM), based on an understanding of shared values and responsibility.[18]

---

[12] European Commission, 'European Commission Confirms Sending a Statement of Objections against Alleged Territorial Restrictions in On-Line Music Sales to Major Record Companies and Apple' (*European Commission*, 2007) MEMO/07/126.
[13] Benjamin Farrand, 'The Case That Never Was: An Analysis of the Apple iTunes Case Presented by the Commission and Potential Future Issues' (2009) 31(10) *European Intellectual Property Review* 508.
[14] European Commission, 'A Digital Agenda for Europe' (2010) COM(2010) 245 final/2 5.
[15] Ibid 7.
[16] Ibid 8.
[17] Explored in Benjamin Farrand, 'The Digital Agenda for Europe, the Economy and Its Impact Upon the Development of EU Copyright Policy' in Irini A Stamatoudi and Paul Torremans (eds), *Copyright Law in the European Union* (Edward Elgar 2014); the EU approach to the financial crisis, which focused on increased privatisation and promotion of private economic activity, while restricting public spending through 'fiscal consolidation' (or austerity) was somewhat influenced by the work of Carmen M Reinhart and Kenneth S Rogoff, 'Growth in a Time of Debt' (2010) 100 *American Economic Review* 573; as well as by the 'Bocconi Boys'; whose ideas helped to shape the European approach of 'expansionary austerity', as discussed in Oddný Helgadóttir, 'The Bocconi Boys Go to Brussels: Italian Economic Ideas, Professional Networks and European Austerity' (2016) 23 *Journal of European Public Policy* 392.
[18] European Commission, 'A Digital Agenda for Europe' (n14) 16–17.

It is of note that in the 2013 Joint Communication on EU Cybersecurity,[19] which served to expand upon the EU's cybersecurity initiatives and reinforce the powers of ENISA, the EU Cybersecurity Agency, there is no specific reference made to online platforms. Instead, the private sector is framed as contributing to a robust and innovative Internet (and by extension, the EU's economic development),[20] as a potential victim of malicious cyber activities,[21] and as partners in combating cybersecurity threats through ensuring the resilience of Internet-connected systems and critical information infrastructure.[22] This Cybersecurity Communication served as the basis for the NIS Directive,[23] which set out the transparency, incident reporting, and cooperative requirements placed upon the providers of critical information infrastructure throughout the EU,[24] which included financial institutions, energy suppliers, and transport providers.[25] It also included digital infrastructure providers in this list of critical infrastructures under Annex II, but this only pertained to Internet exchange points (or IXPs), as well as DNS service providers and TLD registries, not to online platforms.[26]

A perception shift regarding platforms specifically can be identified, however, in Communications from 2015 onwards. In the Digital Single Market Strategy published by the Juncker Commission in 2015, the focus of legislative and policy development was still very much upon economic development, with the Commission arguing that 'by creating a connected digital single market, we can generate up to EUR 20 billion of additional growth in Europe'.[27] In this context, concern was expressed over the market power of platforms, particularly where they act as gatekeepers to other market players dependent upon access to their services.[28] Practices identified by the Commission as requiring scrutiny included promoting own services to the detriment of competitors, non-transparent pricing practices, and restrictions on sale conditions.[29] However, in the context of security, the focus remained upon their role in removing illegal content once it was brought to their attention. In the Digital Single Market Strategy, the Commission

---

[19] European Commission and High Representative of the European Union for Foreign Affairs and Security Policy, 'Cybersecurity Strategy of the European Union: An Open, Safe and Secure Cyberspace' (2013) JOIN(2013) 1.
[20] Ibid 2.
[21] Ibid 3.
[22] Ibid 5.
[23] Directive 2016/1148 concerning measures for a high common level of security of network and information systems across the Union.
[24] For a general overview, see Helena Carrapico and Benjamin Farrand, '"Dialogue, Partnership and Empowerment for Network and Information Security": The Changing Role of the Private Sector from Objects of Regulation to Regulation Shapers' (2017) 67 *Crime, Law and Social Change* 245.
[25] Directive 2016/1148, Annex II.
[26] As discussed in more detail in Chapter 2, and in the context of the NIS2 expansion in Chapter 4.
[27] European Commission, 'A Digital Single Market Strategy for Europe' (2015) COM(2015) 192 2.
[28] Ibid 9.
[29] Ibid 11.

announced it would also be performing an assessment of the activities of online platforms to determine whether they should be required to exercise greater responsibility and due diligence.[30] This assessment came in the form of the Communication on Online Platforms and the Digital Single Market, published in 2016.[31] The 2016 Communication does not strictly frame online platforms as a security threat. Indeed, the focus of this Communication remains upon the economic opportunities and challenges afforded by the rise of large online service providers. Security is considered instead in terms of the 'responsibility' of platforms to take actions concerning illegal content available on their services. In a section of the Communication titles 'Ensuring that online platforms act responsibly', the Commission notes that 'around three quarters of all respondents [to a public consultation on online platforms] called for greater transparency on platform content policy. More than two thirds considered that different categories of illegal content require different policy approaches in respect of notice-and-action procedures'.[32]

At this point in time, a significant focus in discussions regarding platforms and content remained upon the role of online platforms in facilitating copyright infringement and the sale of counterfeit goods. Cases such as *Promusicae*,[33] *Scarlet*,[34] and *Netlog*[35] all made clear that intermediary service providers had obligations to balance between competing rights, such as the protection of intellectual property rights and privacy, and the interests of right-holders and Internet users to have those rights respected, with the CJEU having deference to the right of those service providers to be able to effectively run their businesses. The language used to describe them was very much that of neutral market operators, whose services could potentially be misused by end users to facilitate copyright infringement, and the cases themselves were relatively technical interpretations of the contours of the largely self-regulatory model afforded by the E-Commerce Directive. The pronouncements during the Juncker Commission did not necessarily change this position, with the discussion of the responsibility of intermediaries in this context being limited to a clarification of the rules applicable to online intermediaries in relation to copyright-protected works.[36] The emphasis remained, however, upon devising policies to regulate the economic activities of market players on the basis of their potential economic effects, and not upon a broader geopolitical or security-based logic.

---

[30] Ibid 12.
[31] European Commission, 'Online Platforms and the Digital Single Market: Opportunities and Challenges for Europe' (2016) COM(2016) 288.
[32] Ibid 7.
[33] Case C-275/06 *Promusicae v Telefónica España* EU:C:2008:54.
[34] Case C-70/10 *Scarlet v SABAM* EU:C:2011:771.
[35] Case C-360/10 *SABAM v Netlog* EU:C:2012:85.
[36] European Commission, 'A Digital Single Market Strategy for Europe' (n27) 7.

CAUGHT BETWEEN 'BIG STATES' AND 'BIG TECH': EUROPEAN VULNERABILITY TO PLATFORM POWER

With the change in geopolitical context, however, the position of large tech platforms was subject to renewed scrutiny. Of relevance to these changing perceptions was the issue of disinformation. Disinformation is defined by the Commission as 'verifiably false or misleading information that is created, presented and disseminated for economic gain or to intentionally deceive the public, and may cause harm'.[37] Motivated by concerns over the role of platforms in distributing and promoting disinformation (whether unwittingly or otherwise), the EU labelled disinformation as constituting a form of hybrid threat.[38] A hybrid threat is a type of threat where conventional means of warfare may be combined with unconventional sociological, economic, or technological means in order to destabilise or delegitimise a state government or authority.[39] Hybrid threats are myriad in their forms and applications, as well as in their definition.[40] This is, as the EU's External Action Service argues, as they will continue to evolve 'based on the success of their application, continuing technological developments, changes in potential adversaries' vulnerabilities and developments in measures to counter them'.[41] For the Commission and High Representative for Foreign Affairs and Security Policy, social media platforms were directly implicated in the increased profile of disinformation as a form of hybrid threat, stating that these platforms were being used to spread disinformation in order to 'control the political narrative or to radicalise, recruit and direct proxy actors'.[42] In doing so, these actors could 'undermine fundamental democratic values and liberties'.[43]

The Commission has seized upon disinformation as a key factor in the crises it has faced over recent years, identifying it as influential in influencing the outcome of elections,[44] increasing rates of vaccine hesitancy (even before COVID-19 vaccine disinformation began to proliferate as identified by Europol in 2020,[45] the

---

[37] High Representative of the European Union for Foreign Affairs and Security Policy & the European Commission, 'Action Plan against Disinformation' (2018) JOIN(2018) 36 final 1.
[38] European Commission and High Representative of the Union for Foreign Affairs and Security Policy, 'Joint Framework on Countering Hybrid Threats' (2016) JOIN(2016) 18.
[39] Frank G Hoffman, '"Hybrid Threats": Neither Omnipotent Nor Unbeatable' (2010) 54 *Orbis* 441.
[40] Hanna Smith, 'Countering Hybrid Threats' in Gustav Lindstrom and Thierry Tardy (eds), *NATO and the EU: The Essential Partners* (NATO Defense College 2019).
[41] European External Action Service, 'Food-for-Thought Paper "Countering Hybrid Threats"' (Council of the European Union 2015) EEAS(2015) 731 3.
[42] European Commission and High Representative of the Union for Foreign Affairs and Security Policy, 'Joint Framework on Countering Hybrid Threats' (n38) 2.
[43] Ibid 3.
[44] France 24, 'EU Says "Russian Sources" Tried to Undermine European Vote' (*France 24*, 14 June 2019) <www.france24.com/en/20190614-eu-says-russian-sources-tried-undermine-european-vote> accessed 22 October 2024.
[45] Europol, 'Catching the Virus: Cybercrime, Disinformation and the COVID-19 Pandemic' (2020).

EU was expressing concern over vaccine-related disinformation regarding diseases such as measles[46]) and increased political radicalisation by groups including right-wing extremists.[47] For the EU specifically, disinformation is explicitly recognised as being an external threat, with its central preoccupation being Russia and the use of Russian proxy organisations in the dissemination of disinformation targeting the EU. The EU's 2018 Action Plan on Disinformation refers to Russia throughout the report, going as far as to suggest that other third countries using disinformation tactics have 'been quickly learning from the Russian Federation'.[48] Russian disinformation was seen as being used within its immediate sphere of influence, before expanding to its use in the context of its assaults on South Georgia and then Crimea, at which point it then began targeting the EU, and then the US, with these information-based attacks.[49] However, of particular concern for the EU was that these external threats were mediated through social media platforms.

Social media platforms, particularly Facebook (owned by Meta), were already of concern to the EU due to their perceived *market* power. The potential for these platforms to be used for the spread of disinformation meant that these concerns grew to incorporate security concerns as well as economic ones, with the two being linked in EU policy. In the Communication on Online Disinformation, the Commission indicated that in 2016, 57 per cent of internet users used social media and search engines as one of their main news sources, with one-third of eighteen- to twenty-four-year-olds stating it was their main news source.[50] However, these platforms were assessed as being either unwilling or unable to combat the spread of disinformation, with actions taken voluntarily by the firms deemed as falling far short of the challenges posed.[51] Revelations regarding the use of manipulative algorithms and search engine optimisation in order to promote misleading advertising and news stories further impacted levels of trust in these social media platforms to combat disinformation, prompting policymakers to feel a need to respond.[52] In the case of

---

[46] European Commission, 'Strengthened Cooperation against Vaccine Preventable Diseases' (2018) COM(2018) 245 3.
[47] Francesco Farinelli, 'Conspiracy Theories and Right-Wing Extremism – Insights and Recommendations for P/CVE' (European Commission, Radicalisation Awareness Network 2021).
[48] High Representative of the European Union for Foreign Affairs and Security Policy & the European Commission (n37) 4.
[49] Gregory F Treverton and others, 'Addressing Hybrid Threats' (Center for Asymmetric Threat Studies; The European Centre of Excellence for Countering Hybrid Threats, 2018); Andrew Dawson and Martin Innes, 'How Russia's Internet Research Agency Built Its Disinformation Campaign' (2019) 90 *The Political Quarterly* 245.
[50] European Commission, 'Tackling Online Disinformation: A European Approach' (2018) COM(2018) 236 2.
[51] Ibid.
[52] As discussed in Samantha Bradshaw, 'Disinformation Optimised: Gaming Search Engine Algorithms to Amplify Junk News' (2019) 8 *Internet Policy Review* 1. However, Bradshaw is also careful to argue that the influence of disinformation in search engines may be overstated, and that disinformation may be a reflection of increased polarisation and mistrust in society, rather than causative.

the EU, these actions were explicitly based in a perception that these platforms, increasingly powerful and largely based outside of the EU's sphere of influence, were not neutral arbiters in online governance but a potential threat in themselves, disregarding concerns over safety and not sharing in the EU's values.[53] The EU's immediate response to this was the development in collaboration with platforms of a Code of Practice on Disinformation,[54] intended to minimise the risks of disinformation through processes at platforms aimed at reducing the spreading of inauthentic content by bots, allowing access to fact-checkers, and providing for transparency in the identification and placement of political advertisements.[55] However, the effectiveness of self-regulation in this field was subject to criticism, with the Institute for Strategic Dialogue concluding that voluntary self-regulation was not sufficient to counter these threats,[56] and the Commission's own review admitting that a lack of uniform definitions was leading to divergent approaches in the Member States,[57] and that the self-regulation model was inherently limited as it 'did not establish an independent oversight mechanism for monitoring the completeness and impact of the signatories' actions in tackling disinformation'.[58]

With the von der Leyen Commission, we see a pronounced increase in this framing of platforms as being a potential source of insecurity for the EU. The 'Shaping Europe's Digital Future'[59] policy agenda was published under the 'A Europe Fit for the Digital Age'[60] priority area. Within this agenda, particular attention was paid to an understanding of new technologies bringing risks and costs, with negative impacts upon security interests.[61] Included in these security interests is the need to reduce dependencies on third states,[62] and concerns over the market power of online platforms.[63] In the 2030 Digital Compass Communication, the Commission argues that geopolitical events such as the COVID-19 pandemic have made clear its vulnerabilities in the digital space, requiring it to carefully assess its strategic weaknesses and

---

[53] Helena Carrapico and Benjamin Farrand, 'When Trust Fades, Facebook Is No Longer a Friend: Shifting Privatisation Dynamics in the Context of Cybersecurity as a Result of Disinformation, Populism and Political Uncertainty' (2021) 59 *JCMS: Journal of Common Market Studies* 1160.
[54] European Commission, 'EU Code of Practice on Online Disinformation' (2018).
[55] Paolo Cavaliere, 'From Journalistic Ethics to Fact-Checking Practices: Defining the Standards of Content Governance in the Fight against Disinformation' (2020) 12 *Journal of Media Law* 133.
[56] Chloe Colliver, 'An Evaluation of the EU Code of Practice on Disinformation' (Institute for Strategic Dialogue 2019) 12–13.
[57] European Commission, 'Assessment of the Code of Practice on Disinformation – Achievements and Areas for Further Improvement' (2020) SWD(2020) 180 12–13.
[58] Ibid 17.
[59] European Commission, 'Shaping Europe's Digital Future' (2020).
[60] European Commission, 'A Europe Fit for the Digital Age' (*European Commission*, 7 March 2020) <https://ec.europa.eu/info/strategy/priorities-2019-2024/europe-fit-digital-age_en> accessed 9 March 2020.
[61] European Commission, 'Shaping Europe's Digital Future' (n59) 1.
[62] Ibid 3.
[63] Ibid 5.

high-risk dependencies,[64] particularly on large, non-European tech companies.[65] Reinforcing the role of perceived vulnerability, the 2020 Cybersecurity Strategy for the Digital Decade makes clear the extension of the security dimension of EU technology policy. It states explicitly that it constitutes a key component of the SEDF agenda,[66] and that the digital threat landscape is 'compounded by geopolitical tensions over the global and open Internet and over control of technologies',[67] as well as hybrid threats.[68] Similarly, the EU Security Union Strategy emphasised the proliferation of hybrid threats attacking the economy, society, and democratic structures, with 'what happens outside the EU [having] a critical impact on security inside the EU'.[69]

Central to this was the issue of overreliance, a position inconsistent with a growing emphasis on strategic autonomy. Given the scale of social media platform operations and the lack of effective European competitors, the EU finds its businesses, consumers, and citizens dependent upon non-European platforms in a way that promotes a sense of vulnerability.[70] This vulnerability was framed as being to the very heart of the EU's legitimacy and to the functioning of European democracy. Referring to the direct attacks on the EU's democratic system and institutions, online platforms are explicitly identified in the EU's European Democracy action plan as central to this threat, with the Commission stating that 'online campaigning and online platforms have opened up new vulnerabilities and made it more difficult to maintain the integrity of elections [...] and protect the democratic process from disinformation and other manipulation'.[71] These platforms are identified as gatekeepers, including for online news,[72] reiterating the link between economic dominance and security threat. Whereas these issues were on the agenda because of the tensions and conflict in the late 2010s, these concerns were magnified by the geopolitical tensions of the early 2020s. Responding to the belief that foreign disinformation was being produced by states such as Russia and China concerning the

---

[64] European Commission, '2030 Digital Compass: The European Way for the Digital Decade' (2021) COM(2021) 118 final/2 1.

[65] Ibid 2.

[66] European Commission and High Representative of the Union for Foreign Affairs and Security Policy, 'The EU's Cybersecurity Strategy for the Digital Decade' (2020) JOIN(2020) 18.

[67] Ibid 1.

[68] Ibid 2, 17. The concept of hybrid threats was discussed in the context of security in Chapter 4, and will be expanded upon in the next section of this chapter dealing with political advertising.

[69] European Commission, 'Communication on the EU Security Union Strategy' (2020) COM(2020) 605 1.

[70] See Sebastian Heidebrecht, 'From Market Liberalism to Public Intervention: Digital Sovereignty and Changing European Union Digital Single Market Governance' (2024) 62 JCMS: Journal of Common Market Studies 205; see also Timo Seidl and Luuk Schmitz, 'Moving on to Not Fall behind? Technological Sovereignty and the "Geo-Dirigiste" Turn in EU Industrial Policy' (2023) 31 Journal of European Public Policy 2147.

[71] European Commission, 'Communication on the European Democracy Action Plan' (2020) COM(2020) 790 2.

[72] Ibid 3.

origins of COVID-19 and the safety of vaccines,[73] and the proliferation of disinformation targeting the EU relating to the Russian invasion of Ukraine,[74] President von der Leyen declared that 'these lies are toxic for our democracies [...] we will not allow any autocracy's Trojan horses to attack our democracies from within'.[75] The belief in external threats posed by both state and private actors that threatened the functioning of the state and its institutions in the context of broader geopolitical instability meant that the conditions for regulatory mercantilist policy responses to the identified problems were present. In the next section, 'Reining in Platform Power', we focus on the rationale for action on the part of the Commission considering these vulnerability concerns in order to identify indicators of a regulatory mercantilist reasoning.

REINING IN PLATFORM POWER: 'TAKING BACK CONTROL' AND REASSERTING SOVEREIGNTY OVER REGULATION ONLINE

The rationale for the Commission's interventions into the governance of online platforms is highly compatible with a regulatory mercantilist approach to policy. Regarding the threats posed by disinformation, SEDF stated that 'people are entitled to technologies that they can trust [...] in a world where much of the public debate and political advertising have moved online, we must be prepared to act to forcefully defend our democracies'.[76] In this respect, the policy initiatives aimed at countering the threats posed by disinformation and illegal content online are framed in terms of the exertion of state influence, in this case, for the preservation of European values. We see the element of state-building and reasserting of authority through the statement that the Commission will introduce 'new and revised rules to deepen the for Internal Market for Digital Services, by increasing and harmonising the responsibilities online platforms and information service providers and reinforce the oversight over platforms' content policies in the EU'.[77] The 2021 State of the Union address reinforced the unifying rationale behind interventions in this field, as well as the linkage of economic and security-related policy areas, identified as mutually interdependent. In discussing reforms to the Single Market, von der Leyen stated that 'we have made ambitious proposals in the last year. To contain the gatekeeper power of major platforms [and] to underpin the democratic responsibility of

---

[73] European Commission and High Representative of the Union for Foreign Affairs and Security Policy, 'Tackling COVID-19 Disinformation – Getting the Facts Right' (2020) JOIN(2020) 8 final 3.
[74] EUvsDisinfo, 'Disinformation About the Current Russia-Ukraine Conflict – Seven Myths Debunked' (*EUvsDisinfo*, 24 January 2022) <https://euvsdisinfo.eu/disinformation-about-the-current-russia-ukraine-conflict-seven-myths-debunked/> accessed 22 October 2024.
[75] Ursula von der Leyen, '2022 State of the Union Address by President von Der Leyen: A Union That Stands Strong Together' (European Commission 2022) SPEECH/22/5493 10.
[76] European Commission, 'Shaping Europe's Digital Future' (n59) 6.
[77] Ibid.

those platforms'.⁷⁸ The Commission subsequently made clear that the regulation of online platforms should be based on a common system of public oversight, considering the economic and security concerns that resulted from the reliance and dependence upon online platforms in the EU.⁷⁹ Countering illegal content online, particularly through codifying voluntary codes of conduct in the form of binding legislative requirements, is identified as a priority.⁸⁰

Regarding online advertising, SEDF makes the explicit link between economic and security goals, announcing as part of its package the European Democracy Action Plan, intended to 'improve the resilience of our democratic systems, support media pluralism and address the threats of external intervention in European elections'.⁸¹ The Action Plan discussed the need for increased oversight over political advertising, arguing that new techniques used by intermediaries could be used to tailor and target advertising based on user profiling, referred to as microtargeting.⁸² The Commission expressed concerns that these techniques could be used to increase levels of polarisation and audience manipulation,⁸³ and would therefore propose specific legislation providing additional oversight, including of platforms and advertisers using those platforms, as a means of ensuring protection of European values.⁸⁴ An EU-wide system, creating unified rules for political advertising online, was argued to be the best means of achieving this aim, as it would ensure a fully functional internal market, while at the same time help in the oversight of these activities at the European level, helping to 'increase the overall resilience of the EU to information manipulation and interference in electoral processes, including disinformation'.⁸⁵

The three policy initiatives show clear indications of seeking to rework the sovereignty relations between the public sector and powerful economic actors deemed potential security threats to the EU. The DSA and DMA are 'twin' pieces of legislation proposed as a package intended to reconceptualise the governance of online platforms, with the DSA focused upon the content shared on these platforms and made accessible through search engines, and the DMA focused upon the architecture of these market operators. The PAR is specifically aimed at complementing

---

[78] Ursula von der Leyen, '2021 State of the Union Address by President von Der Leyen: Strengthening the Soul of Our Union' (European Commission 2021) SPEECH/21/4701 4.

[79] European Commission, 'Proposal for a Regulation on a Single Market for Digital Services (Digital Services Act) and Amending Directive 2000/31/EC' (2020) COM(2020) 825 1; European Commission, 'Proposal for a Regulation on Contestable and Fair Markets in the Digital Sector (Digital Markets Act)' (2020) COM(2020) 842 1–2.

[80] European Commission, 'Communication on the EU Security Union Strategy' (n69) 13–14.

[81] European Commission, 'Shaping Europe's Digital Future' (n59) 6.

[82] European Commission, 'Communication on the European Democracy Action Plan' (n71) 4.

[83] Ibid.

[84] Ibid 5.

[85] European Commission, 'Proposal for a Regulation on the Transparency and Targeting of Political Advertising' (2021) COM(2021) 731 7.

these efforts,[86] reorienting sovereignty relations by subjecting private sector actors to increased oversight and regulatory requirements, and 'clarifying their responsibilities and providing legal certainty'.[87] As stated in the SEDF Communication, 'increasing and harmonising the responsibilities of online platforms and information service providers and [reinforcing] the oversight of content platforms' content policies' was central to the Commission's efforts,[88] and was deemed to be a key facilitator of the EU's digital sovereignty.[89] For this reason, implementation of both Acts was linked to achieving digital sovereignty through the adoption of 'strong rules embedding European values [and] being an assertive player in fair and rule-based international trade'.[90] The regulatory mercantilist dimension to this legislative agenda was made clear through the focus on international norm development, in which the EU's digital sovereignty is pursued through the DSA acting as a 'standard-setter at the global level' for content regulation,[91] and in the DMA's objective of pursuing 'public policy goals that go beyond competition or economic considerations'.[92] Where those platforms are considered to be important market players, which is 'characterised by large platforms with significant network effects acting as gatekeepers',[93] then increased oversight is proposed as a means of reasserting the control of the state in shaping the market in which these players are active. As will be explored in more detail in the next section of this chapter, these large platforms are predominantly US or Chinese companies, which account for almost 90 per cent of the global market share of large-scale platforms.[94] The DSA constitutes an attempt by the EU to control the systems that dictate how illegal content and content such as disinformation are treated through increased state oversight.[95] The DMA, according to Heidebrecht, represents an attempt to bring market *structures* under Commission control and in line with EU values, through *ex ante* regulation.[96]

Statements made by Commissioner Thierry Breton at the time when the DSA and DMA entered into force underscored this realignment in the name

---

[86] European Commission, 'Communication on the European Democracy Action Plan' (n71) 5.
[87] Ibid.
[88] European Commission, 'Shaping Europe's Digital Future' (n59) 6.
[89] European Economic and Social Committee, 'Digital Services Act and Digital Markets Act: Stepping Stones to a Level Playing Field in Europe' (European Economic and Social Committee 2021) EESC-2021-33-EN 1.
[90] European Commission, '2030 Digital Compass: The European Way for the Digital Decade' (n64) 1.
[91] European Commission, 'Proposal for a Regulation on a Single Market for Digital Services (Digital Services Act) and Amending Directive 2000/31/EC' (n79) 2.
[92] European Commission, 'Proposal for a Regulation on Contestable and Fair Markets in the Digital Sector (Digital Markets Act)' (n79) 2.
[93] European Commission, 'Shaping Europe's Digital Future' (n59) 5.
[94] Shin-Yi Peng, 'The Uneasy Interplay between Digital Inequality and International Economic Law' (2022) 33 *European Journal of International Law* 205, 212.
[95] Benjamin Farrand, 'How Do We Understand Online Harms? The Impact of Conceptual Divides on Regulatory Divergence between the Online Safety Act and Digital Services Act' (2024) *Journal of Media Law* 1.
[96] Heidebrecht (n70) 13.

of sovereignty, stating that 'big online platforms will no longer behave like they are too big to care',[97] and then four months later describing platforms as regulated entities, that 'online platforms no longer set their own rules [...] the Digital Services Act and Digital Markets Act are part of a wider vision for the online environment [...] they are an expression of European Digital Sovereignty'.[98] However, while reorientation of sovereignty relations with the private sector is a clear and stated aim, there is also an element of reasserting sovereignty vis-à-vis other states. Broeders et al. state that the DSA and DMA 'in imposing controls on large American digital platforms, the larger effect [...] will be once again to send a geopolitical signal to the United States',[99] as an attempt at reasserting its position on digital sovereignty and strategic autonomy.[100] The control of platforms serves as an interesting example of the blurring nature of the external threat, with the EU seeking to assert its digital sovereignty not only against the social media platforms deemed as not conforming to EU values but also against the foreign governments regarded as using these large US platforms for propaganda, disinformation, and sewing discord.[101] As Bernot makes clear, however, this concern increasingly expands beyond the 'usual suspect' of Meta's Facebook platform to the increasing prominence of Chinese-associated platforms such as TikTok.[102] The rationale is therefore one of reining in platform power, both to reassert control over the functioning of technologies made available within the EU's territory by non-EU platforms but also with regard to policy-making vis-à-vis other states, with explicit linkages of economic and security concerns. This results in moves to reshape sovereignty relations, framed in terms of digital sovereignty, indicating that a regulatory mercantilist rationale is present in the EU's attempts to control platform power. In the next section, we will expand upon the means through which the EU has sought to control these actors to demonstrate the regulatory mercantilist policies and actions that have resulted.

---

[97] See Breton's speech at European Commission, 'DSA: Landmark Rules for Online Platforms Enter into Force' (*European Commission*, 2022) <https://ec.europa.eu/commission/presscorner/detail/en/IP_22_6906> accessed 21 February 2023.

[98] European Commission, 'Digital Platforms as Regulated Entities' (*European Commission*, 17 March 2023) <https://ec.europa.eu/commission/presscorner/detail/en/SPEECH_23_1761> accessed 23 October 2024.

[99] Dennis Broeders, Fabio Cristiano and Monica Kaminska, 'In Search of Digital Sovereignty and Strategic Autonomy: Normative Power Europe to the Test of Its Geopolitical Ambitions' (2023) 61 *Journal of Common Market Studies* 1261, 1272.

[100] Ibid 1273.

[101] See Anu Bradford, *Digital Empires* (Oxford University Press 2023) 282–283; see also Jamal Shahin, 'Dancing to the Same Tune? EU and US Approaches to Standards Setting in the Global Digital Sector' (2024) 46 *Journal of European Integration* 1111.

[102] Ausma Bernot, Diarmuid Cooney-O'Donoghue and Monique Mann, 'Governing Chinese Technologies: TikTok, Foreign Interference, and Technological Sovereignty' (2024) 13 *Internet Policy Review* <https://policyreview.info/articles/analysis/governing-chinese-technologies> accessed 25 October 2024.

INTERNATIONAL PLAYERS, BOUND BY EU RULES: USING LAW TO 'LEVEL THE PLAYING FIELD'

How does the Commission seek to give effect to its digital sovereignty agenda in this field? As with our previous case study, it is possible to identify two key characteristics of regulatory mercantilism. In this instance, the first is a shift to a move to heightened oversight by means of binding legislation rather than voluntary codes, creating co-regulatory systems of control rather than permitting self-regulation. The second is an explicit approach of seeking to reinforce a positive regulatory balance of trade, promoting the EU's standards as global standards while seeking to minimise the risk of imported standards, whether market or state facilitated.

From Self-Regulation and Codes to Co-Regulatory Backstops

What are the obligations placed upon online service providers under these Acts, and how do they give effect to the digital sovereignty agenda? The DSA, DMA, and PAR are typified by an increase in oversight that moves the governance model from one of regulated self-regulation to one of co-regulation. Reinforcing the move from light-touch self-regulation is the increasing prescriptiveness of the legal requirements placed on platforms. Article 1 on the subject matter of the DSA makes clear the linking of economic and security goals, framing the Regulation in terms of creating harmonised rules for a safe, predictable, and trusted environment to give effect to the functioning of the internal market. While the intermediary immunity from liability rules for specific instances of illegal activity taking place on their services is maintained from the E-Commerce Directive under Articles 4–6, with Article 8 reaffirming that there is no general obligation to monitor services, Article 7 provides that service providers can conduct their own voluntary investigations without having any impact on this immunity from liability. This does not mean, however, that there is no increased control of platforms and search engines, as there is an increased level of prescriptiveness concerning what is required of service providers.[103] Chapter III of the Act contains due diligence obligations applicable to all online services, ranging from establishing national points of contact[104] and legal representatives based in the EU where the service is not established there,[105] to transparency reporting obligations.[106]

For very large online platforms and search engines, defined under Article 33(1) as those having average monthly active service recipients in the EU of equal to or higher than 45 million, there are additional requirements, such as the obligation to

---

[103] See, for example, Giovanni De Gregorio and Pietro Dunn, 'The European Risk-Based Approaches: Connecting Constitutional Dots in the Digital Age' (2022) 59 *Common Market Law Review* 473.
[104] DSA, Article 11.
[105] Ibid, Article 13.
[106] Ibid, Article 15.

conduct risk assessments under Article 34; pursue risk mitigation strategies on the identification of risks under Article 35; establish crisis response mechanisms under Article 36 in circumstances where a significant threat is identified under Article 36; and facilitate independent audits of their practices under Article 37. Furthermore, heightened obligations concerning recommender systems under Article 38, additional advertising obligations under Article 39, obligations to provide data access and scrutiny under Article 40, the establishment of compliance functions under Article 41, and additional transparency reporting functions under Article 42 all contribute to heightened legislative intervention into the activities of these service providers.[107] The PAR states that it applies to platforms where the political advertising is disseminated in the Union under Article 2, while maintaining an 'internal market' principle under Article 4, which stresses that no divergence in obligations that could fragment the internal market is permitted, reinforcing the 'unifying' dimension of regulatory mercantilism by limiting the ability of Member States to deviate from the required approach. The PAR requires that platforms and advertisers adhere to transparency and due diligence obligations under Article 6 and then expands upon these significant obligations in Articles 7–17. Of particular interest is the creation of a 'European' repository for online political advertisements under Article 13. Key to the PAR is that it takes the voluntary Code of Practice on Disinformation, and through the interaction between it, the revised Strengthened Code of Practice on Disinformation (which remains technically a non-binding instrument),[108] the DSA, facilitates a more comprehensive approach to how platforms should handle disinformation on their platforms while showing regard for the European values concerning freedom of expression.[109]

In the DMA, obligations are placed upon gatekeepers, defined as the providers of core services under Article 2(1), with core services being considered to include online intermediation, search, social networking, video-sharing, operating systems, web browsers, virtual assistants, and cloud computing services.[110] Under Article 3, a service is designated as a gatekeeper if it has a significant impact on the internal market; provides a core service, which is an important gateway for businesses to reach end users, and enjoys an entrenched and durable position, or is likely to do so in the future. Where a service is designated as a gatekeeper, it is required to adhere to obligations concerning the use of data, conditions of access for purposes such as

---

[107] For additional overviews of the substance of these obligations, see Sunniva Hansson, 'The Digital Services Act: Upgrading Liability, Responsibility and Safety Online' (2020) 31 *Entertainment Law Review* 94; Miquel Peguera, 'The Platform Neutrality Conundrum and the Digital Services Act' (2022) 53 *International Review of Intellectual Property and Competition Law* 681; Robert Lister, 'It Is Time to Get to Grips with the Digital Services Act – What This Means for Online Intermediary Service Providers: Part 1' (2023) 34 *Entertainment Law Review* 213.

[108] European Commission, '2022 Strengthened Code of Practice on Disinformation' (2022).

[109] Benjamin Farrand, 'Regulating Misleading Political Advertising on Online Platforms: An Example of Regulatory Mercantilism in Digital Policy' (2024) 45 *Policy Studies* 730.

[110] DMA, Article 2(2).

advertising and the avoidance of service tying under Article 5,[111] the treatment of other businesses' services when in competition with their own under Article 6, interoperability requirements under Article 7, and compliance in the activities under Articles 5–7 with obligations concerning cybersecurity, consumer protection, product safety, and accessibility.[112]

However, control is not only exercised through the imposition of these requirements but also through how adherence to them is assured. The DSA established a co-regulatory system in which the platform can devise its own risk identification and mitigation strategies, which it is then expected to carry out. If this was the limit of what was required, this would appear to be little more than a heightened regulated self-regulation approach. However, not only are the activities of the platform subject to the independent audit specified earlier,[113] but the EU has also created a new oversight system in the form of the Digital Service Coordinators (DSC) and European Board for Digital Services (EBDS). Under Article 49, each Member State is required to designate a DSC, tasked with supervision and enforcement of the DSA. The DSC has the authority to alert a platform to potential infringements of the DSA, carry out inspections and access information related to potential infringements, and question staff.[114] It also has the power to enforce the DSA through binding commitments, penalties, and the adoption of interim measures,[115] as well as to request that a judicial entity temporarily restrict access to a non-compliant platform.[116] Under Article 52, the penalties that can be applied include fines of up to 6 per cent of the annual worldwide turnover of the platform. The EBDS is established under Article 61, which comprises representatives of the DSCs, chaired by the Commission.[117] Under Article 63, the tasks of this board include the facilitation of cross-border investigations by DSCs in different Member States, supporting national authorities in the analysis of platform audits, issuing recommendations, advice, and opinions to DSCs, and advising the Commission on initiating investigations. These powers of investigation are significant, as the Commission is granted direct enforcement powers under Article 65 and, in the initialisation of an investigation under Article 66, can request any information possessed by DSCs or the EBDS

---

[111] A complete breakdown and analysis of these obligations is ultimately beyond the scope of this chapter, but for some excellent accounts, see Giuseppe Colangelo, 'The European Digital Markets Act and Antitrust Enforcement: A Liaison Dangereuse' (2022) 47 *European Law Review* 597; and Natalia Moreno Belloso and Nicolas Petit, 'The EU Digital Markets Act (DMA): A Competition Hand in a Regulatory Glove' (2023) 48 *European Law Review* 391.

[112] DMA, Article 8.

[113] Although it is worth stating that independent audit itself can be subject to forms of capture, as discussed in Johann Laux, Sandra Wachter and Brent Mittelstadt, 'Taming the Few: Platform Regulation, Independent Audits, and the Risks of Capture Created by the DMA and DSA' (2021) 43 *Computer Law & Security Review* 105613.

[114] DSA, Article 49(1).

[115] DSA, Article 49(2).

[116] DSA, Article 49(3).

[117] DSA, Article 62.

in order to facilitate that investigation. It may request information from platforms and search engines under Article 67, conduct interviews and take statements under Article 68, conduct its own inspections of premises under Article 69, and is granted various enforcement powers, including under Article 74 the ability to impose fines. Oversight in the PAR is also delegated to the EBDS and DSCs, under Article 22 of the Regulation.

In the DMA, the European Commission is granted the ability to perform and review the designation of platforms as gatekeepers under Articles 3 and 4. It also has the ability to update gatekeeper obligations through delegated acts under Article 12, and the Commission is empowered to open market investigations into platforms under Article 16, either to designate a core service provider as a gatekeeper,[118] assess non-compliance,[119] and assess new practices or services.[120] Enforcement powers mirror those in the DSA, including powers to request information,[121] carry out interviews and take statements,[122] and conduct site inspections.[123] In the event that infringements are found, the Commission can impose fines of up to 10 per cent of worldwide annual turnover under Article 30. Similar cross-border mechanisms also exist, such as cooperation and coordination between national competition authorities,[124] national courts,[125] and through an established DMA 'high-level group' under Article 40, which as with the EBDS is chaired by the Commission. The control afforded under the DSA, DMA, and PAR goes far beyond what is facilitated by other forms of security cooperation such as in the NIS2 Directive on Cybersecurity,[126] which reinforces the powers of ENISA, the EU's cybersecurity agency, and requires Member States to impose fines on critical information infrastructure providers that do not comply with the Directive's requirements, but without direct enforcement powers on the part of the Commission. In this respect, the move to online platforms has been from one of relatively light-touch self-regulation to a much broader and more prescriptive form of co-regulation, bordering on hierarchical.[127]

Balance of Regulatory Trade: Global Rules, European Values

The platform-regulating legislation implemented by the von der Leyen Commission therefore demonstrates a significant element of taking control, asserted through

---

[118] DMA, Article 17.
[119] DMA, Article 18.
[120] DMA, Article 19.
[121] DMA, Article 21.
[122] DMA, Article 22.
[123] DMA, Article 23.
[124] DMA, Article 38.
[125] DMA, Article 39.
[126] Directive 2022/2555 on measures for a high common level of cybersecurity across the Union.
[127] See also Daniëlle Flonk, Markus Jachtenfuchs and Anke Obendiek, 'Controlling Internet Content in the EU: Towards Digital Sovereignty' (2024) 31 *Journal of European Public Policy* 2316.

legally binding mechanisms, and particularly in the case of the DSA and PAR, motivated by a strong security rationale. That alone would not be enough to indicate that this constitutes regulatory mercantilist law-making, however, and it is important to also consider the aspect of the 'balance of regulatory trade'. The aspect of sovereignty is clear, as both the DSA and DMA were explicitly proposed and developed in the context of the SEDF policy initiative and tied to achieving Europe's Digital Sovereignty, framed in this context as the ability to define its own rules and values in the digital age. In terms of European values, the DSA makes frequent references to fundamental rights throughout its recitals and states in Article 1 that the rules for platforms are to be implemented in such a way that they guarantee the fundamental rights enshrined in the European Charter. That this legislation is intended to 'export' European values through regulation is also made clear in Article 2's statement of the scope of the legislation, which is intended to apply to platforms offering services to users established in the Union, 'irrespective of where the providers of those intermediary services have their place of establishment'. Furthermore, under Article 63, the EDBS is tasked with developing *European* standards, guidelines, reports, templates, and codes of conduct for the activities of platforms and search engines, and the Commission in consultation with the EDBS can 'promote the development and implementation of voluntary standards set by relevant European and international standardisation bodies'. A deeper analysis of the specifics of these legislative interventions, however, can help to reinforce the conclusion that they act as effective case studies of regulatory mercantilism. In the context of the DSA, this is particularly pronounced in the case of the insertion of Article 36 on a crisis response mechanism,[128] after Russia's invasion of Ukraine. This Article requires very large online platforms to, based on a Commission decision, determine to what extent a platform contributes to a serious threat in the context of an ongoing crisis, defined in Article 36(2) as where extraordinary circumstances lead to a serious threat to public security or public health in the EU or significant parts of it. While there is a reference to the use of international standards, this should be read in line with the EU's actions in promoting European standards *as* international standards, as discussed in Chapter 4.

In the DMA, the mentions of fundamental rights are restricted to the recitals, with no operative Articles. However, in terms of European values, it can be argued that the DMA in its entirety reflects those values as they pertain to the EU conceptualisation of competition. Moreno Belloso and Petit have argued that most, if not all, of the obligations imposed under the DMA have their origins in EU competition cases,[129] whereas Ong and Jun Toh trace the origins of the concept of

---

[128] Alain Strowel and Jean De Meyere, 'The Digital Services Act: Transparency as an Efficient Tool to Curb the Spread of Disinformation on Online Platforms?' (2023) 14 *Journal of Intellectual Property, Information Technology and Electronic Commerce Law* 66.

[129] Moreno Belloso and Petit (n111) 394.

'core service' from the Commission's competition investigations undertaken under Article 102 TFEU, which concerns the abuse of dominant positions by market operators.[130] Bachelet reinforces this understanding of the relationship, arguing that the distinction is that while competition law focuses on *ex post* investigations of abuse of dominance, the DMA represents *ex ante* regulation aimed at ensuring that markets where gatekeepers operate are, and continue to be, contestable and fair.[131] In terms of operationalisation, the exporting of these values through the imposition of legal obligations is codified in Article 1's statement of the subject matter and scope, which states that the DMA is applicable to core platform services offered by gatekeepers to businesses or end users located in the EU, 'irrespective of the place of establishment or residence of the gatekeepers and irrespective of the law otherwise applicable to the provision of the service'. Under Article 48, the Commission can mandate that European standardisation bodies facilitate the implementation of the obligations set out in the DMA by developing appropriate standards.

Since the adoption of both Acts, it has become clear that the EU's rules will apply predominantly, if not entirely, to platforms established outside of the EU. In the publication of its first DSA designation decision,[132] out of the twenty-four designated very large online platforms, only two were based in the EU, namely booking.com, a Dutch online travel agency, and Zalando, a German fashion outlet. The remaining twenty-two services, including Facebook, X (referred to by its old name, Twitter),[133] Instagram, Alibaba Express, and TikTok, are either US- or China-based. Similarly, the two very large online search engines identified were both US entities, namely Google and Bing. Similarly, the first gatekeeper designation performed by the Commission identified six gatekeeper entities: Alphabet, Amazon, Apple, ByteDance, Meta, and Microsoft, all of which are either US or Chinese-established entities.[134] In other words, to protect the EU's end users from illegal content and guarantee for end users and business users an environment of fair and contestable markets, it is external entities being regulated by EU rules. For Bradford, this represents an effective external regulatory effect – both regulators in third states carefully consider the usefulness of

---

[130] Burton Ong and Ding Jun Toh, 'Digital Dominance and Social Media Platforms: Are Competition Authorities up to the Task?' (2023) 54 *International Review of Intellectual Property and Competition Law* 527, 555–556.

[131] Vittorio Bachelet, 'The Abuse of Economic Dependence "Digitalization": The Italian Novella in Context' (2023) 44 *European Competition Law Review* 300, 311; see also Tim Paul Thomes and Thomas Weck, 'The Google Android Case and the DMA – Lessons Learned?' (2022) 43 *European Competition Law Review* 52.

[132] European Commission, 'DSA: Very Large Online Platforms and Search Engines' (*European Commission*, 25 April 2023) <https://ec.europa.eu/commission/presscorner/detail/en/IP_23_2413> accessed 16 November 2023.

[133] X is a significant concern to policymakers, and will be returned to in the discussion of the von der Leyen II Commission in Chapter 7 of this book.

[134] European Commission, 'Digital Markets Act: Commission Designates Six Gatekeepers' (*European Commission – European Commission*, 6 September 2023) <https://ec.europa.eu/commission/presscorner/detail/en/ip_23_4328> accessed 16 November 2023.

the EU's approach for their own regulatory interventions, and businesses begin to voluntarily adopt the EU's obligations in territories outside the EU based on reducing complexity and promoting standardisation of their business activities, extending EU rules across the jurisdictions in which they operate.[135] While Bradford describes this as *de jure* Brussels effect, it can also be understood as the effective guarantee of the balance of regulatory trade – embedding European values in legislation that is then exported as global standards, while minimising the risk of 'regulatory import' that may be misaligned with the EU's own values or security interests.

Conclusions: Regulatory Mercantilism and Online Platforms

Platform regulation in the EU serves as an excellent example of regulatory mercantilism. In the DSA, complemented by the PAR and the DMA, we see a hallmark of regulatory mercantilism, namely the interlinking of economic and security goals; not only are the two Acts, one concerning security and the other concerning markets, regarded as 'twins' by the Commission, or alternatively, two complementary halves of the same whole, but they are based on a hybrid policy of promoting a safer, more secure Internet that is based on fairness, growth, and competitiveness that cannot be divorced from its geopolitical context in which the EU feels threatened by the economic power of large tech companies based outside the EU.[136] That these platforms have become so large and have such a prominent role in both social and economic life means that the security risks they present are both social and economic, as well as the medium through which hybrid threats can be realised.[137] This also helps us to understand the emphasis placed in the DSA on 'very large online platforms' and on the 'significant impact' criteria used to determine gatekeepers in the DSA. This is in part influenced by the increasing role of geopolitics and instability upon market activity.[138]

This perception of vulnerability to external players has led to a desire on the part of the Commission to assert its ability to control the internet and the provision of services by large online platforms within it, moving from a system of self-regulation to one of co-regulation,[139] or alternatively, from one of market liberalism to one dominated by state economic-security interventionism.[140] 'Digital sovereignty'

---

[135] See generally Bradford (n101) ch 9.
[136] See Broeders, Cristiano and Kaminska (n99).
[137] Isabella de Vivo, 'The "Neo-Intermediation" of Large on-Line Platforms: Perspectives of Analysis of the "State of Health" of the Digital Information Ecosystem' (2023) 48 *Communications* 420.
[138] For an interesting reflection on the contemporary challenges to competition law orthodoxy, see Oles Andriychuk, 'Between Microeconomics and Geopolitics: On the Reasonable Application of Competition Law' (2022) 85 *The Modern Law Review* 598.
[139] Farrand, 'The Ordoliberal Internet? Continuity and Change in the EU's Approach to the Governance of Cyberspace' (n8).
[140] Heidebrecht (n70).

is the discourse that has been used to justify the actions taken on the part of the Commission, as its desire for state-making and legislative unification in the interests of serving its economic and security interests is motivated by a desire to reorient the sovereignty relationships between itself and private actors, as well as with states that it feels are seeking to either destabilise or delegitimise it. The increase in regulatory oversight, either by the Commission itself or alternatively through bodies such as the EBDS, of which the Commission is a member, underscored by specific legal obligations and sanctions, combined with the emphasis on both exporting these norms as the global 'gold standard'[141] and the fact that the majority of platforms designated under the respective systems are non-European, gives a strong indication that this area of technology control has been significantly impacted by geopolitics, resulting in a distinctly regulatory mercantilist approach.

---

[141] European Commission, 'Digital Platforms as Regulated Entities' (n98).

6

Regulating Data and AI

Europe may have lost the battle to create digital champions capable of taking on US and Chinese companies harvesting personal data, but it can win the war of industrial data.[1]

INTRODUCTION

In this, the last of the case study chapters, the focus moves to the Commission's approach to the control of data and, by extension, artificial intelligence (AI). Data can be conceptualised as being similar in essence to natural resources in the physical realm, particularly as it relates to their exploitation for the purposes of technological development and the promotion of European competitiveness. Yet as with the natural resources essential for semiconductor manufacture discussed in Chapter 4, reliance on data and concerns over who controls it have resulted in a sense of vulnerability on the part of the Commission, which feels that the dependence upon non-EU-owned data servers and processing services has become critical, restraining its strategic autonomy and impacting upon its technological sovereignty. As a set of systems derived from the training of data, this has implications for the development of AI foundational models in the EU and has increased reliance on the models created by increasingly dominant firms in the US and China. For this reason, the Commission has pursued a strategy of interventionist policymaking in this field, with an emphasis on increased regulatory control, data localisation, and seeking to export its approach as global standards, reflective of a regulatory mercantilist approach to furthering its economic and security interests.

This chapter is structured as follows. The first section, 'Personal Data and the Brussels Effect', considers the history of the EU's approach to data, with the emphasis being placed on the control of personal data. In particular, it examines the complexities and challenges that instigated the adoption of the General Data Protection

---

[1] Thierry Breton as cited in Euractiv, 'Europe Can Win Global Battle for Industrial Data, Breton Says' (*Euractiv*, 17 February 2020) <www.euractiv.com/section/digital/news/europe-can-win-global-battle-for-industrial-data-breton-says/> accessed 19 January 2025.

Regulation (GDPR) and the concerns over how personal data of EU citizens was used outside of the EU's jurisdiction, particularly by the US. It considers in this vein the *Schrems* decisions and the norms that they established concerning data protection and equivalency and the belief in a 'Brussels effect' derived from the EU's market position as a 'regulatory superpower', a belief that has motivated the EU's approach to technology regulation vis-à-vis data. The next section, 'Forging Ahead or Falling Behind?', considers the conflictual geopolitical context in which the Commission developed a strategy for data, in which access to personal and non-personal data has become enmeshed with concerns over the market power of large non-EU firms and the disproportionate reliance of European business, industry, and public sector organisations on third-country data servers and processing services. It highlights the sources of dependence and concerns over intersecting economic and security disadvantages, before moving into the next section, 'Virtual(ly) Gold: Industrial Policy for Data-Based Technological Sovereignty', where the Commission's approach, based in promoting data sovereignty in the name of digital/technological sovereignty, is deemed as essential to securing the EU's interests, and in reducing the dependencies that hinder its strategic autonomy, necessitating a regulatory approach based in reasserting control over the data and ensuring its safe use in the context of AI system development. The final substantive section, 'Regulating for Data Sovereignty and a Brussels Effect for AI?', focuses on the specific regulatory initiatives pursued by the Commission, which constitute a form of data industrial policy aimed at facilitating the creation of Common European Data Spaces, securing the localisation of data within the EU's physical territory, ideally on services provided by European firms, and both minimising the export of data while maximising the export of European standards on data and AI, as a means of providing the economic competitiveness and security guarantees seen as vital by the Geopolitical Commission.

PERSONAL DATA AND THE BRUSSELS EFFECT: A PYRRHIC VICTORY?

Data protection is not a new concern on the part of the EU. As was discussed in Chapter 2, how the personal data of Europeans should and could be protected was a subject of policy documents as early as the 1990s.[2] However, data protection had been on the then-EEC's radar since the early 1980s and the adoption of the European Convention on Personal Data.[3] The Convention was framed in terms of human rights and the protection of the right to privacy, while acknowledging commitments to the free flow of information, representing a tension in how data

---

[2] As discussed in European Commission, 'Communication on the Protection of Individuals in Relation to the Processing of Personal Data in the Community and Information Security' (1990) COM(90) 314.
[3] Council of Europe, The Strasbourg Convention for the Protection of Individuals with Regard to Automatic Processing of Personal Data (1981) CETS 108.

was understood; both as a source of individual insecurity for people, who should have their privacy respected, and as a potentially lucrative source of commercial value.[4] Prior to the Convention, individual states in the then EEC had been pursuing their own approaches to data protection as early as the 1970s,[5] but with these efforts at protecting personal data came significant divergences between Member States in how data was treated.[6] The adoption of the Data Protection Directive[7] was intended to achieve two key goals: the first, the effective protection of citizens' privacy in the context of new technologies, and the second, ensuring the effective realisation of the internal market as it related to data.[8] However, despite the adoption of the Directive, issues became immediately clear to policymakers, as well as scholars working in the field of data protection. The first issue was that as a Directive, there was a considerable level of discretion afforded to Member States regarding interpretation of the requirements of the data protection framework. This resulted in significant levels of divergence in the implementation of the Directive in national law, to the detriment of the internal market.[9] The second issue was that global data flows meant that even *if* data was effectively protected in the European Union, the data of Union citizens may not be subject to the same safeguards outside of the EU.[10]

That the US had a somewhat lacklustre approach to personal data protection was not particularly surprising to the EU. The lack of compliance with EU adequacy requirements concerning personal data protection, resulting in negotiations for an EU-US 'safe harbour'.[11] This safe harbour came in the form of a

---

[4] The value of information as a resource and the commercial importance of data is explored in detail in the comprehensive work by Professor Shoshana Zuboff, *The Age of Surveillance Capitalism: The Fight for a Human Future at the New Frontier of Power* (Profile Books 2019).
[5] Viktor Mayer-Schonberger, 'Generational Development of Data Protection in Europe' in Philip Agre and Marc Rotenberg (eds), *Technology and Privacy: The New Landscape* (MIT Press 1998).
[6] European Commission, 'Communication on the Protection of Individuals in Relation to the Processing of Personal Data in the Community and Information Security' (n2) 3; see also Colin Tapper, 'New European Directions in Data Protection' (1992) 3 *Journal of Law and Information Science* 9.
[7] Directive 95/46/EC on the protection of individuals with regard to the processing of personal data and on the free movement of such data.
[8] Two goals that the Commission saw as interlinked, as discussed in European Commission, 'Communication on the Protection of Individuals in Relation to the Processing of Personal Data in the Community and Information Security' (n2) 4.
[9] European Commission, 'First Report on the Implementation of the Data Protection Directive (95/46/EC)' (2003) COM(2003) 265 8; see also Siani Pearson, 'Privacy, Security and Trust in Cloud Computing' in Siani Pearson and George Yee (eds), *Privacy and Security for Cloud Computing* (Springer 2013).
[10] Graham Pearce and Nicholas Platten, 'Achieving Personal Data Protection in the European Union' (1998) 36 *JCMS: Journal of Common Market Studies* 529; Christopher Kuner, 'Extraterritoriality and Regulation of International Data Transfers in EU Data Protection Law' (2015) 5 *International Data Privacy Law* 235.
[11] William J Long and Marc Pang Quek, 'Personal Data Privacy Protection in an Age of Globalization: The US-EU Safe Harbor Compromise' (2002) 9 *Journal of European Public Policy* 325.

Commission Decision,[12] which permitted US-based companies under Article 1 to access and process data on EU citizens so long as they complied with the list of Safe Harbour Principles listed in Annex I, implemented as dictated by Annex II, which would secure adequacy as required under Article 25(1) of the Directive. The Safe Harbour, argued to have been adopted urgently in order to facilitate EU-US trade in the context of the emerging digital economy,[13] was routinely criticised as little more than a public relations exercise routinely ignored by large US companies.[14] In fact, the effectiveness of the regime was so insufficient that it was challenged in a hallmark decision of the CJEU, *Schrems*.[15] In this case, an Austrian data protection advocate brought an action against the Irish Data Protection Commissioner, concerning the transfer of personal data from Facebook Ireland Ltd. to the US and the Data Protection Commissioner's refusal to investigate a complaint concerning this transfer. The Court was scathing in its reasoning, concluding that the US did not ensure an adequate level of protection either with respect to its national laws or its international commitments,[16] concluding that the Commission Decision was invalid.[17] It is worth stating that this case was heard in the aftermath of the Snowden revelations discussed in Chapter 2, something explicitly referred to in the Advocate General's Opinion, with the Commission itself acknowledging that 'all companies involved in the PRISM programme, which grants access to United States authorities to data stored and processed in the United States, appear to be certified under the safe harbour scheme'.[18]

With the Decision invalidated, concerns over the surveillance of EU citizens by US agencies, and the increased levels of divergence between Member States in the application of the Directive, a renewed impetus was given to a reform of the European system for data protection. The salience of data protection as a political issue, rather than a set of technical standards, significantly increased as a result of the concerns over how personal data was being used, and who it was being accessed

---

[12] Commission Decision 2000/520/EC pursuant to Directive 95/46/EC of the European Parliament and of the Council on the adequacy of the protection provided by the safe harbour privacy principles and related frequently asked questions issued by the US Department of Commerce

[13] Subhajit Basu and Amruta Nikam, 'Offshore Outsourcing – How Safe Is Your Data Abroad? Overview of Privacy, Data Protection and Security' (2006) 6 *Global Jurist Topics* 1.

[14] Joel R Reidenberg, 'The Simplification of International Data Privacy Rules Fordham Law School Centennial Issue: Essay' (2005) 29 *Fordham International Law Journal* 1128; Yves Poullet, 'EU Data Protection Policy. The Directive 95/46/EC: Ten Years After' (2006) 22 *Computer Law & Security Report* 206; Daniel R Leathers, 'Giving Bite to the EU-U.S. Data Privacy Safe Harbor: Model Solutions for Effective Enforcement' (2009) 41 *Case Western Reserve Journal of International Law* 193.

[15] Case C-362/14 *Maximillian Schrems v Data Protection Commissioner* EU:C:2015:650.

[16] Ibid, para. 97.

[17] For an excellent overview, see Maria Lorena Flórez Rojas, 'Legal Implications after Schrems Case: Are We Trading Fundamental Rights?' (2016) 25 *Information & Communications Technology Law* 292.

[18] Case C-362/14 *Maximillian Schrems v Data Protection Commissioner*, EU:C:2015:627, para. 157.

by,[19] with the result that the GDPR[20] was significantly strengthened between the initial proposal and the final draft.[21] The EU explicitly set out to have the GDPR act as a global standard for personal data protection,[22] framed in terms of a values-led approach to privacy protection.[23] The GDPR was based on Article 16 TFEU, which provides for the right to data protection, and was central to the aims of the legislation; however, the proper functioning of the internal market was also identified as important in a revision of the data protection rules.[24] Indeed, Recital (3) of the GDPR states that the Regulation 'is intended to contribute to the accomplishment of an area of freedom, security and justice and of an economic union, to economic and social progress, to the strengthening and the convergence of the economies within the internal market, and to the well-being of natural persons'. This interlinking of values-based data protection with internal market development was central to the Brussels effect discussed in Chapter 2, with the global export of the approach to data protection in the GDPR facilitated by the desirability of access to the EU's market.[25] Examples abound of lobbying initiatives by large multinationals to ensure the EU's legal framework became a *de facto* standard to reduce costs of compliance by ensuring a 'one size fits all' approach to personal data protection globally,[26] with notable examples including the California Consumer Privacy Act of 2018, as well as the Indian Digital Personal Data Protection Act of 2023. Also of interest is China's Personal Information Protection Law (PIPL) passed in 2021, which has been stated to have been directly modelled on the GDPR.[27]

---

[19] Nicolas Bocquet, 'Caught Between Privacy and Surveillance: Explaining the Long-Term Stagnation of Data Protection Regulation in Liberal Democracies' (2025) *Regulation & Governance* 1.
[20] Regulation 2016/679 on the protection of natural persons with regard to the processing of personal data and on the free movement of such data, and repealing Directive 95/46/EC (General Data Protection Regulation).
[21] Colin J Bennett, 'The European General Data Protection Regulation: An Instrument for the Globalization of Privacy Standards?' (2018) 23 *Information Polity* 239.
[22] As discussed by Vera Jourova and Didier Reynders, '5th Anniversary of the General Data Protection Regulation' (*European Commission*, 24 May 2023) <https://ec.europa.eu/commission/presscorner/detail/en/statement_23_2884> accessed 31 March 2025.
[23] Described as a right-based model in Anu Bradford, *Digital Empires* (Oxford University Press 2023); or somewhat derisively as the 'Brussels Bourgeois Internet' by Kieron O'Hara and Wendy Hall, *Four Internets: Data, Geopolitics, and the Governance of Cyberspace* (Oxford University Press 2021).
[24] European Commission, 'Proposal for a Regulation on the Protection of Individuals with Regard to the Processing of Personal Data and on the Free Movement of Such Data (General Data Protection Regulation)' (2012) COM(2012) 11 5–6.
[25] As discussed in Anu Bradford, *The Brussels Effect: How the European Union Rules the World* (Oxford University Press 2021) and explored in Chapter 2; see also He Li, Lu Yu and Wu He, 'The Impact of GDPR on Global Technology Development' (2019) 22 *Journal of Global Information Technology Management* 1; Giulio Vittorio Cervi, 'Why and How Does the EU Rule Global Digital Policy: An Empirical Analysis of EU Regulatory Influence in Data Protection Laws' (2022) 1 *Digital Society* 18.
[26] Graham Greenleaf, 'Global Data Privacy Laws 2019: 132 National Laws & Many Bills' (2019) 157 *Privacy Laws & Business International Report* 14.
[27] See, for example, Shujie Cui and Peng Qi, 'The Legal Construction of Personal Information Protection and Privacy under the Chinese Civil Code' (2021) 41 *Computer Law & Security Review* 105560. This shall be returned to in the next subsection of the chapter.

Yet despite the apparent success in norm exporting exemplified by the GDPR, concerns have been raised concerning whether this is something of a pyrrhic victory; questions have been raised over effective compliance with the GDPR, particularly outside of the EU's borders,[28] with continuing divergences between Member States in the internal application of the rules,[29] and potential limitations on the ability of European firms to compete internationally in the commercialisation of data to the detriment of the European economy.[30] Had the EU potentially regulated itself into uncompetitiveness? As will be discussed in the next section, in an environment of heightened geopolitical competition, this became an increasing concern for the EU.

FORGING AHEAD OR FALLING BEHIND? EUROPE'S (LACK OF) COMPETITIVENESS WITH THE US AND CHINA

While the securing of European values regarding personal data protection and the exporting of these values through the EU as a regulatory superpower were ideas with a certain amount of weight in Brussels, the economic benefits of the GDPR were less convincing. Shaping Europe's Digital Future (SEDF) made clear that the Commission saw data as lucrative, stating that 'businesses need a framework that allows them to start up, scale up, pool and use data, to innovate and compete or cooperate on fair terms'.[31] There was a sense, however, that the global terms were not particularly fair; as the Commission argued in its Strategy for Data, 'a small number of Big Tech firms hold a large part of the world's data [...] competitors such as China and the US are already innovating quickly and projecting their concepts of data access and use across the globe'.[32] This power on the part of China and the US was largely related to size, with both countries possessing 'the advantage of scale – large markets and access to massive amounts of data'.[33] The Commission considered this a key source of vulnerability, with considerable market concentration in

---

[28] Joanna Strycharz, Jef Ausloos and Natali Helberger, 'Data Protection or Data Frustration? Individual Perceptions and Attitudes towards the GDPR' (2020) 6 *European Data Protection Law Review (EDPL)* 407; Wenlong Li and others, 'Mapping the Empirical Evidence of the GDPR (In-)Effectiveness: A Systematic Review' (arXiv, 18 July 2024) <http://arxiv.org/abs/2310.16735> accessed 31 March 2025.

[29] See, for example, Giulia Gentile and Orla Lynskey, 'Deficient by Design? The Transnational Enforcement of the GDPR' (2022) 71 *International & Comparative Law Quarterly* 799; Fruzsina Molnár-Gábor and others, 'Harmonization after the GDPR? Divergences in the Rules for Genetic and Health Data Sharing in Four Member States and Ways to Overcome Them by EU Measures: Insights from Germany, Greece, Latvia and Sweden' (2022) 84 *Seminars in Cancer Biology* 271; Filipe Brito Bastos and Przemysław Pałka, 'Is Centralised General Data Protection Regulation Enforcement a Constitutional Necessity?' (2023) 19 *European Constitutional Law Review* 487.

[30] Raised as a potential issue in O'Hara and Hall (n23) 91.

[31] European Commission, 'Shaping Europe's Digital Future' (2020) 3.

[32] European Commission, 'A European Strategy for Data' (2020) COM(2020) 66 3.

[33] Keyu Jin, *The New China Playbook: Beyond Socialism and Capitalism* (Swift Press 2024) 201.

the US, resulting in significant market power,[34] and concerns over the links to the state and the potential for surveillance and lack of regard for safeguards for individuals' rights in the case of China.[35]

Furthermore, the strength of the Brussels effect, even in data, looked somewhat overstated. After the invalidation of the Safe Harbour Decision, the EU and US concluded a new agreement facilitating personal data transfers to the US called the Privacy Shield.[36] While acknowledged as being more robust in its obligations than the Safe Harbour, the Privacy Shield was nevertheless regarded as not amounting to effective adequacy for protection of personal data in the US,[37] and shared the same vulnerabilities as the previous attempt at facilitating these data transfers, particularly as regards the effective self-regulation of large US multinationals and Big Tech firms.[38] Ultimately, and with a certain amount of foreseeability, the validity of the Privacy Shield was effectively challenged at the CJEU in the *Schrems II* sequel.[39] In this case, the CJEU declared that neither the respect afforded to personal data through the potential that it could be accessed by national intelligence agencies in the context of surveillance under the Foreign Intelligence Surveillance Act (FISA) nor the lack of effective redress mechanisms in the US meant that it was possible to state that US efforts at data protection were sufficient to be considered as adequate under Article 45 of the GDPR.[40] Similarly, while China's PIPL was based on the GDPR, it had significant divergences as a result of a strategic instrumentalisation that adapts to China's distinct legal culture while also working to influence the states in its periphery.[41] In particular, and related to China's pursuit of its own cyber sovereignty and its own concerns regarding the Snowden revelations over the PRISM programme,[42] one of the hallmarks of the PIPL was a requirement firstly that the PIPL would apply to the data of Chinese citizens regardless of where in the world it was being processed under Article 3, and under Article 40, requires that both critical

---

[34] As discussed in Chapter 5 in the context of platform governance.
[35] European Commission, 'A European Strategy for Data' (n32) 3.
[36] Commission Implementing Decision 2016/1250 pursuant to Directive 95/46/EC of the European Parliament and of the Council on the adequacy of the protection provided by the EU-U.S. Privacy Shield.
[37] Xavier Tracol, 'EU–U.S. Privacy Shield: The Saga Continues' (2016) 32 *Computer Law & Security Review* 775.
[38] Emily Linn, 'A Look into the Data Privacy Crystal Ball: A Survey of Possible Outcomes for the EU-U.S. Privacy Shield Agreement Notes' (2017) 50 *Vanderbilt Journal of Transnational Law* 1311.
[39] Case C-311/18 *Data Protection Commissioner v Facebook Ireland Limited and Maximillian Schrems (Schrems II)* EU:C:2020:559.
[40] For more on Schrems II, see Xavier Tracol, '"Schrems II": The Return of the Privacy Shield' (2020) 39 *Computer Law & Security Review* 105484; Maria Helen Murphy, 'Assessing the Implications of Schrems II for EU–US Data Flow' (2022) 71 *International & Comparative Law Quarterly* 245.
[41] Wenlong Li and Jiahong Chen, 'From Brussels Effect to Gravity Assists: Understanding the Evolution of the GDPR-Inspired Personal Information Protection Law in China' (2024) 54 *Computer Law & Security Review* 105994.
[42] Yi Shen, 'Cyber Sovereignty and the Governance of Global Cyberspace' (2016) 1 *Chinese Political Science Review* 81.

information infrastructure providers and personal information processors above a certain threshold are required to ensure that data is stored on servers physically located within the territory of the People's Republic of China, with transfers out of China permitted only on the basis of a security assessment conducted by the State cyberspace administration, a requirement known as data localisation.[43]

These twin issues, namely a lack of competitiveness when compared to the US and China in the commercialisation of data and the relatively weak impact of the GDPR on those states, combined to create a perceived vulnerability on the part of the EU as it relates to data and revealed a significant strategic dependency. Not only was the EU less able to commercialise personal data, but it also suffered from an inability to use non-personal data for economic benefit[44] and was heavily dependent on US and Chinese data servers for its storage and processing. In its Data Strategy, the Commission argued that 'the EU needs to reduce its technological dependencies in these strategic infrastructures, at the centre of the data economy'.[45] It continued that EU-based firms only possessed a small market share for data servers,[46] with the European Council on Foreign Relations identifying that the EU and its Member States were particularly weak in cloud computing.[47] As of the end of 2024, Amazon's AWS had a worldwide market share of 30 per cent, followed by Microsoft's Azure at 21 per cent, Google Cloud at 12 per cent, and Alibaba had 4 per cent, with Tencent Cloud at 2 per cent.[48] The EU, by way of comparison, has no companies in the top ten cloud service providers and has been heavily dependent on cloud services provided by companies based in third countries. According to the Commission's Industrial Strategy[49] the Commission saw the EU as lagging behind its global competitors on cloud and data applications,[50] identified as a key dependency in the strategic dependencies report.[51] Of note to the Commission was the fact that public cloud infrastructure was converging around four non-European firms,[52] with the EU

---

[43] Luca Belli, Water B Gaspar and Shilpa Singh Jaswant, 'Data Sovereignty and Data Transfers as Fundamental Elements of Digital Transformation: Lessons from the BRICS Countries' (2024) 54 *Computer Law & Security Review* 106017.
[44] European Commission, 'A European Strategy for Data' (n32) 6–8.
[45] Ibid 9.
[46] Ibid 8.
[47] Jana Puglierin and Pawel Zerka, 'European Sovereignty Index' (European Council on Foreign Relations, 2022) 28.
[48] Felix Richter, 'Infographic: Amazon and Microsoft Stay Ahead in Global Cloud Market' (*Statista Daily Data*, 27 February 2025) <www.statista.com/chart/18819/worldwide-market-share-of-leading-cloud-infrastructure-service-providers> accessed 1 April 2025.
[49] European Commission, 'A New Industrial Strategy for Europe' (2020) COM(2020) 102 final, also discussed in Chapter 4.
[50] Ibid 2.
[51] European Commission, 'Strategic Dependencies and Capacities: Accompanying the Communication Updating the 2020 New Industrial Strategy: Building a Stronger Single Market for Europe's Recovery' (2021) SWD(2021) 352.
[52] Ibid 92.

having an investment gap with the US and China of €11 billion annually,⁵³ able to scale up and form agreements faster than European firms, further creating barriers to entry.⁵⁴ As President von der Leyen stated in the 2020 State of the Union, 'On personalized data [...] Europe has been too slow and is now dependent on others. This cannot happen with industrial data.'⁵⁵

This technological dependency and lack of economic competitiveness presented further security threats; not only could personal data based on US and Chinese-firm-owned data servers present the potential for improper use or surveillance under the US CLOUD Act, or through the transfer of data from Chinese apps to data servers in China,⁵⁶ but it also opened up potential opportunities for states or state-affiliated firms to surreptitiously access sensitive industrial data without authorisation, or alternatively, argue that access was permitted under their own laws, such as China's Cybersecurity Law of 2017.⁵⁷ However, this was not only a concern due to the commercial value of data in its own right but also its potential use in the context of AI. AI had periodically appeared in policy documents of the Commission prior to the von der Leyen Commission,⁵⁸ but had not featured prominently in the work of the Juncker Commission. One exception was the publication of the AI Strategy⁵⁹ with the associated Coordinated Action Plan on Artificial Intelligence published in 2018,⁶⁰ which discussed the transformative potential of AI, but framed it in almost entirely economic terms⁶¹ – geopolitically, this was framed in terms of economic competition, in which 'AI start-ups do not find the resources and talent they need in Europe, and international competition is fiercer than ever with massive investments in the US and China'.⁶² In SEDF, in comparison, the EU identified AI as a strategic interest, and one with links to security and trust.⁶³ The subsequent White Paper on AI framed the technology in more explicit security terms, including with respect to its use for criminal purposes,⁶⁴ but also ensuring that it is used in a way that ensures and respects human and ecosystem safety and security.⁶⁵ However, the White Paper

---

[53] Ibid 94.
[54] Ibid 94–95.
[55] Ursula von der Leyen, '2020 State of the Union Address by President Von Der Leyen: Building the World We Want to Live In' (*European Commission*, 2020) 12.
[56] European Commission, 'A European Strategy for Data' (n32) 9.
[57] Ibid.
[58] Being mentioned as early as 1979 in European Commission, 'European Society Faced with the Challenge of New Information Technologies: A Community Response' (1979) COM(79) 650.
[59] European Commission, 'Artificial Intelligence for Europe' (2018) COM(2018) 237.
[60] European Commission, 'Coordinated Plan on Artificial Intelligence' (2018) COM(2018) 795.
[61] See European Commission, 'Artificial Intelligence for Europe' (n59) 5–8.
[62] European Commission, 'Coordinated Plan on Artificial Intelligence' (n60) 1.
[63] European Commission, 'Shaping Europe's Digital Future' (n31) 4.
[64] European Commission, 'White Paper on Artificial Intelligence: A European Approach to Excellence and Trust' (2020) COM(2020) 65 1.
[65] As discussed throughout European Commission, 'Artificial Intelligence for Europe' (n59); see also Jozef Andraško, Matúš Mesarčík and Ondrej Hamuľák, 'The Regulatory Intersections between

also acknowledged that compared to the €12.1 billion invested in AI in North America and €6.5 billion in Asia in 2016, the EU area had only invested €3.2 billion, another significant investment gap.[66] The impact of the lower level of investment in AI specifically was compounded by the lower investment in cloud computing and data servers in Europe, as the former heavily depended upon the latter.[67] The EU was therefore in a 'big data race' with the US and China, particularly as regards the development of AI systems,[68] as the unlocking of access to personal and non-personal data would provide larger datasets for the training of AI systems.

This of course presented additional security concerns; the dependence on foreign data servers and cloud services also created a related dependency on non-European firms for AI compute, and the largest AI firms, particularly in the context of Foundational Models and Generative Artificial Intelligence, are based in the US and China.[69] Put in regulatory mercantilist terms, these strategic dependencies put the EU in a position where data could be considered a critical digital resource for AI in the same way as silicon is a critical natural resource for semiconductors. The EU's reliance and dependence upon access to data stored, processed, and utilised outside of its geographical reach places the EU at a competitive economic and security disadvantage to the US and China. The concentration of power in a relatively small set of non-European players, such as AWS, Microsoft, Alibaba, and Baidu, combined with new players such as OpenAI, Anthropic, and later Deepseek, also presents similar concerns to the regulation of platforms discussed in Chapter 5. For example, the misuse of AI, either by state or non-state actors, can have significant security ramifications for Europe – the spread of algorithmically generated disinformation, for example,[70] as well as presenting significant cybersecurity threats such as exposing vulnerabilities or facilitating cyberattacks,[71] or being used in the context of

---

Artificial Intelligence, Data Protection and Cyber Security: Challenges and Opportunities for the EU Legal Framework' (2021) 36 *AI & SOCIETY* 623; Jon Truby and others, 'A Sandbox Approach to Regulating High-Risk Artificial Intelligence Applications' (2022) 13 *European Journal of Risk Regulation* 270.

[66] European Commission, 'White Paper on Artificial Intelligence: A European Approach to Excellence and Trust' (n64) 4.

[67] European Commission, 'Strategic Dependencies and Capacities: Accompanying the Communication Updating the 2020 New Industrial Strategy: Building a Stronger Single Market for Europe's Recovery' (n51) 92.

[68] Jamal Shahin, 'Dancing to the Same Tune? EU and US Approaches to Standards Setting in the Global Digital Sector' (2024) 46 *Journal of European Integration* 1111, 1119.

[69] Fabian Ferrari, 'State Roles in Platform Governance: AI's Regulatory Geographies' (2024) 28 *Competition & Change* 340; David Matthews, 'EU Companies in Danger of AI "Dependence" on US and China | Science|Business' (*Science Business*, 3 November 2022) <https://sciencebusiness.net/news/eu-companies-danger-ai-dependence-us-and-china> accessed 1 April 2025.

[70] Christopher Marsden, Trisha Meyer and Ian Brown, 'Platform Values and Democratic Elections: How Can the Law Regulate Digital Disinformation?' (2020) 36 *Computer Law & Security Review* 105373.

[71] Andrea Calderaro and Stella Blumfelde, 'Artificial Intelligence and EU Security: The False Promise of Digital Sovereignty' (2022) 31 *European Security* 415.

military conflict.[72] These were concerns identified by President von der Leyen in her 2023 State of the Union address, in which, influenced by increased geopolitical instability and the war in Ukraine, she stated that 'general technology that is accessible, powerful and adaptable for a vast range of uses – both civilian and military. And it is moving faster than even its developers anticipated.'[73] This fast-moving nature, combined with the EU's comparatively weak position in AI development, therefore constituted a key geopolitical vulnerability.

VIRTUAL(LY) GOLD: INDUSTRIAL POLICY FOR DATA-BASED TECHNOLOGICAL SOVEREIGNTY

As with technological systems and platform governance, the EU's response to these perceived vulnerabilities was based in securing its technological sovereignty and ensuring strategic autonomy. As SEDF made clear, the regulation of data on the EU's own terms was central to the Commission's technological sovereignty ambitions,[74] with the publication of the Data Strategy framed as ensuring the EU was a global leader in the 'data-agile economy'.[75] Linking to the Industrial Strategy, the Data Strategy stated that in order to guarantee technological sovereignty in the context of data, the EU would be required to invest more in new technologies and infrastructures, with the purpose of creating European data spaces that could be leveraged to boost the European economy.[76] As was stated in SEDF, data was 'a key factor of production [...] we need to build a genuine European single market for data – a European data space based on European rules and values'.[77] For the Commission, the reliance on third-country service providers in this field was a key source of risk, negatively impacting upon its strategic autonomy,[78] necessitating regulatory action. The EU would therefore support the development of key enabling technologies strategically important for Europe's industrial future, thereby ensuring its technological sovereignty, in fields including 'high-performance computing and data cloud infrastructure'.[79]

Ultimately, the aim of action in this area by the Commission was to ensure that its digital/technological sovereignty equally applied to data in the form of 'data

---

[72] Daniel Mügge, 'The Securitization of the EU's Digital Tech Regulation' (2023) 30 *Journal of European Public Policy* 1431.
[73] Ursula von der Leyen, '2023 State of the Union Address by President von Der Leyen: Answering the Call of History' (2023) SPEECH/23/4426 9.
[74] European Commission, 'Shaping Europe's Digital Future' (n31) 3.
[75] Ibid 5.
[76] European Commission, 'A European Strategy for Data' (n32) 5.
[77] European Commission, 'Shaping Europe's Digital Future' (n31) 5.
[78] European Commission, 'Strategic Dependencies and Capacities: Accompanying the Communication Updating the 2020 New Industrial Strategy: Building a Stronger Single Market for Europe's Recovery' (n51) 97.
[79] European Commission, 'A New Industrial Strategy for Europe' (n49) 13.

sovereignty'.[80] This data sovereignty is ultimately about the ability to exert control over data,[81] whether through existing legal frameworks such as for cybersecurity[82] or through the establishment of new regimes. Data sovereignty is therefore intended to offset the lack of competitiveness and subsequent dependence on third-country resources as part of an 'industrial policy agenda to catch up in the development and deployment of enabling technologies'.[83] In order to ensure that this would be effective and avoid divergences between Member States, the Commission proposed introducing regulations to create frameworks to shape the context and provide the conditions for the realisation of common European data spaces (or CEDSs) to be facilitated through a Data Act.[84] The intention behind this would be to reduce the dependency on non-European data spaces, which would be complemented with increased funding and support for initiatives such as European cloud federations around topics such as industrial data, health data, and financial data,[85] and Member State initiatives such as Gaia X.[86] Through these measures, the Commission hoped that by 2030 the EU's share of the data economy would correspond to its economic weight, 'not by *fiat* but by choice'.[87] This strategy therefore had both internal industrial policy dimensions and external regulatory export dimensions, captured by Commissioner for the Internal Market Breton's statement that:

> In the face of growing tensions between the United States and China, Europe will not be a mere bystander, let alone a battleground. It is time to take our destiny into our own hands. This also means identifying and investing in the digital technologies that will underpin our sovereignty and our industrial future.[88]

The Data Strategy resulted in two interlinked legislative proposals, one for a Data Governance Act[89] and the other for a Data Act.[90] The Data Governance Act was

---

[80] Patrik Hummel and others, 'Data Sovereignty: A Review' (2021) 8 *Big Data & Society* 1.
[81] Mark Ryan, Paula Gürtler and Artur Bogucki, 'Will the Real Data Sovereign Please Stand up? An EU Policy Response to Sovereignty in Data Spaces' (2024) 32 *International Journal of Law and Information Technology* eaae006.
[82] Anupam Chander and Haochen Sun, 'Introduction: Sovereignty 2.0' in Anupam Chander and Haochen Sun (eds), *Data Sovereignty: From the Digital Silk Road to the Return of the State* (Oxford University Press 2023) 7.
[83] Filippo Gualtiero Blancato, 'The Cloud Sovereignty Nexus: How the European Union Seeks to Reverse Strategic Dependencies in Its Digital Ecosystem' (2024) 16 *Policy & Internet* 12, 14.
[84] European Commission, 'A European Strategy for Data' (n32) 12–13.
[85] Ibid 22.
[86] Ibid 17–18.
[87] Ibid 4.
[88] Thierry Breton, 'Speech by Commissioner Thierry Breton at Hannover Messe' (*European Commission*, 15 July 2020) <https://ec.europa.eu/commission/presscorner/detail/fr/speech_20_1362> accessed 1 April 2025.
[89] European Commission, 'Proposal for a Regulation on European Data Governance (Data Governance Act)' (2020) COM(2020) 767.
[90] European Commission, 'Proposal for a Regulation on Harmonised Rules on Fair Access to and Use of Data (Data Act)' (2022) COM(2022) 68.

intended to 'unlock' the value of data through making public sector data available for reuse, encouraging sharing of data between businesses, allowing personal data to be used with the assistance of 'personal data-sharing intermediaries' to give effect to data subject rights under the GDPR while allowing for commercial use of personal data, and allowing data use for altruistic purposes.[91] In the accompanying impact assessment, this was framed as ensuring the EU was competitive in the data economy, ensuring its data sovereignty as an alternative to the business model 'dominated by Big Tech platforms'.[92] For European businesses seeking to boost their economic productivity, data was a 'critical resource',[93] discussed in similar terms throughout the document in a similar way that other policy documents discussed raw materials.[94] The Proposal for a Data Act had a more explicit focus on security as opposed to 'just' industrial policy. In its approach to industrial policy by way of regulating for the promotion of CEDSs, the Data Act aimed to facilitate access to and the use of data by consumers and businesses, with incentives to invest in CEDSs, while facilitating the easier switching of cloud service providers and by implementing safeguards to prevent the unlawful access of non-personal data by third countries and companies based within them.[95] Interestingly, the impact assessment accompanying the Proposal indicated that it saw the issues of switching providers and unlawful access to data as linked, with the dependence on third-country data servers increasing security threats, which could be alleviated by encouraging the switch to European providers.[96] Furthermore, there is an element of minimising the risk of regulatory import. The impact assessment states that 'specific laws with extraterritorial effect of several third countries have raised concerns […] the third country may oblige certain […] providers to grant its authorities access to data from EU organisations that are customers of the cloud providers, even if the data is processed in the EU'.[97] This was particularly concerning for the Commission as despite EU-based private initiatives like Gaia-X, dependence on non-EU 'hyperscalers' such as AWS and Tencent was growing.[98] For this reason, the sector could not be governed by systems of self-regulation but had to be subject to increased regulatory oversight.[99]

---

[91] European Commission, 'Proposal for a Regulation on European Data Governance (Data Governance Act)' (n89) 1.
[92] European Commission, 'Impact Assessment Accompanying the Proposal for a Regulation on European Data Governance (Data Governance Act)' (2020) SWD(2020) 295 11.
[93] Ibid 2.
[94] As discussed in Chapter 4.
[95] European Commission, 'Proposal for a Regulation on Harmonised Rules on Fair Access to and Use of Data (Data Act)' (n90) 2.
[96] European Commission, 'Impact Assessment Accompanying the Proposal for a Regulation on Harmonised Rules on Fair Access to and Use of Data (Data Act)' (2022) SWD(2022) 34 13–15.
[97] Ibid 21.
[98] Ibid 24.
[99] Ibid 23.

Finally, sovereignty and reduced dependency in data are explicitly linked to ensuring technological sovereignty vis-à-vis AI. The Strategic Dependencies report highlighted that cloud servers were key to AI as transformational services,[100] arguing that the Data Governance Act would provide the environment in which a healthy AI ecosystem could develop to the benefit of the European economy.[101] The impact assessment accompanying the Proposal for the Data Governance Act (DGA) identified access to data as being essential for the EU's ability to invest and deploy AI,[102] with the impact assessment accompanying the Data Act Proposal stating that 'data is the basis for many new digital products and services, in particular for developing artificial intelligence'.[103] While data sovereignty was seen as important for realising the EU's AI ambitions, AI itself was also linked to the EU's technological sovereignty.[104] As a technology identified as strategic by the Commission, action would require significant investment in industrial and technical capacities, positioning the EU as a global data hub, with regulation implemented in order to ensure that AI systems were implemented in ways that minimise risk[105] and export European standards and values as global standards.[106] Comprehensive regulation was determined to be the best way to achieve this, with the publication of a Proposal for an AI Act.[107] This Proposal identified a lack of a unified Union response as being a threat to the realisation of the EU's digital sovereignty and regulation as a way of shaping global rules and standards.[108] By creating common standards applicable to all AI systems used in the EU, the EU could avoid a situation in which companies from third countries possessed a competitive advantage over European firms, upholding its digital sovereignty and preventing the offering of services 'from foreign companies [that] might not completely comply with European values and/or legislation or [that] might even pose security risks and make the European infrastructure more vulnerable'.[109] In its justification for action in the field of data and AI, a clear regulatory mercantilist

---

[100] European Commission, 'Strategic Dependencies and Capacities: Accompanying the Communication Updating the 2020 New Industrial Strategy: Building a Stronger Single Market for Europe's Recovery' (n51) 92.
[101] Ibid 102.
[102] European Commission, 'Impact Assessment Accompanying the Proposal for a Regulation on European Data Governance (Data Governance Act)' (n92) 1.
[103] European Commission, 'Impact Assessment Accompanying the Proposal for a Regulation on Harmonised Rules on Fair Access to and Use of Data (Data Act)' (n96) 2.
[104] European Commission, 'White Paper on Artificial Intelligence: A European Approach to Excellence and Trust' (n64) 3.
[105] Ibid 25.
[106] Ibid 8.
[107] European Commission, 'Proposal for a Regulation Laying down Harmonised Rules on Artificial Intelligence (Artificial Intelligence Act)' (2021) COM(2021) 206.
[108] Ibid 6.
[109] European Commission, 'Impact Assessment Accompanying the Proposal for a Regulation Laying down Harmonised Rules on Artificial Intelligence (Artificial Intelligence Act)' (2021) SWD(2021) 84 27.

approach is discernible, based in concerns over sovereignty and external dependencies in the face of geopolitical competition. As will be demonstrated in the next section, this has resulted in legislative frameworks aimed at promoting industrial strategy *within* Europe while seeking to both minimise regulatory import and maximise regulatory export in the form of global standards.

REGULATING FOR DATA SOVEREIGNTY AND A BRUSSELS EFFECT FOR AI?

As the previous sections have identified, the EU's approach to data and AI during the first von der Leyen Commission was heavily influenced by the geopolitical conditions in which Europe found itself and the sense of dependency that arose as a result. In response to these perceived vulnerabilities, the EU pursued an approach that highlighted the need for increased regulatory intervention in order to ensure its strategic autonomy and technological sovereignty, with an emphasis on data sovereignty specifically as a means of achieving this. This crystallised into two distinct but interrelated goals that demonstrate a regulatory mercantilist approach to lawmaking. The first was the pursuit of a data-focused industrial policy based in incentivising the creation of CEDSs and promoting the storage and use of data within the EU's geographical territory by Europe-based firms. The other was maximising regulatory export both in terms of the EU requirements for data territorialisation and AI safety, while minimising the risk of European data export as a means of achieving a positive regulatory balance of trade.

Industrial Policy for Data: Creating the Conditions for CEDSs

The DGA was successfully adopted in June 2022,[110] and the Proposal for the Data Act (DA) in December 2023.[111] Recital (3) of the DGA states that it is 'necessary to improve the conditions for data sharing in the internal market, by creating a harmonised framework for data exchanges and laying down certain basic requirements for data governance, paying specific attention to facilitating cooperation between Member States', further developing the internal market and a 'human-centric, trustworthy and secure data society and economy'. Recital (2) states that this can be achieved through giving effect to the Data Strategy's goal of creating CEDSs,[112] competing on quality of service rather than volume of data possessed (in essence a rebuke to the large tech providers of the US in particular), with strong oversight at

---

[110] Regulation 2022/868 on European data governance and amending Regulation (EU) 2018/1724 (Data Governance Act).
[111] Regulation 2023/2854 on harmonised rules on fair access to and use of data and amending Regulation (EU) 2017/2394 and Directive (EU) 2020/1828 (Data Act).
[112] See also Olga MC van der Valk and Mark Ryan, 'Data for the Common Good in the Common European Data Space' (2025) 7 *Data & Policy* e32.

the EU level. Recital (27) explains the reasoning behind the DGA's establishment of data intermediaries, which are services that the Commission expected to play a significant role in bolstering the data-driven economy, supporting and promoting voluntary data sharing practices between undertakings or facilitating data sharing.[113] Recital (27) adds that they could have a 'facilitating role in the emergence of new data-driven ecosystems independent from any player with a significant degree of market power, while allowing non-discriminatory access to the data economy for undertakings of all sizes', again indicating alignment with the goals of the Digital Markets Act, as well as the goal of reducing dependency on third-country data services. Oversight of the function of these different data-handling organisations should be provided by a newly established European Data Innovation Board (EDIB).[114]

The DA emphasises the intersection of economic and security interests reflected in the Geopolitical Commission's approach to market-building, with Recital (4) arguing that in order to respond to the needs of the digital economy and 'to remove barriers to a well-functioning internal market for data, it is necessary to lay down a harmonised framework specifying who is entitled to use product data or related service data, under which conditions and on what basis'. The Recital argues therefore for a common European approach, without Member States adopting additional requirements that could hinder pan-European activity; this includes actions to facilitate the ease of switching between data processing services and ensuring interoperability.[115] As discussed earlier, this switching is also intended to reduce EU dependency on third-country data processing services as a means of promoting strategic autonomy.[116] The desire to incentivise the creation of European-based data-based services as an element of industrial strategy can be seen in Recital (26), where it is stated that in order to 'foster the emergence of liquid, fair and efficient markets for non-personal data, users of connected products should be able to share data with others, including for commercial purposes, with minimal legal and technical effort', removing internal barriers to trade that are reflective of processes of state unification while, as will be discussed later, securing the state through the erection of external barriers. This is compounded by the explanation in Recital (32) that the purpose of the DA 'is not only to foster the development of new, innovative connected products or related services [...] but also to stimulate the development of entirely novel services making use of the data concerned, including based on data from a variety of connected products or related services'. The aspect of increased regulatory oversight is also present in the Recitals to the DA, with a reference to the role of the EDIB in this capacity.[117]

---

[113] See also Jukka Ruohonen and Sini Mickelsson, 'Reflections on the Data Governance Act' (2023) 2 *Digital Society* 10.
[114] Data Governance Act, Recital (21).
[115] Data Act, Recital (5).
[116] See also Blancato (n83) 16.
[117] DA, Recitals (103), (109), and (110).

The AI Act[118] also has an element of industrial policy facilitation behind it, albeit not to the same extent as the DGA or DA. The reasons for this are twofold; the first is that the aim of creating the market conditions for AI exploitation revolves around the issues of access to data covered by the DGA and DA, and the second is that the key to the AI Act was the issue of system safety based on European values.[119] As Recital (8) makes clear, the rationale of the AI Act in this respect is that 'harmonised rules on AI is therefore needed to foster the development, use and uptake of AI in the internal market that at the same time meets a high level of protection of public interests, such as health and safety and the protection of fundamental rights, including democracy, the rule of law and environmental protection'. The AI Act's rationale, as far as the internal market goes, therefore, is harmonising standards regarding trust and safety to facilitate the digital single market by removing the barriers to trade that could arise through Member States taking divergent approaches to safety standards.[120] Again, increased regulatory oversight is a clear goal in the AI Act, with Recital (138) stating the need for 'strict regulatory oversight' for testing innovative AI systems and the establishment of regulatory networks of competent national authorities in Recital (138).

What do these legal obligations look like in practice? Article 1(1) of the DGA states that the purpose is to lay down conditions for reuse of data held by public sector bodies, establish a notification and supervisory framework for the provision of data intermediation services, set the conditions for altruistic data use, and establish a framework for the establishment of the EDIB, and Article 3 states that the data relevant to the development of a unified data economy in the context of the DA is data held by public sector bodies that may be covered by commercial confidentiality, third-party IP rights, statistical confidentiality, or personal data. Article 10 establishes the role of the data intermediation services, and while Article 11 allows for the possibility that these services may be offered by companies outside of the EU, they will be required to assign a legal representative in an EU Member State. Article 14 outlines the compliance mechanisms for these services, with the possibility of fines or suspension of activities under Article 14(4). The EDIB is established under Article 29 and has representatives of the competent bodies for the data intermediation services as well as ENISA, the European Data Protection Board, the European Data Protection Supervisor, and other sector experts, with the Commission chairing the Board, providing for a co-regulatory structure that increases Commission control of this area of technology.[121]

---

[118] Regulation 2024/1689 laying down harmonised rules on artificial intelligence and amending Regulations 300/2008, 167/2013, 168/2013, 2018/858, 2018/1139, and 2019/2144 and Directives 2014/90/EU, 2016/797, and 2020/1828 (Artificial Intelligence Act)
[119] AI Act, Recital (1) provides an overview of these goals.
[120] See, for example, Troels Krarup and Maja Horst, 'European Artificial Intelligence Policy as Digital Single Market Making' (2023) 10 *Big Data & Society* 20539517231153811.
[121] Herwig CH Hofmann, 'New Regulatory Approaches under the EU's Legislation on Digitalisation: Introduction to the Special Edition of the EJRR "Charting the Landscape of Automation of Regulatory Decision-Making"' (2025) 16 *European Journal of Risk Regulation* 1.

Of the competences of EDIB listed under Article 30 are those relating to the design, identification, and promotion of standards for, and guidelines for running CEDSs, furthering EU industrial policy in this field.

The DA goes further in this respect. Article 33 lays out interoperability requirements intended to facilitate data sharing and the creation of CEDSs, with the Commission empowered to adopt delegated acts further specifying essential requirements. Article 23 provides the conditions for switching between different data processing providers, stating that they 'shall not impose and shall remove pre-commercial, commercial, technical, contractual and organisational obstacles', which are covered in more detail in Articles 25, 26, 27, 29, and 30.[122] In order to make data accessible for use by enterprises to develop data-driven businesses, Article 3 promotes obligations to make product data and related service data derived from Internet of Things devices accessible to the user and creates a right under Article 5 to share data with third parties upon request by a user or by a party acting on behalf of a user. Article 4 defines how these rights are to operate, ensuring that trade secrecy confidentiality in particular is maintained, and that data is not used for the purposes of entering into direct competition with the data holder. The purpose behind these Articles is to facilitate data reuse on the basis that the data itself is non-rivalrous and can be used by diverse companies to develop distinct commercial offerings,[123] promoting the innovation that is behind the Data Strategy and the EU's pursuit of data-driven industrial policy. The element of reasserted control, particularly in the context of the 'Big Tech' firms discussed in Chapter 5, is the specific exclusion of 'gatekeepers' as defined under the Digital Markets Act from being able to request access to this data.[124] As with the DGA, the EDIB is empowered with oversight competences under Article 42, including advising and assisting the Commission with the development of consistent practices under the DA and liaising with competent national authorities, as well as recommending the harmonisation of standards regarding interoperability and the facilitation of CEDSs, as well as making recommendations regarding penalties to be applied for infringements of the DA under Article 40.

Finally, the AI Act seeks to improve the functioning of the internal market and promote the uptake of human-centric and trustworthy AI under Article 1(1), laying down rules for placing on the market, putting into service, and using AI systems, prohibiting certain practices, making specifications for high-risk systems, with harmonised rules on transparency and enforcement, and with measures to

---

[122] For an overview, see Pieter Wolters, 'The Influence of the Data Act on the Shifting Balance between Data Protection and the Free Movement of Data' (2024) 15 *European Journal of Law and Technology* <www.ejlt.org/index.php/ejlt/article/view/991> accessed 4 April 2025.

[123] Wolfgang Kerber, 'EU Data Act: Will New User Access and Sharing Rights on IoT Data Help Competition and Innovation?' (2024) 12 *Journal of Antitrust Enforcement* 234.

[124] Article 5(3) states that gatekeepers are not to be considered eligible third parties; see also Federico Casolari, Carlotta Buttaboni and Luciano Floridi, 'The EU Data Act in Context: A Legal Assessment' (2023) 31 *International Journal of Law and Information Technology* 399.

support innovation in this field. Article 5 provides an overview of the prohibited practices, including the use of subliminal techniques or systems that exploit user vulnerabilities, while Article 6 provides for the classification of systems as high risk.[125] Annex III, which Article 5 refers to, lists services always considered as high risk, such as where they are used in biometric information systems and critical infrastructure. For high-risk systems, while permitted, their use requires compliance with risk management systems under Article 9, and on the basis of established principles of data governance under Article 10. Article 16 extends obligations to those deploying these systems, ensuring compliance along the AI supply chain.[126] Article 21 requires entities in the supply chain[127] to comply with competent national authorities, through officially designated representatives of providers of high-risk AI systems established in the Union under Article 22. Each Member State is required to have a notifying body that performs assessments for and monitoring of AI systems under Article 28, with a full schedule of obligations and tasks under Section 4 of Chapter III of the AI Act. Under Article 65, a European Artificial Intelligence Board (EAIB) is established, with the attendance of a representative of the Commission's AI Office. Its tasks under Article 66 include identifying best practices and ensuring coherent and consistent application of the principles of the AI Act by the national authorities. Ultimately, in the context of geopolitics, the key purpose of this Act is to create a unified approach to AI in the Member States, to ensure that European firms are not at a competitive disadvantage when compared to the large AI developers based in the US and China, and to establish principles that can be exported as global standards, as discussed in the next subsection.

Minimising Data Export, Maximising Regulatory Export

The Commission's activities in data and AI reflect regulatory mercantilist logic insofar as they seek to ensure a positive regulatory balance of trade. As well as harmonising *internally*, the EU's regulatory interventions in this field seek to ensure barriers are erected *externally* to minimise data export,[128] while seeking to export the EU's standards, particularly on AI.[129] The DGA at Recital (20) states that data should only be exported outside of the EU where appropriate safeguards are in place for

---

[125] For more, see Isabel Kusche, 'Possible Harms of Artificial Intelligence and the EU AI Act: Fundamental Rights and Risk' (2024) *Journal of Risk Research* 1.
[126] See Nathalie A Smuha, 'Regulation 2024/1689 of the Eur. Parl. & Council of June 13, 2024 (Eu Artificial Intelligence Act)' (2025) *International Legal Materials* 1.
[127] Reinforced by the responsibilities provided for in Article 25.
[128] See Samuele Fratini and Francesca Musiani, 'Data Localization as Contested and Narrated Security in the Age of Digital Sovereignty: The Case of Switzerland' (2024) *Information, Communication & Society* 1. https://doi.org/10.1080/1369118X.2024.2362302.
[129] Daniel Mügge, 'EU AI Sovereignty: For Whom, to What End, and to Whose Benefit?' (2024) 31 *Journal of European Public Policy* 2200.

non-personal data, with Recital (21) adding that 'appropriate safeguards should be considered to be implemented where, in the third country to which non-personal data is being transferred, there are equivalent measures in place which ensure that data benefit from a level of protection similar to that applicable by means of Union law', namely around intellectual property rights and trade secrets. The DA makes data localisation central to its efforts, with Recital (101) stating that data transfers or access by the governments of third countries should only be permitted in line with the DA, and that providers should provide for robust cybersecurity as a means of preventing unauthorised access from private or public actors in third countries under Recital (102). The AI Act intends that its principles have extraterritorial effect, as Recital (21) highlights that the rules are to apply to AI providers 'irrespective of whether they are established within the Union or in a third country'. Furthermore, under Recital (141), 'as regards transfer of data, it is also appropriate to envisage that data collected and processed for the purpose of testing in real-world conditions should be transferred to third countries only where appropriate and applicable safeguards under Union law are implemented', reinforcing the data localisation principles established in the DGA and DA.

This is given legal effect through distinct yet complementary means: Article 31 of the DGA regulates international transfers of data, stating that all entities covered by the DGA 'shall take all reasonable technical, legal and organisational measures, including contractual arrangements, in order to prevent international transfer or governmental access to non-personal data held in the Union where such transfer or access would create a conflict with Union law'. The DA has a more expansive provision under Article 32(1), reiterating the position under Article 31 of the DGA, and then adding at Article 32(2) that any decision or judgement by national authorities or judicial bodies based outside the Union will only be recognised and enforceable if based on an international agreement such as a mutual agreement treaty, as a means of reinforcing the EU's control over data within its borders, or alternatively ensuring it is governed by international standards that are based on EU values. In this respect, Article 32 acts as a legal reassertion of the EU's data sovereignty.[130] Under Article 32(3), transfers outside of these strict parameters will be prevented unless criteria are met that establish that there is a request on the basis of a specific allegation of infringement of law, there is a review by a competent third-country court or tribunal, and that that court or tribunal takes into account the relevant legal interests of the provider of the data. EDIB is tasked with drawing up guidance on performing these assessments, once again establishing the Commission as a controlling entity in this context. With regard to the AI Act, Article 2(1)(a) makes clear that the legislation applies to all AI providers offering AI services in the EU regardless of their establishment in the EU or a third country, and that conformity assessments

---

[130] See Mariavittoria Catanzariti, *Disconnecting Sovereignty: How Data Fragmentation Reshapes the Law* (Springer International Publishing 2024) 112–116.

performed by third-country bodies will only be recognised under Article 39 when done in compliance with the requirements of notification bodies covered by Article 31. Under Article 60(4)(e) data may only be transferred outside of the EU in the context of system testing where appropriate and applicable safeguards under Union law are implemented.

An element of cyber-diplomacy, as well as hope in a regulatory Brussels effect for (non-personal) data and AI, is also identifiable in the EU's attempts to engage in regulatory export and the setting of global norms and standards aligned with EU values.[131] The Commission hoped that through its promotion of CEDs and 'its effective regulatory and policy framework',[132] it could encourage non-European firms to engage with the CEDs subject to them adopting European standards for data, while also actively promoting these standards throughout the world, using references to the 'adoption of rules modelled on the GDPR by Brazil and Kenya'.[133] One example of this approach can be seen in the Global Gateway EU-Africa investment package on digital transition, which includes a 'Team Europe Initiative on Data Governance in Africa', which includes EU support for developing data policy frameworks with the African Union Commission, Regional Economic Communities, and African Union Member States.[134] Similarly, the EU has concluded a Joint Declaration on a Digital Alliance with Latin America and the Caribbean, which covers topics such as data governance, data protection, and AI.[135] With regard to AI specifically, the EU intended to promote its rules as global standards working through international bodies to promote the European approach to AI regulation, working with bodies such as the OECD, UN, UNESCO, and standardisation bodies such as ISO.[136] It has also pursued bilateral dialogues with countries such as the US through the EU-US Trade and Technology Council in order to promote EU AI standards.[137] In the hope that the combination of robust rules *in* Europe, which are then exported as global standards *from* Europe, a variant of the Brussels Effect believed to have been effective in setting global personal data protection standards, can be achieved for AI,[138] which effectively interlinks its economic and security goals in the context of geostrategic competition.[139]

---

[131] European Commission, 'A European Strategy for Data' (n32) 23.
[132] Ibid.
[133] Ibid.
[134] European Commission, 'EU-Africa: Global Gateway Investment Package – Digital Transition' (2023) 4.
[135] European Commission, 'Joint Declaration on a Digital Alliance: European Union – Latin American and Caribbean' (2023) 1.
[136] European Commission, 'Annex to the Communication Fostering a European Approach to Artificial Intelligence' (2021) COM(2021) 205 34–35.
[137] Ibid 35–36.
[138] Cristiano Codagnone and Linda Weigl, 'Leading the Charge on Digital Regulation: The More, the Better, or Policy Bubble?' (2023) 2 *Digital Society* 4.
[139] Mügge (n72).

CONCLUSIONS

The concerns and strategically disadvantageous dependencies identified in Chapters 4 and 5, such as regarding technological systems in Chapter 4 and platform service providers in Chapter 5, are equally present in the control of data. As a 'critical digital resource' upon which further economic and technological innovations such as AI depend, control over and access to data is identified by the Commission as being essential to the EU's technological sovereignty, introducing the concept of data sovereignty into its discourse on technology regulation as a means of underscoring its vital nature for economic competitiveness and security. The reliance on cloud data servers and processing provided by large tech firms mirrored to an extent its reliance on large social media platforms and gatekeepers, and correspondingly the same concerns for loss of regulatory control. European strategic autonomy and the ability to choose its own rules and values were therefore hindered by the dependence upon technologies provided by states that may not necessarily respect those rules or share those values.

For the Geopolitical Commission, these dependencies were magnified by uncertainties regarding the economic and security implications of the race for AI; particularly given that the EU was at a strategic disadvantage with the US and China in the development of AI technologies such as foundational models, with an increased risk therefore of increasing dependence, and by extension vulnerability, through their reliance on both models and compute provided by external players. As with the fields of activity explored in Chapters 4 and 5, the Commission reasoned that the way to remedy this would be by using its position as a 'regulatory superpower' to regain control over these technologies by way of legislative interventions. Domestically, this entailed creating the optimal market conditions for investment in European technologies through a form of data industrial policy, facilitating the creation of CEDSs as ways of creating new data-driven services, and by extension, the data that could be useful for AI. It also required creating the conditions for businesses and consumers, as well as the public sector, to more easily switch cloud providers, as part of an attempt to encourage them to bring their data more effectively within Europe's territory, jurisdiction, and control. This data localisation policy is intended to achieve both economic and security goals and, in particular, limit the risks of sensitive non-personal data such as confidential industrial information from being accessed without authorisation by governments of third countries. In this respect, the combination of industrial policy internally, the promotion of data localisation, and the erection of barriers to data transfers out of the EU for non-personal data unless adequate protections were adopted by the other state combined to create a regulatory mercantilist approach in which data import and regulatory export are maximised, while data export and regulatory import are minimised. Through this approach, the EU could ensure a positive regulatory balance of trade.

The use of cyber-diplomacy in order to promote EU standards as global standards was combined with a strong belief in the Brussels Effect, and that by virtue of the EU's position as a regulatory superpower and the size of its market, adoption of the EU's rules and values for new technologies could be facilitated. Particularly in the context of AI, where the EU was an importer rather than an exporter, regulatory export was regarded as essential, ensuring that EU laws would apply regardless of where those models were devised and deployed, should those services be offered in Europe. By seeking a regulatory first-mover advantage and then working through international organisations such as the UN and ISO and regional partnerships such as the Global Gateway, the EU sought to ensure that in the adoption of new rules around data governance and AI system safety, the EU approach could be regarded as a default to which all nations should adapt. Through these means, EU standards and global standards would be one and the same.

With this chapter, the case studies explored in this book of the von der Leyen Commission's technology policies are complete. It has demonstrated the regulatory mercantilist approach to policy and lawmaking adopted by the Commission and the resulting proliferation of regulatory activity as a result. With Chapter 7, we will explore what the future holds for the von der Leyen II Commission. With a new Commission and Commission structure, in a world that is even more geopolitically fractured, unstable, and arguably belligerent than during the von der Leyen I Commission, can the Geopolitical Union still succeed in its ambitions to gain control over technology regulation?

PART III

The Future of the Geopolitical Union

7

The von der Leyen II Commission and the Future of the Geopolitical Union

We need to be lucid, and recognise that our Europe is mortal. It can die. It all depends on the choices we make, and those choices need to be made now.[1]

INTRODUCTION

Chapters 4–6 have focused on what the Commission *has* done in pursuit of its technological ambitions. This chapter is focused on what the Commission *plans* to do in its strengthening of the Geopolitical Union under the von der Leyen II Commission. If the period 2019–2024 was one of significant turbulence, with COVID-19 and the Russian invasion of Ukraine in particular having destabilising effects on Europe, 2025–2029 looks as of April 2025 to be even more chaotic. Geostrategy is likely to be typified by incredibly high levels of uncertainty, and traditional allies are no longer perceived as trustworthy or even particularly aligned with the EU's values. In order to understand how the Geopolitical Union may seek to regulate technology during Commission President von der Leyen's second term, and whether the approach of regulatory mercantilism will be maintained during this period, this chapter explores the new geopolitical context the Commission finds itself in and how this may lead to an expansion and reinforcement of regulatory mercantilism on the Union's part.

The chapter is structured as follows. The chapter outlines the new Commission structure in 'Von der Leyen II: Europe's Choice(s)', beginning with von der Leyen's announcement of her candidature, the political guidelines outlined as part of her election campaign, and the significant changes to the Commission structure and portfolios that demonstrate that the concept of technological sovereignty is being mainstreamed into Commission lawmaking. It highlights the publication of the Letta and Draghi Reports as a means of focusing EU economic strategy and

---

[1] President Emmanuel Macron, as cited by Hugh Schofield, 'Europe Risks Dying and Faces Big Decisions – Macron' (*BBC News*, 25 April 2024) <www.bbc.com/news/world-europe-68898887> accessed 7 April 2025.

how it has become even more interlinked with security policy in the setup of the Commission's activities. The next section, 'The Geopolitical Context', focuses on the current geopolitical context, and in particular the uncertainty brought by the re-election of US President Donald Trump. It considers the EU's 'cold' trade war with China, particularly around electric vehicles, and the increasingly 'hot' trade war that the US is pursuing not only with China but, at the time of writing, with the entire world. It highlights how the concerns that the US raises for Europe are not purely economic, or due to the bad behaviour of its large tech firms, but due to the explicit statements and actions undertaken by the US Administration that directly threaten Europe's stability, security, and territorial integrity. Due to these concerns, the EU's priorities are focusing even more on defence than in previous Commissions, as is explored in the next substantive section, 'Technology, Competitiveness, Security: A Compass for Commission Action', which outlines the strengthening of interdependence between the EU's economic and security policies, which are reinforced as being mutually reinforcing of the EU's democracy and sovereignty. It expands upon how these linked economic and security concerns, framed in terms of reducing dependencies and increasing strategic autonomy, are found in the key priorities and actions of the new Commission published between January and early April 2025. The final substantive section, 'The Future of the Geopolitical Union: Regulatory Mercantilism as the New Normal?' expands upon what this means for the Geopolitical Union and regulatory mercantilism as an approach to law and policymaking.

VON DER LEYEN II: EUROPE'S CHOICE(S)

It was apparent late in 2023 that President von der Leyen intended to pursue a second term as Commission President, with the launch of her campaign beginning in February 2024.[2] At a European Parliament Plenary, President von der Leyen argued for the need for Europe to strengthen its defence in a volatile geopolitical landscape, making a statement that is worth reproducing in full here:

> European sovereignty is about taking responsibility ourselves for what is vital, and even existential, for us. It is about our ability but also about our willingness to defend our interests and values ourselves. This is what Leaders agreed with the Versailles agenda just after the start of the [Ukraine] war to reduce our strategic dependencies in critical areas like energy, key technologies – you remember the semi-conductors –, economic capacities and of course defence.[3]

---

[2] Henry Foy and Guy Chazan, 'Ursula von Der Leyen Kick Offs Campaign for Second Term at Brussels' Helm' (*Financial Times*, 19 February 2024) <www.ft.com/content/6498da43-fd18-47ef-be3c-05d46ee51e5c> accessed 7 April 2025.

[3] Ursula von der Leyen, 'Speech by President von Der Leyen at the European Parliament Plenary on Strengthening European Defence in a Volatile Geopolitical Landscape – European Commission'

Throughout this speech, President von der Leyen frequently referred to the need for economic and security interests to be aligned, talking about spending more (and 'spending European'), boosting its industrial capacity, and focusing on technology innovation in order to support its security and defence aims. Insecurity, particularly geopolitically, was also foregrounded in the speech, with references to the unpredictability of other states and regions and the impetus for Europe to look to its own security interests. These interests were made clearer in the published political guidelines for a 2024–2029 Commission agenda published in July 2024, titled 'Europe's Choice'.[4] This choice was framed as a number of sub-choices: whether to be disunited and alone, or united in European values; to be dependent, or ambitious and sovereign; to ignore the scale of change and new realities, or to be clear-eyed about the threats and dangers faced by Europe; and whether to let extremists and appeasers prevail, or to ensure the EU's democracy remained strong.[5] The core ambitions underlying these choices were framed in a way that is clearly aligned with regulatory mercantilism, as 'Defence and security. Sustainable prosperity and competitiveness. Democracy and social fairness. Leading in the world and delivering in Europe'.[6]

Within these four priority areas, key actions related to technology were identified. On defence and security, this included increased spending on defence and the establishment of a European Defence Union, with an emphasis on cyber, hybrid, and space-related threats, a Single Market for Defence, and Internal Security Strategy, in which cyber and digital threats would be an area of focus.[7] On prosperity and competitiveness, the political guidelines highlighted the need to reduce strategic dependencies, referring to 'Putin's energy blackmail [and] China's monopoly on raw materials',[8] with measures to boost business investment and innovation, a Clean Industrial Deal with an emphasis on 'clean' technologies, boosting productivity through digital technologies and scaling up its efforts in fields such as AI and data, including with a proposal for a European Data Union Strategy, and reconsidering public procurement rules as they relate to vital technologies.[9] Technology regulation also featured in the section on democracy. Social media was identified as a risk to democratic systems, with the proposal for a European Democracy Shield akin to the European Cyber Shield discussed in Chapter 4, along with proposals to boost enforcement of the Digital Services Act and address

---

(*European Commission*, 28 February 2024) <https://enlargement.ec.europa.eu/news/speech-president-von-der-leyen-european-parliament-plenary-strengthening-european-defence-volatile-2024-02-28_en> accessed 7 April 2025.

[4] Ursula von der Leyen, 'Europe's Choice: Political Guidelines for the Next European Commission' (*European Commission*, 18 July 2024).
[5] Ibid 4.
[6] Ibid 5.
[7] Ibid 13–15.
[8] Ibid 6.
[9] Ibid 7–12.

AI-generated deepfakes.[10] Finally, as a global leader, President von der Leyen would seek to promote the Geopolitical Union, arguing that 'Europe needs to be more assertive in pursuing its strategic interests'.[11] This section of the guidelines revealed the increasing disillusion with the global system as discussed in Chapter 3, with von der Leyen describing the international system as being characterised by geostrategic rivalries and having moved from cooperation to competition.[12] This would entail strategic enlargement, on the basis that 'a larger and stronger Union gives us greater geopolitical weight and influence [...] it helps reduce our dependencies, enhances our resilience and strengthens our competitiveness'.[13] Of particular relevance was the proposal for a new economic foreign policy, explicitly framed in terms of the interdependence of geopolitics and geoeconomics and 'an increasingly thin line between economy and security',[14] particularly as it related to new technologies.[15] Global leadership in this field would entail 'derisking' and protecting the EU's technological and security concerns, reforming the international trading system, and engaging in diplomacy and outward investment through the Global Gateway programmes, with the EU leading in reshaping multilateralism, particularly around digital technologies.[16]

With the European Parliament elections in June 2024, both populist right and centrist elements of the Parliament were strengthened, resulting in a difficult balancing act for President von der Leyen to maintain while seeking support for her candidature.[17] Ultimately, however, President von der Leyen secured the support of most Member States (excluding Italy's Georgia Meloni and Hungary's Viktor Orbán),[18] and a majority in the European Parliament with the EPP, S&D, Renew, and the Greens supporting her candidature and the ECR voting against.[19] President von der Leyen immediately started her work with a restructuring of the European Commission in light of her new agenda. Internal Market Commissioner Thierry Breton, who had been steadfast in pursuing European strategic autonomy and pursuing US tech giants,[20] resigned in an acrimonious dispute with von der Leyen over

---

[10] Ibid 23.
[11] Ibid 25.
[12] Ibid.
[13] Ibid.
[14] Ibid 27.
[15] Ibid.
[16] Ibid 27–28.
[17] For discussion of this as it relates to the rise in 'populist right' political parties, see Mustafa Demir and Amelia Hadfield, 'The Challenge of the Populist Right in Democratic Europe in the 2024 European Parliamentary Elections' (2024) 48 *Fletcher Forum of World Affairs* 93.
[18] Euractiv with Reuters, 'Analysts: Meloni Put Domestic Concerns First in Rejecting von Der Leyen' (*Euractiv*, 22 July 2024) <www.euractiv.com/section/politics/news/analysts-meloni-put-domestic-concerns-first-in-rejecting-von-der-leyen/> accessed 7 April 2025.
[19] Gilsun Jeong, 'European Parliament Elections 2024 – A New Trend?' (2024) 15 *Political Insight* 22.
[20] Ana E Juncos and Sophie Vanhoonacker, 'The Ideational Power of Strategic Autonomy in EU Security and External Economic Policies' (2024) 62 *JCMS: Journal of Common Market Studies* 955.

governance in the Commission.²¹ Interestingly, traditional Commission positions such as 'Internal Market' and 'Competition' disappeared in this reshuffle, with activities undertaken under these portfolios dispersed between briefs, with a focus instead on topics such as 'Trade and Economic Security' under Maroš Šefčovič, 'Economy and Productivity' under Valdis Dombrovskis, an entirely new Commission portfolio for Defence and Space under Andrius Kubilius, and the somewhat interesting combination of 'Democracy, Justice, the Rule of Law and Consumer Protection' under Michael McGrath.

Of direct relevance for this chapter, a new Vice Presidency position was created for 'Tech Sovereignty, Security and Democracy', with Henna Virkkunen appointed to the role. This role is noteworthy for two reasons; the first is that while technological sovereignty was not explicitly mentioned in the political guidelines, the establishment of this Vice Presidency makes it clear that it is not a concept that ended with the first von der Leyen Commission but instead appears mainstreamed within Commission policymaking. The second reason is that the linking of technological sovereignty, security, and democracy within one role indicates the understanding of these areas as being mutually constitutive, reinforcing the regulatory mercantilist approach that the Commission appears to be adopting in its relation to technology governance. Indeed, in an outline of the role, it is stated that Commissioner Virkkunen will be tasked with promoting technological innovation around AI, data, and online platforms to ensure Europe's competitiveness and security while 'maintaining or attaining leadership in strategic digital technologies'.²² In the Mission Letter written to her as Vice-President Designate, von der Leyen outlined an expansive portfolio centred around technology in all areas: economic and industrial competitiveness, security and defence, and protecting Europe's democracy and exporting its norms and values.²³ A new Vice Presidency for 'Prosperity and Industrial Strategy' was assigned to Stéphane Séjourné, which concerns strategic investments in new technologies and maximising the EU's efforts in fields such as securing critical raw materials,²⁴ and one for 'Clean, Just and Competitive Transition', with the position assigned to Teresa Ribeira, which interestingly links environmental policy to competition but frames competition in terms of 'modernising the EU's competition policy to support European companies in innovating, competing, and leading

---

[21] Jorge Liboreiro, 'Breton Quits as EU Commissioner, Directly Blames von Der Leyen' (*euronews*, 16 September 2024) <www.euronews.com/my-europe/2024/09/16/breton-quits-as-eu-commissioner-blames-von-der-leyens-questionable-governance> accessed 7 April 2025.

[22] European Commission, 'Henna Virkkunen: Executive Vice President (2024–2029) Tech Sovereignty, Security and Democracy' (*European Commission*, 1 April 2025) <https://commission.europa.eu/about/organisation/college-commissioners/henna-virkkunen_en> accessed 7 April 2025.

[23] See generally Ursula von der Leyen, 'Mission Letter to Henna Virkkunen, Executive Vice-President-Designate for Tech Sovereignty, Security and Democracy' (*European Commission*, 2024) 5–9.

[24] European Commission, 'Stéphane Séjourné: Executive Vice President (2024–2029) Prosperity and Industrial Strategy' (*European Commission*, 11 December 2024) <https://commission.europa.eu/about/organisation/college-commissioners/stephane-sejourne_en> accessed 7 April 2025.

worldwide'.²⁵ Finally, the position of High Representative for Foreign Affairs and Security Policy was awarded to former Estonian Prime Minister Kaja Kallas, a 'hawk' on Russia and vocal in support for Ukraine after the Russian invasion.²⁶ In this capacity, High Representative Kallas is predominantly responsible for the 'regulatory export' dimension of the EU's technology policies; building a European Defence Union reacting to hybrid and cyber threats, and tasked with giving effect to the new foreign economic policy as well as 'responding to concerns of partners impacted by European legislation'.²⁷

Perhaps influential upon the Commission's thinking on technology in the development of its specific policy actions were two reports produced in 2024, one by former Prime Minister of Italy Enrico Letta in April,²⁸ and the other by Matteo Draghi, who served both as Italian Prime Minister and as President of the European Central Bank, published in September.²⁹ Both reports are highly significant and significantly dense works on the state of the European economy, and it is not possible to summarise the entirety of their contents here. Very briefly, the Letta Report emphasis is on the effectiveness of the single market as a mechanism for ensuring Europe's prosperity and competitiveness, albeit with an emphasis on bringing down barriers that may hinder the ability of European companies to be adaptable to new technologies and situations. By way of comparison, while also focusing on the value of the single market, the Draghi Report is more ambitious and proposes a common fiscal policy, emphasising the need for increased capital investment, closing the innovation gap with China and the US, decarbonising the economy, and increasing Europe's security through reducing its dependencies. Regarding technology, the key focus of this book, the Reports make specific arguments. The Letta Report discussed a potential Fifth Freedom of research, innovation, and education, stating that 'it's vital to stimulate innovation and foster the development of leading industrial ecosystems capable of producing entities of global importance within Europe. Establishing a strong European technological infrastructure poses a strategic challenge, necessitating a shift in governance'.³⁰ Economy and security are explicitly linked in this argument, with industrial policy being considered an effective means of producing European technological corporations, without which Europe will be

---

²⁵ European Commission, 'Teresa Ribera: Executive Vice President (2024–2029) Clean, Just and Competitive Transition' (*European Commission*, 11 March 2025) <https://commission.europa.eu/about/organisation/college-commissioners/teresa-ribera_en> accessed 7 April 2025.
²⁶ Kaja Kallas, 'No Peace on Putin's Terms' (2022) *Foreign Affairs* <www.foreignaffairs.com/russia/no-peace-putin-terms-kaja-kallas> accessed 7 April 2025; see also Sandra Hagelin and Catherine Gibson, 'Renegotiating Estonia's Marginality in the Imagined Geography of Europe: Kaja Kallas' Tweets about Russia's War in Ukraine' (2024) *Territory, Politics, Governance* 1–18.
²⁷ European Commission, 'Kaja Kallas: High Representative/Vice President (2024–2029) Foreign Affairs and Security Policy' (*European Commission*, 19 March 2025) <https://commission.europa.eu/about/organisation/college-commissioners/kaja-kallas_en> accessed 7 April 2025.
²⁸ Enrico Letta, 'Much More than a Market: Speed, Security, Solidarity' (2024).
²⁹ Mario Draghi, 'The Future of European Competitiveness' (2024).
³⁰ Letta (n28) 20.

'susceptible to cybersecurity threats, misinformation campaigns, and potential military confrontations'.[31] The Draghi Report was more cautious, stating that in many areas of technological innovation, Europe was facing widening gaps in its competitiveness, including in cloud computing. Nevertheless, the Draghi Report maintained that Europe should not give up on developing its domestic technology sector, arguing that it was important 'that EU companies maintain a foothold in areas where technological sovereignty is required, such as security […] a weak tech sector will hinder innovation [… and that] AI, particularly generative AI is an evolving technology in which EU companies still have an opportunity to carve out a leading position'.[32] However, the Draghi Report was perhaps more committed to, or at the very least confident in, the liberal international economic order than the Commission. While sovereignty was important, Mario Draghi argued that while having some 'sovereign cloud' projects was important, it was just as important to 'negotiate a low barrier "digital transatlantic marketplace", guaranteeing supply chain security and trade opportunities for EU and US tech companies on fair and equal conditions'.[33] Should Kamala Harris have won the US election in November 2024, such a move may not have been outside of the realm of possibility. However, if the geopolitical climate was febrile before November, the outcome of the US election has made geopolitics more central to the EU's preoccupations than perhaps ever before.

THE GEOPOLITICAL CONTEXT: EUROPE CAUGHT BETWEEN CHINESE INDUSTRY AND US INIMICALITY

In the run-up to the start of the von der Leyen II Commission in December 2024, it was clear that the geopolitical situation had considerably worsened. The Russian war on Ukraine was continuing with little in the way of respite, with increasing impacts upon the EU's energy security, as well as the cost of that energy given a dependence upon Russian gas.[34] This has not only had implications for energy for heating for civilian populations but has also significantly increased industrial output costs, making European manufacturing output less competitive internationally.[35] This hit Germany particularly hard, with consequences for the automobile industry, one of Germany's

---

[31] Ibid.
[32] Draghi (n29) 24.
[33] Ibid 34.
[34] An issue that has had security implications for some time: see Tom Casier, 'The Rise of Energy to the Top of the EU-Russia Agenda: From Interdependence to Dependence?' (2011) 16 *Geopolitics* 536; with the beginning of the conflict, this has become a crisis quite quickly for the EU, which has not reduced its dependency on Russian natural gas as much as some would hope, as discussed in Francesco Sassi, 'The (Un)Intended Consequences of Power: The Global Implications of EU LNG Strategy to Reach Independence from Russian Gas' (2025) 198 *Energy Policy* 114494.
[35] Miguel Á Martínez-García, Carmen Ramos-Carvajal and Ángeles Cámara, 'Consequences of the Energy Measures Derived from the War in Ukraine on the Level of Prices of EU Countries' (2023) 86 *Resources Policy* 104114.

most important industrial sectors. A significant decrease in exports to Russia,[36] along with a decrease in sales of German cars in China combined with China's emergence as a systemic competitor in the automobile sector for electric vehicles,[37] has resulted in a perceived competitiveness crisis in Germany, commonly seen as the engine of European industry.[38] This crisis, coupled with the inability of Chancellor Scholz to hold together the governing coalition, resulted in the first early election in twenty years in Germany, placing Friedrich Merz of the CDU in line to be the next Chancellor.[39]

For the EU, however, the struggles of the German automobile sector were an aspect of a broader geostrategic concern around the rise of Chinese car manufacturers, who were becoming the largest electric car manufacturers in terms of export volume in the world.[40] In the 2023 State of the Union, President von der Leyen highlighted the geopolitical concerns regarding Chinese battery manufacture and electric vehicle production, arguing that 'the future of our clean tech industry has to be made in Europe'.[41] However, according to this speech, while electric vehicles were critical for Europe and its economic potential, 'global markets are now flooded with cheaper Chinese electric cars and their price is kept artificially low by huge state subsidies'.[42] That the Chinese state is heavily influential in the development of the electric vehicle sector is generally accepted; the majority of these direct subsidies, including trade-in incentives for Chinese citizens to replace their combustion-engine vehicles with electric ones, were significantly reduced in 2016, with many ending by 2022.[43] However, indirect subsidies around production, including around access to critical raw materials and battery supply, have continued, resulting in the Commission initiating an investigation into China's subsidies for battery electric vehicles (BEVs) in October 2023 and resulting in a finding that the Chinese government provides for 'unfair subsidization which is causing threat of economic injury to EU producers of BEVs'.[44] This resulted in the use of a trade

---

[36] For more on this, see Wolfgang Münchau, *Kaput: The End of the German Miracle* (Swift Press 2024) 108–110.
[37] Ibid 136–140.
[38] Piotr Arak, 'Germany's Economy Has Gone from Engine to Anchor. Here's What the next Chancellor Faces' (*Atlantic Council*, 19 February 2025) <www.atlanticcouncil.org/blogs/new-atlanticist/germanys-economy-has-gone-from-engine-to-anchor/> accessed 8 April 2025.
[39] Liana Fix and Peter Sparding, 'In Germany, the Center Can Hold' (*Foreign Affairs*, 2025) <www.foreignaffairs.com/germany/germany-center-can-hold> accessed 8 April 2025.
[40] Lorenzo Bencivelli and others, 'The Rise of the Electric Vehicle in China and Its Impact in the EU' (Banco de España, 2024) Economic Bulletin 2024/Q4.
[41] Ursula von der Leyen, '2023 State of the Union Address by President von Der Leyen: Answering the Call of History' (2023) SPEECH/23/4426 3.
[42] Ibid 4.
[43] Wei Li, Yue Zou and Caihua Zhu, 'The Electric Vehicle Revolution: A New Track for Industrial Competition among Major Countries' (2024) 14 *Journal of WTO and China* 3.
[44] European Commission, 'Definitive Duties on BEV Imports from China' (*European Commission*, 29 October 2024) <https://ec.europa.eu/commission/presscorner/detail/en/ip_24_5589> accessed 8 April 2025.

defence instrument in the form of an Implementing Regulation applying tariffs to Chinese vehicle producers, including 17 per cent on BYD Group, 18.8 per cent on Geely Group, and 35.3 per cent on SAIC Group.[45] Justification for the measures included findings by the Commission that BEVs produced in China benefited from preferential state financing including through state-owned financial institutions,[46] grant programmes,[47] and governmental provision of goods and services for less than adequate remuneration.[48] China's response to the imposition of these tariffs has been argued to have strengthened the Commission's belief that 'de-risking' by reducing dependence on China for both raw materials and advanced technologies is essential.[49]

However, if geopolitical relations with China were strained by the end of 2024, relations with the US after the re-election of President Donald Trump have increasingly become torn altogether, in ways that impact the EU's interdependent economic and security concerns. During the election campaign, President Trump made it clear that he would take a much more assertive line on trade, particularly around tariffs, with the EU being a prime target for increased rates alongside China.[50] Furthermore, President Trump repeatedly criticised NATO, the EU, and Ukraine for taking advantage of the US's security guarantees,[51] with his Vice President JD Vance repeating arguments about President Zelenskyy's actions that have been largely dismissed as false.[52] The initial actions of the Trump Administration in January 2025 immediately began to cause concern for Europe. In a fractious speech given at the World Economic Forum at Davos, President Trump stated that NATO spending should be increased to 5 per cent of GDP for all nations, arguing that anything less was 'unfair to the United States. But many, many things have been unfair for many years to the United States'.[53] Furthermore, he singled out the EU as acting

---

[45] Commission Implementing Regulation 2024/2754 of 29 October 2024 imposing a definitive countervailing duty on imports of new battery electric vehicles designed for the transport of persons originating in the People's Republic of China, Article 1(2)
[46] Ibid, Section 3.5.
[47] Ibid, Section 3.6.
[48] Ibid, Section 3.7.
[49] Alicia García-Herrero, 'European Union Duties on Electric Vehicles Point to New Era of EU-China Relations' (*Bruegel*, 9 October 2024) <www.bruegel.org/first-glance/european-union-duties-electric-vehicles-point-new-era-eu-china-relations> accessed 9 April 2025.
[50] Camille Gijs, 'EU's Trade War Nightmare Gets Real as Trump Triumphs' (*POLITICO*, 6 November 2024) <www.politico.eu/article/eu-trade-war-donald-trump-elections-triumphs-board-tariffs-transatlantic-relations/> accessed 9 April 2025.
[51] Ian Bond and others, 'Can Europe Navigate Trump 2?' (Centre for European Reform, 2024) CER Insight 1–3.
[52] Veronika Melkozerova, 'Fact-Checking J.D. Vance's Statements on Ukraine' (*POLITICO*, 16 July 2024) <www.politico.eu/article/jd-vance-europe-russia-ukraine-donald-trump-kyiv-vp-pick-policy-us-elections-ohio-aid-war/> accessed 9 April 2025.
[53] The White House, 'Remarks by President Trump at the World Economic Forum' (*The White House*, 23 January 2025) <www.whitehouse.gov/remarks/2025/01/remarks-by-president-trump-at-the-world-economic-forum/> accessed 9 April 2025.

in ways detrimental to the US's economic interests, claiming that 'the EU treats us very, very unfairly, very badly. They have a large tax that we know about and – a VAT tax – and it's a very substantial one. They don't take our far – essentially, don't take our farm products and they don't take our cars. Yet, they send cars to us by the millions.'[54] This speech was a sign of geopolitical trouble to come, rather than empty rhetoric. February 2025 brought a meeting at the White House that can only be described as disastrous; accusing Zelenskyy of being ungrateful for US support, both the President and Vice President signalled an end to support for Ukraine while seeking an agreement for access to Ukrainian critical natural resources in a deal described by Ukrainian sources as akin to extortion.[55] Wolfgang Ischinger, former German Ambassador to the United States and former Chair of the Munich Security Conference, described the meeting as having 'called into question some of the bedrock assumptions that have undergirded the transatlantic relationship since World War II'.[56] He continued that 'In European Capitals, panic has set in. Some policymakers and analysts are speaking of the end of NATO, or the end of the West'.[57] While US military aid to Ukraine resumed after talks that took place in Saudi Arabia in March,[58] this did little to allay concerns in Europe about the capriciousness of US support and engagement with Europe.

These concerns have been exacerbated by repeated statements by President Trump concerning the future of Greenland and assertions that the US will claim the island as US territory by whatever means necessary due to significant economic and security concerns in the Atlantic, including control of mineral resources.[59] The President's rhetoric around Greenland's sovereignty and Denmark's territorial integrity has sparked an unusually united response from the EU and its Member States, with President von der Leyen stating that 'To all the people of Greenland – and of Denmark as a whole – I want to be clear that Europe will always stand for sovereignty and territorial integrity'.[60] Threats to the territorial integrity of Europe *from* the United States, rather than *responded to* by the United States, were unprecedented in Europe's recent history. This has resulted in a subtle shift in Commission discourse

---

[54] Ibid.
[55] Andrew Bogrand, 'Mineral Diplomacy or Modern-Day Extortion in Ukraine?' (*The Kyiv Independent*, 7 April 2025) <https://kyivindependent.com/mineral-diplomacy-or-modern-day-extortion-in-ukraine-2/> accessed 9 April 2025.
[56] Wolfgang Ischinger, 'Europe's Moment of Truth' (*Foreign Affairs*, 2025) <www.foreignaffairs.com/ukraine/volodymyr-zelensky-trump-europes-moment-truth> accessed 9 April 2025.
[57] Ibid.
[58] Joe Stanley-Smith, Seb Starcevic and Eli Stokols, 'US Resumes Military Aid to Ukraine after Saudi Ceasefire Talks' (*POLITICO*, 11 March 2025) <www.politico.eu/article/us-ukraine-russia-saudi-ceasefire-talks-after-talks-in-jeddah/> accessed 9 April 2025.
[59] Michelle Del Rey, 'JD Vance Admits That He Wasn't Sure Why Trump Wanted Greenland' (*The Independent*, 29 March 2025) <www.independent.co.uk/news/world/americas/us-politics/jd-vance-greenland-b2723850.html> accessed 9 April 2025.
[60] Ursula von der Leyen, 'Speech by President von Der Leyen on European Defence at the Royal Danish Military Academy' (*European Commission*, 2025) 1.

concerning the US that has implicitly (rather than explicitly) framed the US as a potential security threat for the US, rather than a security ally (while admittedly being an economic rival). However, at the time of writing, this threat has increased and permeated the EU's economic security concerns with the application of potentially ruinous blanket tariffs by the US on the EU of 20 per cent,[61] and the ratcheting up of tariffs against China in a 'tit-for-tat' battle that as of 9 April 2025 stand at 104 per cent with China responding with blanket tariffs on US goods of 84 per cent.[62] The EU has now responded to US tariffs with strategically placed tariffs of 10–25 per cent on goods such as tobacco, steel, aluminium, and poultry.[63] At the time of writing, it remains to be seen whether we will see further tariff increases for both the EU and China as a result of the expanding trade war between the US and its geopolitical rivals.

Finally, the role of 'Big Tech' needs to also be considered in terms of the current geopolitical challenges facing the EU. With the takeover of Twitter by Elon Musk and its reconstruction as X, Commissioner Thierry Breton raised concerns over Musk's conduct in a Statement of Objections regarding potential breaches of the Digital Service Act in December 2023.[64] A preliminary investigation by the Commission determined that there had been breaches of the Act, including misleading users under Article 25, the transparency of advertising under Article 39, and failures to allow access to data for researchers investigating systemic risks under Article 40(12),[65] and at the time of writing, the Commission is still weighing up the possibility of issuing fines and ordering changes to the structure of the platform.[66] This has been complicated by Musk's pseudo-governmental role in the US Administration due to his involvement with the Department of Government Efficiency (DOGE),[67] with an alignment of public and private power that has been

---

[61] Described by the Commission President as 'a major blow to the world economy'; Ursula von der Leyen, 'Statement by President von Der Leyen on the Announcement of Universal Tariffs by the US' (*European Commission – European Commission*, 3 April 2025) <https://ec.europa.eu/commission/presscorner/detail/en/statement_25_964> accessed 9 April 2025.

[62] Ian Aikman, 'Trump's Top Tariffs for "Worst Offenders" Take Effect' (*BBC News*, 9 April 2025) <www.bbc.com/news/articles/cgkgg1krg63o> accessed 9 April 2025.

[63] Thomas Moller-Nielsen, 'EU Greenlights €22 Billion Retaliatory Tariffs against US' (*Euractiv*, 9 April 2025) <www.euractiv.com/section/economy-jobs/news/eu-greenlights-e22-billion-retaliatory-tariffs-against-us/> accessed 9 April 2025.

[64] European Commission, 'Commission Opens Formal Proceedings against X under the DSA' (*European Commission*, 18 December 2023) <https://ec.europa.eu/commission/presscorner/detail/en/ip_23_6709> accessed 10 April 2025.

[65] European Commission, 'Commission Sends Preliminary Findings to X for Breach of DSA' (*European Commission*, 12 July 2024) <https://ec.europa.eu/commission/presscorner/detail/en/ip_24_3761> accessed 10 April 2025.

[66] Adam Satariano, 'E.U. Prepares Major Penalties Against Elon Musk's X' (*The New York Times*, 3 April 2025) <www.nytimes.com/2025/04/03/technology/eu-penalties-x-elon-musk.html> accessed 10 April 2025.

[67] As discussed in Ana Faguy and James FitzGerald, 'What Is the Department of Government Efficiency?' (*BBC News*, 13 November 2024) <www.bbc.com/news/articles/c93qwn8poloo> accessed 9 January 2025; Musk holds something of a 'Schrödinger's position' as both head and not head of DOGE, with statements both confirming and denying his leadership role.

active in shaping the current US administration.[68] Similarly, as head of Meta, Mark Zuckerberg has rowed back on commitments to the EU regarding system safety of the Facebook platform, appointing US Republican Joel Kaplan as Meta's new chief of global affairs at the Oversight Board, replacing former UK MP Nick Clegg,[69] and appointing long-term Trump supporter Dana White (owner of UFC) to Meta's Board of Directors.[70] As part of this pivot away from European regulation and to US norms, Zuckerberg announced both a downsizing of its content moderation teams, revisions to its community guidelines around user safety and the intention to ensure 'more speech, fewer mistakes', including around politically sensitive topics, allowing for more political targeting[71] in a way that may breach its obligations under the Digital Services Act and Political Advertising Regulation.[72] With this pivot, both Musk and Zuckerberg have publicly argued for non-compliance with the Digital Services Act, and their intention to 'fight back' against European 'censorship', comments that have been responded to approvingly by right-wing parties in Europe.[73] As such, reconfigurations of hybrid power in the US, with the merging of business and state interests, and the ability of the EU to exert influence over businesses deemed non-compliant with European values appear to have been considerably weakened.

TECHNOLOGY, COMPETITIVENESS, SECURITY: A COMPASS FOR COMMISSION ACTION

Regulatory mercantilism has not waned with the von der Leyen II Commission, but instead it has been reinforced by geostrategic dependencies. The Competitiveness Compass Communication published in January 2025[74] was stark in its recognition of the geopolitical challenges facing the EU. Acknowledging the EU's economic strengths, the Competitiveness Compass nevertheless argued that the EU needed to act quickly in order to guarantee its economic competitiveness and future prosperity, identifying the failure to catch up with US advanced technological innovation as a major challenge, compounded by China overtaking the US in certain technological fields.[75] It continued with the pronouncement that:

---

[68] Adam Tooze, 'Elon Musk's First Principles' (*Foreign Policy*, 23 March 2025) <https://foreignpolicy.com/2025/03/25/elon-musk-trump-doge-physics-principles/> accessed 10 April 2025.
[69] Cecilia Kang, 'Who Is Joel Kaplan, Meta's New Global Policy Chief?' (*The New York Times*, 7 January 2025) <www.nytimes.com/2025/01/07/business/joel-kaplan-meta.html> accessed 9 January 2025.
[70] João da Silva, 'UFC Boss Dana White and Two Others to Join Meta Board' (*BBC News*, 7 January 2025) <www.bbc.com/news/articles/c627p8leww10> accessed 9 January 2025.
[71] Joel Kaplan, 'More Speech and Fewer Mistakes' (*Meta*, 7 January 2025) <https://about.fb.com/news/2025/01/meta-more-speech-fewer-mistakes/> accessed 9 January 2025.
[72] Discussed in Chapter 5.
[73] See Pieter Haeck, 'Musk, Meta Fuel Far-Right Attack against EU Tech "Censorship"' (*POLITICO*, 10 January 2025) <www.politico.eu/article/elon-musk-x-mark-zuckerberg-meta-fuel-far-right-attack-against-eu-tech-censorship/> accessed 10 April 2025.
[74] European Commission, 'A Competitiveness Compass for the EU' (2025) COM(2025) 30.
[75] Ibid 1.

What is at stake for Europe is not just economic growth, but the future of its model. If Europe does not increase its productivity, it risks to be stuck on a low growth path [...] Europe faces a world of great power rivalry, competition for technological supremacy, and a scramble for control over resources. In this world, Europe's competitiveness and what Europe stands for are inseparable. Our freedom, security and autonomy will depend more than ever on our ability to innovate, compete and grow.[76]

Perhaps more than any other statement made by the Commission since 2019, this paragraph is reflective of an approach to state-market relations most akin to the driving motivation of 'power and plenty' identified in Chapter 1 as central to mercantilist thought. Europe's external dependencies are considered vulnerabilities, and its competition with other nations in the context of great power politics means that the securing of technological advantage and economic prosperity is key to its continued survival and the survival of its values. A regulatory mercantilist approach to policy is clear with the identification of the three 'flagship' measures identified as central to Commission action: closing the innovation gap; decarbonisation and competitiveness; and reducing excessive dependencies and increasing security'.[77]

The first flagship measure around closing the innovation gap entails measures intended to promote an innovation-intensive industrial policy in Europe, aimed at facilitating greater investment including through venture capital, and the introduction of a European Innovation Act promoting access to European research and technology infrastructures as a means of promoting further private sector innovation.[78] In another set of measures characteristic of the 'removing barriers internally while providing for greater external security' approach of regulatory mercantilism, the Commission proposes measures to remove barriers to the development of innovative technologies through acts of simplifying regulatory environments (which some observers have referred to as being tantamount to deregulation).[79] These efforts, the Commission reasons, 'will enhance technological sovereignty and competitiveness'[80] and propose an EU Cloud and AI Development Act that will incentivise the establishment of 'AI Gigafactories', complemented by a Data Union Strategy, Quantum Strategy, and Quantum Act.[81] The focus on technology moves beyond the purely digital to include proposals for new regulatory initiatives to boost innovation

---

[76] Ibid 1.
[77] Ibid 3.
[78] Ibid 4.
[79] See, for example, Nikolaus J Kurmayer, 'EU Countries Embrace New Deregulation Agenda in Spirit and Word' (*Euractiv*, 12 March 2025) <www.euractiv.com/section/eet/news/eu-countries-embrace-new-deregulation-agenda-in-spirit-and-word/> accessed 10 April 2025; Corporate Europe Observatory, 'Deregulation Watch' (*Corporate Europe Observatory*, 28 March 2025) <https://corporateeurope.org/en/2025/03/deregulation-watch> accessed 10 April 2025.
[80] European Commission, 'A Competitiveness Compass for the EU' (n74) 5.
[81] Ibid 5–6.

and investment including a Biotechnology Act, Advanced Materials Act, Space Act, and Digital Networks Act.[82]

The second flagship measure focuses on policies making this technological innovation easier to achieve, including the adoption of a Clean Industrial Deal 'aimed securing the EU as an attractive location for manufacturing, including for energy intensive industries, and promoting clean tech and new circular business models, in order to meet its agreed decarbonisation objectives'.[83] This flagship introduces measures to reduce the cost of energy supply for households and industries under an Affordable Energy Action Plan,[84] with a focus on electric vehicles and 'greening' transport through an industrial action plan for the automotive sector complemented by a Sustainable Transport Investment Plan, all intended to improve the competitiveness of the EU through providing confidence in affordable, renewable energy and reducing dependency on externally sourced natural resources to fuel the European economy.[85] The final flagship area also reinforces a regulatory mercantilist approach, starting with the statement that 'In a global economic system fractured by geopolitical competition and trade tensions, the EU must integrate more tightly security and open strategic autonomy considerations in its economic policies'.[86] In other words, there is an explicit recognition that security and economy go hand-in-hand, rather than being the source of potential trade-offs, and the actions proposed under this measure reinforce this position. Trade policy is explicitly framed as being built around reducing critical dependencies, diversifying trade routes and sources (particularly for critical natural resources), with proposals for deepening relations with countries through the Global Gateway programme and the conclusion of agreements with Mercosur and Mexico, and expanding its Digital Trade Agreements with countries such as Korea.[87] Under the heading of 'unfair competition and levelling the playing field', the Commission expands on plans to enhance the use of trade defence instruments, modernise the WTO, and promote a system of coordination between Member States for the promotion of domestic production, stockpiling, and diversification for critical resources such as raw materials, as well as medicines under a Critical Medicines Act.[88]

Interestingly, and in line with mercantilist thinking, the Commission proposes a reform of public procurement to introduce a policy of 'European preference in public procurement for strategic sectors and technologies [...] reinforcing technological security and domestic supply chains'.[89] Furthermore, the Commission seeks

[82] Ibid 6–8.
[83] Ibid 8.
[84] Ibid 9.
[85] Ibid 10–11.
[86] Ibid 12.
[87] Ibid 12–14.
[88] Ibid 14.
[89] Ibid 14–15.

to establish a defence industrial policy, with research and innovation in weapons and security systems, with the defence sector as 'a driver of innovation for the entire economy'.[90] A White Paper on the Future of European Defence is proposed as a way of outlining how the EU can develop an integrated defence-oriented industrial capacity with a Single Market for defence,[91] a Preparedness Strategy on protecting the European economy and citizens,[92] and an Internal Security Strategy as a means of ensuring that security is integrated into EU legislation and policies by design with an emphasis on hybrid threats and the risk of cyberattacks.[93] Ultimately, the Competitiveness Compass is demonstrative of a perception on the part of the Commission that technology, competitiveness, and security are intimately connected, and that joined-up policy bridging these interconnected fields is essential for the EU's continued survival.

These themes occur throughout the policy documents produced by the Commission since the publication of the Competitiveness Compass. The Preparedness Strategy[94] published in March 2025 is framed in terms of risks and growing uncertainties, referencing the Russian invasion of Ukraine, rising geopolitical tensions, state-sponsored hybrid and cyberattacks, and foreign information manipulation and interference.[95] The Strategy highlights a need to ensure resilience, which is categorised as protecting democratic functioning, ensuring economic and financial resilience through ensuring the integrity of the internal market, protecting the environment and ensuring sustainable use of natural resources, and strengthening strategic autonomy and reducing external dependencies, while reinforcing industrial competitiveness and technological leadership.[96] Similarly, the Joint White Paper on Defence Readiness[97] is perhaps obviously framed in terms of geopolitical risk, particularly in the context of Russia's invasion, but also links this concept of defence readiness to the economic realm, arguing that 'transnational challenges such as rapid technological change, migration and climate change could put immense stress on our political and economic system. Authoritarian states like China increasingly seek to assert their authority and control in our economy and society. Traditional allies and partners, such as the United States, are also changing their focus away from Europe'.[98] The White Paper frames its discussion of conflicts and tensions with other regions as intersections between economic and traditional

---

[90] Ibid 15.
[91] Ibid.
[92] Ibid.
[93] Ibid 15–16.
[94] European Commission and High Representative of the Union for Foreign Affairs and Security Policy, 'European Preparedness Union Strategy' (2025) JOIN(2025) 130.
[95] Ibid 1.
[96] Ibid 6.
[97] European Commission and High Representative of the Union for Foreign Affairs and Security Policy, 'Joint White Paper for European Defence Readiness 2030' (2025) JOIN(2025) 120.
[98] Ibid 2.

security concerns, concluding this assessment by stating that 'Geopolitical rivalries have not only led to a new arms race but have also provoked a global technology race',[99] and identifies both economic competition *and* military use as the security threats the EU is presented with, necessitating a defence industrial policy to promote innovation in new defence technologies while seeking to reduce dependence on externally sourced technologies and resources.[100] Even ProtectEU, the Internal Security Strategy[101] published in April 2025, is framed in terms of the *external* geopolitical risks facing the EU.[102] As with the Competitiveness Compass, the approach to tackling internal security threats (that are discussed in terms of arising from external geopolitical tensions) is based on the combination of a whole-of-society approach ensuring public and private sector coordination, the mainstreaming of security in all EU legislative and policy actions, investing in the EU's industries to ensure competitiveness in the provision of security, and assisting in the guarantee of strategic autonomy.[103]

Even as the security-focused policy documents have an economic dimension running through them, the more 'economy'-oriented documents have a corresponding security dimension serving as a rationale for action. At the time of writing, the EU's Data Union Strategy has not yet been published, being expected in the third quarter of 2025, nor have the Quantum Strategy, EU Cloud and AI Development Act, or Quantum Act. However, April 2025 saw the publication of the AI Continent Action Plan.[104] This Action Plan focuses on economic activities aimed at facilitating the development of Europe-based AI production, albeit with a strong security focus. As the Action Plan states:

> The EU lags behind the US and China in terms of available data centre capacity, relying on infrastructure installed in and controlled by other regions of the world, that EU users access via the cloud. While access to innovative and affordable cloud services is vital for EU competitiveness, an excessive dependence on non-EU infrastructure may bring economic security risks and is a concern for European industry, key economic sectors and public administrations. To adequately serve the AI and general computing needs of businesses and public administrations across the entire EU, and to ensure competitiveness and sovereignty, it is essential for the EU to increase its current cloud and data centre capacity in a geographically balanced manner.[105]

While this is a somewhat lengthy extract, it is an important one. It demonstrates that while economic competitiveness drives the EU's actions in this sphere of activity,

---

[99] Ibid 4.
[100] Ibid 4–5.
[101] European Commission, 'ProtectEU: A European Internal Security Strategy' (2025) COM(2025) 148.
[102] Ibid 1.
[103] Ibid 2.
[104] European Commission, 'AI Continent Action Plan' (2025) COM(2025) 165.
[105] Ibid 9.

it is a drive for competitiveness motivated by a sense of vulnerability. Strategic autonomy is hindered as the EU's ability to act is hindered by its dependence on foreign-owned and controlled technologies, with significant impacts upon its security. Technological sovereignty, increasingly linked to the EU's sovereignty more generally, can only be maintained through investments aimed at building domestic capacity in these technologies, thereby increasing control and guaranteeing security. The Cloud and AI Development Act is framed explicitly in these terms, with the AI Continent Action Plan arguing that its speedy adoption will incentivise large investments in cloud capacity, essential to facilitating highly secure EU-based AI applications.[106] Of particular relevance is the conclusion to the Action Plan, where it is stated that there is an intention on the part of the Commission to published, in the second quarter of 2025, a Strategy for Digital Sovereignty, Security and Democracy, intimately linked to the boosting of European technological industries while promoting external partnerships aligned with EU values.[107] The approach the Geopolitical Commission has taken to the advancement of its goals around technology would therefore not appear to be waning with the von der Leyen II Commission; rather, they are being reinforced.

THE FUTURE OF THE GEOPOLITICAL UNION: REGULATORY MERCANTILISM AS THE NEW NORMAL?

Some reflection on how the EU appears to be operationalising these ambitions can help us to better understand the future of the Geopolitical Union and the approach that may characterise law and policymaking for the remainder of von der Leyen's second term as Commission President. Given the interweaving of economic, security, and democracy-related rationales for action, an approach aligned with regulatory mercantilism is likely to remain for the foreseeable future. If we focus on the dimensions of increased regulatory control, the facilitation of state-making and industrial policy internally, and the maximisation of regulatory export as dimensions of a regulatory mercantilist approach, it is possible to identify how the EU's measures are described in its recent policy outputs. In particular, the expansion of this logic of regulation into the realm of defence represents an expansion rather than a contraction of the approach.

On regulation, the Competitiveness Compass is interesting in its approach to the role of regulation in the EU. In the section of the Communication that followed the actions outlined earlier, the Commission outlines its approach, in which regulation is intended to ensure Europe's competitiveness and must be simplified in pursuit of this goal, arguing that excessive regulatory burden is

---

[106] Ibid 10.
[107] Ibid 1, 23–24.

hindering innovation.[108] The emphasis is placed on reducing administrative and reporting burdens on European firms, combined with an approach focused on full harmonisation and enforcement in the Single Market as a means of avoiding fragmentation, indicating a stronger role for the Commission in these activities.[109] This is complemented by a focus on removing barriers to the functioning of the internal market through the adoption of a Horizontal Single Market Strategy that will 'modernise the governance framework, removing intra-EU barriers and preventing the creation of new ones'.[110] As of yet, this Strategy has not yet been published. Nevertheless, in terms of regulation, the commitments identified in the Competitiveness Council are reflective of an approach that aims to remove barriers to the functioning of the market through establishing unified and standard approaches to rulemaking and enforcement that provide for a singular approach akin to the traditional mercantilist approaches of removing the byelaws and local ordinances that hindered trade between localities in France and the German city-states. To provide some evidence for this in the absence of the defined strategy, it is useful to turn to the Mission Letters sent by the Commission President to relevant Commissioners, such as the previously discussed Stéphane Séjourné, Vice-President for Prosperity and Industrial Strategy.

In his letter, it is stated that he should pursue a strategy for internal market governance that 'allows business and innovation to thrive by tackling fragmentation and remaining barriers and ensuring that rules are easy to implement and report on'[111] and that he should build a growth-conducive regulatory framework, including through a Single Market Strategy that should include consideration of a Single Market Barriers Act that would help to further bring down barriers and reinforcement of the Single Market Enforcement Taskforce.[112] Very interestingly, as Commissioner for Democracy, Justice and the Rule of Law, Michael McGrath was tasked in his Mission Letter[113] with adding a Single Market dimension to Rule of Law Reports, 'to address rule of law issues affecting companies [...] operating across borders'.[114] On the technology front, this also includes the adoption of a Digital Fairness Act, aimed at ensuring that practices such as influencing on social media platforms, the use of dark patterns, and other measures aimed at exploiting consumer and citizen vulnerabilities online would be tackled through a common EU response.[115] Yet perhaps the clearest statement of intent in this vein comes from the Competitiveness Compass itself, where the Commission proposes a '28th legal regime', which would 'simplify applicable rules and reduce the

---

[108] European Commission, 'A Competitiveness Compass for the EU' (n74) 16–17.
[109] Ibid 17–18.
[110] Ibid 19.
[111] Ursula von der Leyen, 'Mission Letter: Stéphane Séjourné' (2024) 5.
[112] Ibid 7.
[113] Ursula von der Leyen, 'Mission Letter: Michael McGrath' (2024).
[114] Ibid 6.
[115] Ibid 7.

cost of failure, including any relevant aspects of corporate law, insolvency, labour and tax law'[116] for companies, allowing them to rely on a common European framework for these issues rather than upon one of the existing twenty-seven Member State regimes, creating something almost like a federal-level set of Single Market rules to foster European competitiveness.[117] In this respect, the Commission's planned approach appears to reflect a regulatory mercantilist approach of state-and-market building in its internal focus, actively regulating in order to remove barriers in the pursuit of competitiveness, linked explicitly to issues of security.

Similarly, the actions speak clearly to the desire to establish a much more integrated and interventionist industrial policy in Europe. Industrial strategy is at the heart of the Competitiveness Compass, referred to throughout the entirety of the document. The approach is largely reflected in the statement in the Compass that 'Europe must be the place where tomorrow's technologies, services, and clean products are invented, manufactured and marketed'.[118] In addition to measures discussed in the previous section, the Compass identified the development of a TechEU investment programme in conjunction with the European Investment Bank Group and private investors in order to facilitate 'disruptive innovation, strengthen Europe's industrial capacity and scale up companies that invest in innovative technologies such as AI, clean tech, critical raw materials, energy storage, quantum computing, semiconductors, life sciences, and neurotechnology',[119] broadening the scope of technologies that it wished to develop from the von der Leyen I Commission, and also announcing a European Research Area Act, which would be used to strengthen R&D investment with a 3 per cent GDP target, focused on Europe's strategic priorities.[120] This will further be reinforced with the Competitiveness Coordination Tool, which, in acknowledging divergences in Member State approaches to R&D and industrial development, would 'align industrial and research policies and investments at the EU and the national levels'.[121] The AI Continent Action Plan highlights the desire for an industrial policy for AI, with the €10 billion investments into infrastructure for the development of AI centres, with a plan for nine AI supercomputers being established in Europe, distributing compute throughout the EU for Member States through 'AI Factory Antennas'.[122] This is complemented by the AI Gigafactories-focused 'InvestAI Facility', a platform for public-private partnership

---

[116] European Commission, 'A Competitiveness Compass for the EU' (n74) 4.
[117] This is an idea that has been floated before by the Commission, albeit in much more discrete areas, rather than as a general approach; see Zdenek Kudrna, 'Cross-Border Resolution of Failed Banks in the European Union after the Crisis: Business as Usual' (2012) 50 JCMS: Journal of Common Market Studies 283; Giesela Rühl, 'The Common European Sales Law: 28th Regime, 2nd Regime or 1st Regime?' (2012) 19 Maastricht Journal of European and Comparative Law 148.
[118] European Commission, 'A Competitiveness Compass for the EU' (n74) 2.
[119] Ibid 5.
[120] Ibid.
[121] Ibid 23.
[122] European Commission, 'AI Continent Action Plan' (n104) 4–5.

in investing in developing the Gigafactories and required infrastructure as part of a dedicated industrial policy for AI.[123]

The Defence White Paper expands upon this desire for coordinated, interventionist industrial policy, with an EU-wide Market for Defence proposed as a means of achieving 'key objectives such as global competitiveness, readiness, and greater industrial scale'.[124] In discussing defence transformations, the Commission highlights the potential military applications of technologies such as AI and quantum, as well as already weaponised technologies such as drones, with Europe needing to establish its own military defence technology industry to reduce strategic dependencies.[125] The stated aim of this is to be able to mobilise its industrial capacity on the basis of direct investments, combining the expertise of private sector civilian innovation with the knowledge base and operational capacity of the military sector, overseen by the Commission to leverage this potential to achieve technological military superiority.[126] In order to facilitate this, the Commission is going as far as to suggest how this can be achieved within the context of the Stability and Growth Pact,[127] traditionally perceived as a barrier to investment by Member States after the Eurozone Crisis.[128] In its guidance, it promotes flexibility in the application of the fiscal framework so long as it is done in order to boost investment in defence industrial capacity,[129] and reinforces a regulatory mercantilist understanding of the purpose of industrial strategy by stating that in procuring new equipment or services by Member States they are 'invited to privilege European industry and service providers so as to ensure that this increased spending contributes to the EU's autonomy and competitiveness, instead of reinforcing any excessive dependencies'.[130] Finally, a Regulation for a Security Action for Europe (SAFE) Act was proposed, which would legislate to provide the framework for increased spending for defence in the context of a European Defence Technological and Industrial Base (known as EDTIB).[131]

---

[123] Ibid 7–8.
[124] European Commission and High Representative of the Union for Foreign Affairs and Security Policy (n97) 14.
[125] Ibid 15–16.
[126] Ibid 15.
[127] European Commission, 'Accommodating Increased Defence Expenditure within the Stability and Growth Pact' (2025) C(2025) 2000.
[128] See, for example, Orsola Costantini, 'Political Economy of the Stability and Growth Pact' (2017) 14 *European Journal of Economics and Economic Policies* 333; Séverine Menguy, 'Reform of the Stability and Growth Pact: Which Changes for the Governments?' (2024) 15 *Journal of Government and Economics* 100120; on the legal restrictiveness of the fiscal rules, see Benjamin Farrand and Marco Rizzi, 'There Is No (Legal) Alternative: Codifying Economic Ideology into Law' in Eva Nanopoulos and Fotis Vergis (eds), *The Crisis Behind the Eurocrisis* (Cambridge University Press 2019).
[129] European Commission, 'Accommodating Increased Defence Expenditure within the Stability and Growth Pact' (n127) 2.
[130] Ibid 5.
[131] European Commission, 'Proposal for a Regulation Establishing the Security Action for Europe (SAFE) through the Reinforcement of European Defence Industry Instrument' (2025) COM(2025) 122 4.

Article 1 of the proposed Regulation states that SAFE is intended to provide financial assistance to Member States allowing them to carry out urgent and major public investments in support of the European defence industry, with Article 7 allowing for the grants of money to build capacity in the production of category one technologies including small drones, critical information infrastructure protection, and cyber, and category two technologies such as artificial intelligence and electronic warfare. In this respect, technology in the context of security and defence is where we see clear reflections of the concept of 'power and plenty' expanded upon in Chapter 1.

Given the geopolitical instabilities facing the EU, internal consolidation needs to be combined with external action. Global leadership remains a strategic ambition for the Commission, and as discussed in the preceding section, the Competitiveness Compass identified a number of avenues for expanding this leadership, including through agreements with Mercosur and Mexico, as well as its Digital Trade Agreements. Its Clean Trade and Investment Partnerships proposal is interesting, insofar as it seeks to both secure access to critical raw materials, clean energy, and clean tech from throughout the world on the basis of European investments in those third countries,[132] indicating an approach aimed at maximising the import of critical materials while exporting its norms and values through its agreements. As the Mission Letter to Vice President Virkkunen states, part of the brief for Technological Sovereignty, Security and Democracy entails working with 'the Commissioner for International Partnerships to support Global Gateway projects in partner countries, such as trustworthy digital communications networks',[133] identified in Chapters 4–6 as a key aspect of EU cyber-diplomacy. While in the context of defence in the White Paper, there is less emphasis on regulatory export but instead on pursuing multilateralism based in (and promoting) European values.[134] It concludes the White Paper by stating that 'Europe must make bold choices and build a Defence Union that ensures peace on our continent through unity and strength',[135] reinforcing a more assertive approach to its partnerships and security interests. Similarly, the AI Continent Action Plan concludes by arguing that AI policy requires international engagement, and that the EU will lead global engagements on AI, helping to support innovation and development of AI solutions in third countries, but within a framework of good AI global governance promoting European values such as human rights.[136] While we do not yet have sufficient detail on the regulatory outputs that von der Leyen II will produce in the context of the Data Union Strategy or Quantum Strategy, it is likely given the trajectory of lawmaking in this field that

---

[132] Ibid 13.
[133] von der Leyen, 'Mission Letter to Henna Virkkunen, Executive Vice-President-Designate for Tech Sovereignty, Security and Democracy' (n23) 8.
[134] European Commission and High Representative of the Union for Foreign Affairs and Security Policy (n97) 19–21.
[135] Ibid 22.
[136] European Commission, 'AI Continent Action Plan' (n104) 23.

the EU will attempt to export the norms it develops in these areas as global values, relying on the Brussels Effect as a means of influencing international norms.

CONCLUSIONS

The von der Leyen II Commission has considerable challenges to face in a world in which geopolitics and geostrategic positioning are likely to take precedence for all states and regions for the foreseeable future. The vulnerabilities and dependencies identified by the Commission in 2019 have only become more pronounced, and the tensions with the United States and China more profound. The conflict on Europe's eastern borders is being compounded by threats to its territorial integrity and sovereignty on its western borders. Old alliances and faith in NATO (and by extension the US) as a guarantor of European security are shaken. China continues its technological race against the US and Europe, leading in key fields such as electric vehicles, which are increasingly essential for meeting goals concerning the climate. Internationally, tariffs as a form of economic warfare, applied with seeming capriciousness, create new economic and regulatory uncertainties, with consequences for economic policy. And in all this, the EU perceives itself as more alone than ever.

In this context, then, it is perhaps not surprising that the Geopolitical Commission has reinforced its regulatory mercantilist approach. The Commission structure is now strongly built around defence both as a concept and as a policy area, linking to its industrial and economic policies, underscored by a unified Vice Presidency for Technological Sovereignty, Security, and Democracy. The Competitiveness Compass acts as a strategic linchpin for the actions the Commission is planning to take over the course of its mandate, a document that stresses the interdependence of economic and security ambitions as both mutually reinforcing and mutually vulnerable in the current climate. Rather than a waning of a discourse of dependencies, strategic autonomy, and the EU's need for technological sovereignty, this discourse is being maintained and expanded into fields such as defence, with a stated ambition of securing vital military technologies in a way that was reserved in the previous Commission for technologies such as microchips, guaranteeing cybersecurity, regulating platforms, and protecting data. The approach of 'security in all things' being reflected through the Commission's stated goal of incorporating security into all legislative endeavours is clearly reflective of a more mercantilist mindset, insofar as economic policies are seen as guarantors of security, and security as a guarantor of future prosperity. In other words, power and plenty are drivers of action for the Commission.

Operationally, this means that the approach identified in Chapters 4–6, of reinforcing regulatory control, engaging in state-and-market-making practices centred around removing barriers to trade internally and coordinating industrial policy in pursuit of European competitiveness, is complemented by efforts aimed at accruing critical raw materials (or guaranteeing supply-chain control and access where geographical control is not possible) and maximising regulatory export. The Commission hopes, in its new defence industrial policies and its pursuit of the AI Continent agenda, that this can be done through bilateral and regional partnerships and uploading European standards as global standards through international forums, theoretically relying on the Brussels effect to more effectively achieve these goals, complemented with cyber-diplomacy and engagements with non-rival states through its Global Gateway programme. While the feasibility of the technological supremacy the EU desires may potentially be open to question, its pursuit of it is not and is strongly reflective of the broader strategic aims of the Geopolitical Commission and, by extension, the Geopolitical Union. The next chapter of this book is the conclusion to this work, which draws the distinct threads of the book together and reflects upon the changing nature of regulation in the twenty-first century.

Conclusions

The Geopolitical Union as an Approach to Governance and the Utility of Regulatory Mercantilism for Regulation and Governance Studies

It is important to state that economic strength and Europe's plan to REARM are two sides of the same coin. Europe's economic and innovative potential is an asset for its security. Vice versa, Europe's defence efforts can give a massive boost to a more competitive Single Market in the mid and long term.[1]

The past five years have seen a substantial change in the EU's approach to the regulation of technology, which has been characterised by a move from a logic of efficiency to a logic of security. The early period of European integration in this field was focused upon the removal of barriers to trade that existed within the internal market, and more recently on ensuring the protection of European personal data and intellectual property rights in global markets, with cybersecurity provision being a related yet distinct area of policymaking. As the case studies presented in this book have shown, however, it is not just that the lines between economic policy and security have blurred, but that the two are now perceived as mutually constitutive and reinforcing goals. Security is no longer something that acts as a trade-off for economic goals, but economic goals are dependent upon achieving security goals. Achieving security goals is inherently and explicitly linked to economic prosperity.

These trends appear to be accelerating in the EU, as the perceptions of Europe's vulnerability in the context of broader geopolitical instabilities and uncertainties grow, serving as an impetus for a renewed push for European integration in technology control. In a world in which allies are unpredictable and where rivals appear to have a considerable competitive advantage in new and emerging technologies, relying on old ways of working is seen as courting disaster. In technology sectors where the owners of information infrastructures no longer appear to be aligned with

---

[1] Ursula von der Leyen, 'Press Remarks by President von Der Leyen on the First 100 Days of the 2024–2029 Commission' (*European Commission*, 10 March 2025) <https://enlargement.ec.europa.eu/news/press-remarks-president-von-der-leyen-first-100-days-2024-2029-commission-2025-03-10_en> accessed 22 April 2025.

European values or even willing to be bound by Europe's rules, relying on self-regulatory regimes or voluntary agreements and viewing technology governance as a largely neutral activity taking place in efficient global markets appears naïve. Where data becomes a critical raw material for the next-generation information economy services, allowing that data to rest in the hands of those same states, regions, and private sector actors that no longer seem aligned with Europe's values is counterintuitive. In this broader context, self-sufficiency is a strategic objective and reducing external dependencies is a way of promoting both sovereignty and autonomy. As discussed throughout this work, the response to these concerns was the establishment of the Geopolitical Commission, which promised open relations with its allies and those states aligned with its values, while acknowledging that geostrategy and the need for European self-protection would be key to the EU's success in a more competitive, less cooperative global order. In these concluding sections of the book, I will expand briefly on where the Geopolitical Union could go over the remainder of the von der Leyen II Commission in 'The Future of the Geopolitical Union', the relevance and utility of the regulatory mercantilism framework for regulation and governance studies in 'Regulatory Mercantilism as an Approach to the Study of Regulation and Governance', and possible directions for future research in 'Future Directions for Research'.

THE FUTURE OF THE GEOPOLITICAL UNION

The Geopolitical Union as a concept does not appear to be going away, but it is being reinforced as the Commission's understanding of the role of the EU in the world appears confirmed by the continuing insecurities Europe faces. One way of putting this is that Europe is assertive, yet not necessarily confident; it is actively regulating, yet from a position of perceived threat rather than one of a self-assured regulatory superpower. The emphasis placed on technological sovereignty and on strategic autonomy, including in the most recent policy outputs covered in Chapter 7, suggests that those goals are not yet being obtained. Indeed, as the US becomes seen as less of an ally and more of a geopolitical threat, China as a technological rival surpassing even the US in fields such as AI and drone technologies, and Russia as an explicit military threat on its immediate borders, geopolitics is likely to remain central to the EU's understandings of and interactions with the public and private sectors external to its territory.

The Geopolitical Commission is highly likely to continue to act as an engine for this geostrategic positioning, even as defence becomes more of a priority for Europe. With the closer coordination between economic and defence goals, and President von der Leyen's commitment to 'security in all things', the identification of security interests and concerns is incorporated into legislative activity in the same way as economic impact assessments. The 'mainstreaming' of security into Commission activity is such that 'legislation, policies and programmes will need to be prepared, reviewed and implemented with a security perspective in mind, making sure that the necessary security considerations are addressed so as to promote a coherent and comprehensive approach to security'.[2] Proactivity on the Commission's part can be seen in a range of very recent announcements,[3] such as the confirmation of investigations into the conduct of large tech firms such as Apple and Google, with President von der Leyen reiterating that rules will be applied regardless of the power of the firms involved, stating that 'we don't care where a company's from, and who's running it'.[4] There is an acknowledgement on the part of the Commission that these exercises, which could once have been argued to be technical, take on a dimension of the political in the face of US opposition to these investigations and their pursuance in light of a broader trade war.[5] For Commission Vice President Virkkunen, a proactive Commission is essential in promoting the EU's interests, both economic and security-related, stating in an April 2025 speech that 'No Member State can tackle these challenges alone. We need a powerful, coordinated European response.'[6]

Technology is highly likely to remain at the centre of these geopolitical struggles for control. As was touched upon in Chapter 7, both the Letta[7] and Draghi[8] reports placed a heavy emphasis on the importance of technology in guaranteeing Europe's future. Letta argued that 'Europe will be better suited to position itself not only as a global leader in ethical standards for innovation and knowledge diffusion, but **a creator and a maker of new technologies**.'[9] Draghi similarly stated that 'technological change is accelerating rapidly. Europe largely missed out on the digital revolution led by the internet and the productivity gains it brought: in fact, the productivity gap between the EU and US is largely explained by the tech sector. The EU is weak in the emerging technologies that will drive future growth.'[10] These two perspectives on Europe harness the twin desires of regulatory mercantilist approaches to governance: the first, the desire for self-sufficiency and strength in economic state-making, and the second, a desire for security and competitiveness with a recognition of the interplay between the two. And while the ink has now dried on regulatory interventions in the fields of standards, cybersecurity,

---

[2] European Commission, 'ProtectEU: A European Internal Security Strategy' (2025) COM(2025) 148 2.
[3] As of the time of writing in April 2025.
[4] Nicholas Vincour, 'Von Der Leyen Warns X, Meta, TikTok to Play by the Rules in Europe – No Matter Who's CEO' (*POLITICO*, 21 April 2025) <www.politico.eu/article/european-commission-ursula-von-der-leyen-warns-x-meta-tiktok-rules-ceo/> accessed 21 April 2025.
[5] Francesca Micheletti and Jacob Parry, 'Big Tech Fines Just Got Political, Whether the Commission Likes It or Not' (*POLITICO*, 14 April 2025) <www.politico.eu/article/big-tech-fines-digital-markets-act-political-european-commission-meta-apple-donald-trump-tariffs/> accessed 21 April 2025.
[6] Henna Virkkunen, 'Remarks by Executive Vice-President Virkkunen and Commissioner Brunner' (*European Commission*, 1 April 2025) <https://ec.europa.eu/commission/presscorner/detail/en/speech_25_954> accessed 21 April 2025.
[7] Enrico Letta, 'Much More than a Market: Speed, Security, Solidarity' (2024).
[8] Mario Draghi, 'The Future of European Competitiveness' (2024).
[9] Letta (n7) 20.
[10] Draghi (n8) 5.

semiconductor supply chains, platform governance, and data governance, there is more work yet to be done.

At the time of writing the Data Union Strategy, Quantum Union Strategy, and Quantum Act have not yet been published, nor have the Biotechnology Act, Advanced Materials Act, Space Act, or Digital Networks Act. However, the intention to do so demonstrates that the Geopolitical Union's technology governance focus is expanding to incorporate a wider range of technologies moving beyond those that could be more easily categorised as 'digital'. The plans in these fields indicate interests in medical and space technologies, where the Commission hopes that the EU will be able to catch up with the developments occurring in competitors such as the US and China.[11] The approach to governance in these sectors is likely to mirror that already adopted in the regulations produced by the von der Leyen I Commission, as well as that proposed by von der Leyen II in areas discussed in Chapter 7. Internally, we are likely to see efforts directed towards market unification measures, with an emphasis on industrial policy, incentives for investment in critical sectors, and encouragement of bringing sectors into European territory. These measures are likely to be combined with greater oversight, with pan-European boards with Commission membership or leadership, as a way of ensuring a unified European response. Externally, the emphasis will be on securing access to the critical resources required for these initiatives, exporting regulatory approaches as global standards, or relying on cyber-diplomacy as a means of securing bilateral agreement on cooperation in these sectors, albeit based on European rules and values, as in the approach adopted in the Global Gateway programme. In all instances, however, I would expect to see that the rationale for action is clearly expressed in the dual urgencies of promoting European sovereignty and securing its strategic autonomy. In this, at least, the Geopolitical Union is likely to be consistent.

REGULATORY MERCANTILISM AS AN APPROACH TO THE STUDY OF REGULATION AND GOVERNANCE

One of the central aims of the book has been to expand upon the regulatory mercantilism concept and how it has utility for the study of regulation and governance beyond the scope of the EU's technology governance regime. I believe that regulatory mercantilism works effectively as a framework for analysing governance regimes, which in turn demonstrate characteristics of regulatory mercantilism in action. One of the key dimensions of its utility is in its recognition of contingency in policymaking, and the way that policymakers respond to uncertainty. As

---

[11] Ricardo Filipe, 'EU Overregulation Is Stifling Innovation in Biotechnology' (*EU Reporter*, 3 April 2025) <www.eureporter.co/business/research/2025/04/03/eu-overregulation-is-stifling-innovation-in-biotechnology/> accessed 21 April 2025.

we currently find ourselves in times in which traditional modes of governance are either being questioned or, alternatively, appear ill-equipped to respond to current geopolitical instabilities, policymakers appear to be moving away from relatively long-standing assumptions about how regulation should operate, and to what ends.

In the case of this book, the focus has been on the EU and the Commission's changing approach to technology regulation in light of its perceived vulnerability. Ideational constants, such as the idea of market efficiency and light-touch regulation being the most effective means of promoting economic development, have been challenged by the actions of large tech operators. This means that the model of networked regulatory capitalism discussed in Chapter 1 no longer appears appropriate, when significant questions are raised about the values of those private sector actors and therefore their suitability for steering policy formulation as well as rowing for operationalising those policies. In fact, in sectors deemed critical, regulatory capitalism in general, with its approach to governance based in a logic of efficiency and private sector expertise, appears to create potential security risks for the EU, which it has sought to remedy through the incorporation of a security logic into its market regulation, its increased preference for 'European' solutions, whether in terms of territorial location or company origin, and a desire for increased top-down control, based in systems of strong state oversight and co-regulatory regimes; in other words, more 'state' in the 'regulatory state'.

The proliferation of different oversight bodies, ranging from the European Board for Digital Services, the European Artificial Intelligence Board, and the European Data Innovation Board, all with Commission membership or leadership, is indicative of a changed approach to technology governance in which 'letting markets decide' is being caveated with 'according to our economic and security interests'. Regulatory mercantilism as a framework allows for analysis of the conditions, rationale, and operationalisation of a regulatory approach in order to determine the extent to which it seeks to increase control based on an economic and security rationale, in conditions of uncertainty or vulnerability, resulting in regulatory structures that emphasise increased control, measures such as industrial policy, and external norm promotion. What this also means is that this framework can be used to determine when an approach taken by policymakers *does not* appear to be regulatory mercantilist in nature – absent a security logic, or when conditions appear to be such that the policymaker is reinforcing particular strengths or engaging in minor technical adjustments, and public–private relations are not subject to reassessment or alternatively oriented around self-regulation, then regulatory mercantilism is unlikely to be the approach to governance adopted in that given situation.

The focus of this book has been on technology governance and at the level of the EU. However, regulatory mercantilism as an approach can be applied to a much broader swathe of policies and regions. It could be applied to energy policies, for example, or environmental and climate change-related developments, in order to determine whether they are increasingly framed in economic and security terms, with a preference for increased regulatory oversight and state control rather than more informal and self-or-market regulatory mechanisms such as benchmarking, ranking, or voluntary and non-binding commitments.[12] It could be applied in the context of other regional blocs, such as Mercosur, in order to assess the extent to which trade and economic policy[13] are being complemented by a security logic through the incorporation of the Union of South American Nations (UNASUR) and the South American Council of Defence,[14] in order to determine whether regulatory outputs are demonstrating characteristics of a regulatory mercantilist approach. It could also be used in order to assess external actions or foreign policy initiatives, in order to determine the extent to which states seek to promote a positive regulatory balance of trade, engaging in cyber-diplomacy or norm uploading to promote their own standards as global standards, albeit on a security-based logic. In the next and final section of this chapter and book, some potential future directions for research are outlined.

DIRECTIONS FOR FUTURE RESEARCH

The main focus of this book has been in understanding the changing governance model of technology regulation in the EU, in terms of identifying the characteristics of regulatory mercantilism, when it is likely to be visible as an approach, and applying it to the developments taking place within the actions of the Geopolitical Commission. As such, the emphasis of the book has been on the 'why', the 'how', and the 'what' of the Commission's policymaking in this field – the 'why' being the underlying geopolitical conditions motivating action, the 'how' digital/technological sovereignty and strategic autonomy as rationales *for* action, and the 'what' being the operationalisation of this rationale through increased legislative intervention emphasising control, industrial policy, and ensuring a positive regulatory balance of trade. What this book has not covered in detail but would constitute a highly useful contribution to understanding of the actions of the Commission in this field would be an assessment of the success of these actions. Are digital sovereignty and strategic autonomy being effectively promoted? Are the measures adopted to incentivise industrial policy in technology being successful, or are their scope and level of investments such that the goals are not being realised? Is true reduced

---

[12] See, for example, B Guy Peters, 'Forms of Informality: Identifying Informal Governance in the European Union' (2006) 7 *Perspectives on European Politics and Society* 25; Mareike Kleine, 'Informal Governance in the European Union' (2014) 21 *Journal of European Public Policy* 303.

[13] Which is currently expanding into consideration of social policies, as discussed in Andrea C Bianculli, 'From Free Market to Social Policies? Mapping Regulatory Cooperation in Education and Health in MERCOSUR' (2018) 18 *Global Social Policy* 249.

[14] Katharina L Meissner, 'Regional Security in the Twenty-First Century's South America: Economic, Energy, and Political Security in MERCOSUR and UNASUR' in Paweł Frankowski and Artur Gruszczak (eds), *Cross-Disciplinary Perspectives on Regional and Global Security* (Springer International Publishing 2018).

dependency on external suppliers and European solutions for AI gigafactories or Common European Data Spaces feasible, or even realistic as goals? It is my hope that this book has provided a useful foundation for pursuing these questions about the Commission's technology policies specifically.

Similarly, what about other facets of the Geopolitical Union? The 2019–2024 von der Leyen Commission was marked by developments around environmental issues, framed as the 'twin transitions' around technology and green/environmental, which were also discussed in geopolitical terms.[15] This book has only touched upon energy and environmental policies pursued by the Commission as they directly relate to technology policy – however, it is probable that a regulatory mercantilism approach may be seen in the policies adopted during this period, and they are likely to become even more pronounced in the von der Leyen II Commission, particularly as a result of increased trade tension with China around electric vehicles and the increasingly politicised nature of environmental action. Further research, both around how energy and environmental policies are developed by the Geopolitical Commission, the extent to which they demonstrate regulatory mercantilist characteristics, and the extent to which we see divergences, either in scope of action, forms of regulatory oversight, or feasibility of the approach, would be hugely beneficial. It may be possible to identify 'optimal conditions' for regulatory mercantilist approaches to be successful, for example, or to undertake comparative work that may help us to identify varieties of regulatory mercantilism.

Finally, the application of the approach to different states or regions could be an interesting avenue for future research. The US's current actions in terms of trade policy could be argued to be a return to more clear-cut, traditional mercantilism, rather than actions of a regulatory mercantilist nature. Furthermore, the actions internally that appear to be efforts at the deconstruction of the state, rather than its further unification under centralised oversight, appear to be incompatible with the regulatory mercantilist approach to internal industrial policy, or indeed traditional mercantilist industrial policy, regardless of the stated ambitions of 'bringing manufacturing home'.[16] However, the actions of the Biden Administration during his term as President may be more amenable to analysis using the regulatory mercantilism approach. Similarly, in the context of China, which on the one hand is demonstrating hugely significant advancements in technology and AI, with dedicated policies and state intervention in order to promote industrial policy and growth in critical sectors, on the other hand is facing demographic concerns, declining manufacturing, and years of economic stagnation following the

---

[15] European Commission, '2022 Strategic Foresight Report: Twinning the Green and Digital Transitions in the New Geopolitical Context' (2022) COM(2022) 289.
[16] Talmon Joseph Smith, 'Trump Is Promising a Manufacturing Renaissance. Is That Even Possible?' (*The New York Times*, 3 April 2025) <www.nytimes.com/2025/04/03/business/economy/trump-tariffs-us-manufacturing-economy.html> accessed 22 April 2025.

COVID-19 pandemic.[17] Could it be that a perceived sense of vulnerability in the Chinese state apparatus could also result in a changed governance approach, more akin to that of regulatory mercantilism? In particular, actions aimed at boosting domestic production and consumption, along with engaging in efforts at regional cyber-diplomacy through initiatives such as the Digital Silk Road, could be means by which China seeks to promote its own standards and norms as regional and global standards.[18] Further research on these initiatives, the utility of the regulatory mercantilism approach in studying them, and considerations of their feasibility could also help to further understanding, not only of technology governance specifically but also of the shifting dynamics in global regulation during times of geopolitical instability more broadly.

It is here that this book draws to a close. To quote Gramsci, it is in the time that the old world is dying and the new world is not yet born, this interregnum period, that a great variety of morbid symptoms appear. With the old liberal international economic order appearing to be ending, globalisation under threat, and the future model not yet easily able to be seen, it may be that we are in this interregnum period. Is the linking of economic and security issues as interdependent and mutually constitutive, with the EU concerned for its sovereignty and strategic autonomy, something of a symptom? Is it something that may be short lived, and pass as global conditions ease? Or is it instead the new, and a shape of the regulatory world to come? While it may be too soon to tell, for now at least, the Geopolitical Union as both ambition and ideation may not be disappearing at any point soon.

---

[17] William Langley and Haohsiang Ko, 'China Is Suffering Its Own "China Shock"' (*Financial Times*, 25 March 2025) <www.ft.com/content/7640fe64-006a-4d46-9564-cbb2bd89ebd4> accessed 22 April 2025.
[18] Fakhar Hussain and others, 'The Digital Rise and Its Economic Implications for China through the Digital Silk Road under the Belt and Road Initiative' (2024) 9 *Asian Journal of Comparative Politics* 238.

Index

AI Continent Action Plan, 182–183, 187
AI Strategy, 150
Area of Freedom, Security, and Justice, 62, 146
artificial intelligence (AI), 8, 15, 103, 115, 142–143, 150–152, 154–158, 159–164, 169, 171, 173, 179, 182, 185–186, 189, 191, 194, 196
   Anthropic, 151
   Deepseek, 151
   foundational models, 142, 151, 163
   Gigafactories, 15, 179, 185, 196
   OpenAI, 151

Biden, Joe, 85, 108
Big Tech, 2, 9, 13, 15, 65, 122–123, 147–148, 154, 159, 177, 192
Breton, Thierry, 120, 132–133, 142, 153, 170–171, 177
Brussels effect, 8, 13, 51, 66–67, 140, 143, 146–149, 162, 164, 188–189
Bush, George W, 81

China, 1–2, 9–10, 14–15, 34, 50, 67, 82, 95, 108, 118, 129, 139, 142, 153, 160, 163, 168–169, 172, 177–178, 182, 188, 191, 193
   cyber sovereignty, 9, 148
   Cybersecurity Law, 150
   Digital Silk Road, 153, 197
   global influence of, 1, 72–73, 84–85, 100–101
   intellectual property rights enforcement, 79, 98–99
   Personal Information Protection Law, 146, 148
   resource wealth, 103–104, 107–108
   response to Global Financial Crisis, 87–89
   state subsidisation of technology, 99, 108, 175
   technological acceleration, 82–84
Chips for Europe, 113
Clinton, Bill, 78
Cold War, 13, 31, 71–76
Comecon, 13, 73

Committee for Multilateral Export Controls (COCOM), 13, 73–75
Common European Data Spaces (CEDSs), 143, 153–154, 157, 159, 162–163, 196
Common Security and Defence Policy (CEDP), 11, 89
Competitiveness Compass, 15, 178–181, 183–185, 187–188
Court of Justice of the European Union (CJEU), 13, 50–55, 69, 97, 125, 145, 148
Covid-19, 2, 34, 58, 61, 63, 101, 106, 126, 128, 130, 167, 197
critical raw materials, 7, 47, 88, 109, 117, 142, 171, 180–181, 185, 187–188
Cybercrime Convention, 61
cyber-diplomacy, 8, 95, 115–116, 119, 162, 164, 187, 189, 193, 195, 197
cybersecurity, 2, 4, 6, 8, 13, 25–27, 33, 39, 47, 51, 58, 61, 69–70, 87, 96, 101–104, 106–107, 110–112, 115–116, 119, 124, 128–129, 136–137, 150–151, 161, 173, 188, 192
   critical information infrastructure, 26, 47, 63–64, 70, 96, 102, 107, 111, 118, 124, 137, 149, 187
   cybercrime, 13, 61, 63
   reflective of regulatory capitalism, 63–64
   as supportive of internal market, 61–62, 64
Cybersecurity Strategy (2020), 63, 102, 107, 111, 124, 129

data
   cloud, 100, 111, 135, 144, 149, 152–154, 163, 173, 179, 182–183
   as critical raw material, 151, 163
   industrial, 142, 150, 153
   lack of European competitiveness, 149–150
   localisation, 149, 161, 163
   strategy, 149, 152–154, 156, 159
   unauthorised access to, 61, 154, 161

200

Index

defence, 11–12, 15, 60, 66, 68, 70, 74, 89, 102, 107, 168–171, 175, 180–183, 186, 188–191, 195
digital compass, 128
Digital Service Coordinators (DSC), 136
Digital Single Market Strategy, 60, 124
digital sovereignty, 6, 9–12, 64, 66, 90, 118, 133, 138, 140, 155, 183, 195
disinformation, 1, 14, 65, 87, 103, 120–121, 135, 151
  code of practice on, 135
  political advertising and, 14, 130–132, 135
  Strengthened Code of Practice on, 135
Dombrovskis, Valdis, 68, 171
Draghi Report, 167, 172, 192

economy, security, mutually constitutive nature, 3, 12–13, 20, 90, 102, 105, 171, 190, 197
ENISA, 27, 62–64, 106, 112, 124, 137, 158
EU Directives
  Copyright in the Information Society Directive, 59
  Data Protection Directive, 58, 144
  E-Commerce Directive, 58, 122, 125, 134
  Network and Information Security 2 Directive (NIS2 Directive), 110–112, 115–116, 119, 137
  Network and Information Security Directive (NIS Directive), 63, 124
EU Regulations
  AI Act, 155, 158–159, 161
  Chips Act, 108, 113, 116
  Critical Raw Materials Act, 109, 117–118
  Cyber Resilience Act, 107, 112, 116, 119
  Cyber Solidarity Act, 112–113, 116, 119
  Cybersecurity Act, 106
  Data Act, 153–157, 159–162
  Data Governance Act, 153–162
  Digital Markets Act, 120, 131–140, 157, 159
  Digital Services Act, 120, 131–140, 169, 178
  General Data Protection Regulation (GDPR), 70, 121, 145–150, 154, 162
  Political Advertising Regulation, 131–132, 134–135, 137–138, 140
  Regulation Amending the Standardisation Regulation, 110
EU State of the Union, 5, 65–66, 89, 99, 107, 108, 130, 150, 152, 174
European Artificial Intelligence Board (EIAB), 160
European Board for Digital Services (EBDS), 136–137, 141
European Coal and Steel Community, 51
European Commission, Geopolitical Commission, 1, 3, 9, 64, 118, 143, 157, 163, 183–189, 191, 195

European Committee for Standardisation (CEN), 97
European Data Innovation Board (EDIB), 157–159, 161
European Data Protection Board, 158
European Economic Community (EEC), 51–55, 60, 69, 76, 144
European integration
  negative integration, 13, 50, 53, 55
  positive integration, 51–52, 56, 59, 69
European standardisation organisations (ESOs), 97–98, 100
European Telecommunications Standards Institute (ETSI), 59, 66, 97, 101, 110, 114, 118–119
European Union
  Eurozone crisis, 1, 60, 65, 85–91, 97, 123, 186
  polycrisis, 13, 65, 87
  rules and values, 10, 130–132, 135, 137–140, 147, 155, 158, 169, 178, 187, 191
  vulnerability, 2–3, 51, 85–90, 100–104, 126–130, 147–152
Europol, 63, 102, 126
EU-US Trade and Technology Council (TTC), 115

free movement of goods and services, 52–53, 58, 67, 69, 121, 144, 146

gatekeepers, 124, 129, 132, 135, 137, 139–140, 159, 163
GAMAM, 122
General Agreement on Trade and Tariffs (GATT), 73, 77–78, 90
Geopolitical Union, 1, 15, 19, 49–50, 68, 90, 95, 109, 164–165, 167–168, 170, 183–189, 191–193, 196
geopolitics, 1, 9, 13, 17, 36, 73, 88, 100, 108, 112, 115, 140, 146, 173
Germany, 9, 28, 36, 45, 51, 53–54, 65, 74, 76, 79–80, 86, 147, 173–174
Global Gateway, 8, 115, 118–119, 162, 164, 170, 180, 187, 189, 193
globalisation, 20, 24, 31, 46, 72, 77–81, 90–91, 98–100, 197
  crisis of, 81–85
grounded theory, 3–5

Huawei, 84, 85, 100–101, 103, 116

industrial policy, 3, 7–9, 11, 13–15, 20, 69, 98, 116, 118, 143, 188, 193–196
  data, 152–154, 156–160
  defence technology, 178–188

mercantilism in, 41–43
regulatory mercantilism, in, 45–46
technology, 95–96, 108, 110–114
intellectual property rights (IPRs), 78, 98–100
Internal Security Strategy (2010), 63
Internal Security Strategy (2025), 169, 182
International Telecommunication Union (ITU), 100–101, 115, 119

Japan, 42, 51, 53, 78, 84, 104
Joint White Paper on Defence Readiness, 181
Juncker, Jean-Claude, 60, 65, 67, 87, 89, 99–100, 124–125, 150

Kallas, Kaja, 172
Kubilius, Andrius, 171

Letta Report, 167, 172–173, 192

Macron, Emmanuel, 167
McGrath, Michael, 171, 184
mercantilism, 6–7, 21–23, 29–31, 34–37, 41–43
Merkel, Angela, 82
Merz, Friedrich, 174
microchips, 2, 14, 75, 103–104, 107–108, 118, 188
Musk, Elon, 120, 177

North Atlantic Treaty Organization (NATO), 31, 126, 175, 188

Obama, Barack, 81, 84, 88, 99
ordoliberalism, 28, 45, 57, 87, 122, 140

personal data
 EU-US safe harbour, 144–145
 PRISM, 145, 148
 Privacy Shield, 148
 Schrems I, 143, 145, 148
 Schrems II, 148
political guidelines of the European Commission, 1, 5, 68–70, 72, 90, 96, 167, 169–171
populism, 13, 65, 84, 87
Preparedness Strategy, 15, 181
private sector, 1, 7, 28, 51
 power of, 13, 44
 relations with, 8, 11, 12, 26, 36–37, 48, 57, 63–64, 67, 70, 121, 132–133, 182, 191
 role of, 19, 25, 37–40, 46, 48, 51, 57, 64, 80, 122, 124, 179, 186
 trust in, 20, 32–33, 49, 115, 191, 194
Putin, Vladimir, 88, 169, 172

Reagan, Ronald, 24, 76, 77
regulation

co-regulation, 3, 7, 20, 44, 80, 134, 137, 140
oversight, 7, 11–12, 14, 20, 33, 38, 40, 45, 96, 107, 110–114, 119–121, 128, 130–137, 141, 154–160, 193–196
self-regulation, 13, 20, 32, 37, 39, 44, 46, 80, 111, 121–122, 128, 134, 136–137, 140, 148, 154, 194
state-based, 10, 25, 121
regulatory capitalism, 25–28, 31–33, 37–39, 46–47
regulatory export, 8, 13, 46, 96, 153, 156, 163–164, 172, 183, 189
 data, 160–162
 platforms, 137–140
 technology, 114–118
regulatory mercantilism, 7–9
 balance of regulatory trade, 47–48
 conditions, 33–34
 increased control, 45–46
 mainstreaming in European Commission policy, 183–188
 rationale, 38–40
 relevance of approach, 195
regulatory state, 13, 19–20, 23–25, 27, 37, 48–49, 57, 194
Ribeira, Teresa, 171
Russia, 1, 10, 33, 65, 76, 79–80, 83, 87–90, 103–104, 109, 113, 127, 129, 138, 167, 172–173, 181, 191

Scholz, Olaf, 174
Schroeder, Gerhard, 80
security, economy, mutually constitutive nature, 3, 12–13, 20, 90, 102, 105, 171, 190, 197
Šefčovič, Maroš, 171
Séjourné, Stéphane, 171, 184
semiconductors, 14, 71, 75, 85, 95–96, 103–109, 113, 116–119, 142, 151, 185, 193
Shaping Europe's Digital Future, 5, 105–106, 128, 130–132, 138, 147, 150, 152
Single European Act, 56
social media platforms
 Meta, 120, 122, 127, 133, 139, 178, 192
 X, 120, 139, 153–154, 177, 192
social media platforms, illegal content, 122, 124, 130, 132, 139
Soviet Union, 13, 71–76, 78, 83
strategic autonomy, 5, 7, 9, 11–12, 14–15, 48, 64, 66, 70, 72, 89–91, 99, 105, 109, 114, 157, 168, 170, 180–183, 188, 191, 193, 195, 197
 data, 142–143, 152, 156, 163
 platforms, 129, 133
 technology, 89–90, 95–96, 111, 113, 115, 117
supply chains, 2, 12, 15, 46, 95–96, 105–110, 116, 119, 160, 173, 180, 193
Syrian refugee crisis, 65, 87

Taiwan, 103
Taiwanese Semiconductor Manufacturing Company (TSMC), 103
technological sovereignty, 3, 5, 9–12, 64, 68, 70, 90, 95–96, 105–108, 113, 142–143, 152–153, 155–156, 163, 167, 171, 173, 179, 183, 188, 191, 195
technological standards, 47, 66, 96–98, 100–101, 105–106, 110, 114, 118, 138–140, 162
trade
  free, 6, 14, 19, 28, 30, 77, 89
  protectionism, 14, 29, 72
  tariffs, 42, 52–53, 85, 103, 174–177, 188
trade war, 43, 72, 91, 103, 168, 177, 192
Trade-Related Aspects of Intellectual Property Rights Agreement (TRIPS), 78–79
Treaty of Rome, 52
Trump, Donald, 1, 3, 15, 84, 88, 91, 99, 103, 108, 168, 175–178

Ukraine, 1, 87, 102, 104, 108, 118, 130, 138, 152, 167–168, 172–173, 175, 181
United Kingdom, 1, 30
United Nations (UN), 8, 80, 100, 162, 164
United States (US), 1–3, 9, 11, 13, 24, 71, 73, 76, 78, 87, 90–91, 95, 108, 115, 127, 139, 142–143, 147, 151, 153, 160, 163, 168, 170, 172, 182, 188, 192–193, 196

EU lack of competitiveness with, 51, 53, 103–104, 147, 149, 178
Global Financial Crisis, 81–83
impact on geopolitics, 15, 84, 88, 99–100, 133, 175–178, 191
power of private tech, 132, 156
role in global order, 31
state surveillance, 65, 144–145, 150
technology control, 74
US Export Control Act, 75

Virkkunen, Henna, 171, 187, 192
von der Leyen, Ursula, 1, 3–4, 64, 67–69, 71, 90–91, 104, 107–109, 130–131, 150, 152, 168–170, 174, 176, 183, 191

Wandel durch Handel, 79, 90
Wassenaar Arrangement, 79
White Paper on the Future of European Defence, 181
World Trade Organization (WTO), 78–82, 84–85, 90–91, 99–100, 180

Xi Jinping, 84

Zelenskyy, Vladimir, 175
ZTE, 85, 100
Zuckerberg, Mark, 178

For EU product safety concerns, contact us at Calle de José Abascal, 56–1°, 28003 Madrid, Spain or eugpsr@cambridge.org.

www.ingramcontent.com/pod-product-compliance
Ingram Content Group UK Ltd.
Pitfield, Milton Keynes, MK11 3LW, UK
UKHW040001020326
468546UK00013B/595